Sam has written an immensely practical
that will help anyone who longs to experie
see those gifts meaningfully integrated int

JACK DEERE, former professor of Old Testament Exegesis and Semitic Languages at Dallas Seminary; pastor; and author of *Surprised by the Power of the Spirit*

I am an elder in a church that engages with God in genuine worship, seeks maturity through dynamic preaching, loves compassionately in community, expresses mercy to the disenfranchised, and multiplies through intentional missionality. Thankful for God's many blessings, we long for more of his grace, especially through an outpouring of the Spirit's gifts. But how can our church experience this renewing power? It seems Sam Storms wrote this book to guide our church in this quest. I think it is for your church too!

GREGG R. ALLISON, Professor of Christian Theology, The Southern Baptist Theological Seminary; elder, Sojourn Community Church; secretary, the Evangelical Theological Society; author, *Historical Theology*; *Sojourners and Strangers*; *Roman Catholic Theology and Practice*

Sam Storms has done it again. This book combines sound theology with inspiring personal examples, together with practical ways to express the compassion of Jesus to others by partnering with him in spiritual gifts. Sam successfully demystifies what it means to obey the apostle Paul's injunction to earnestly desire spiritual gifts (1 Cor. 12:31; 14:1). I highly recommend this book for anyone seeking to grow in this dimension of the grace of God, and especially pastors seeking to lead their flock into a deeper experience as empowered evangelicals who want all that Jesus provides for us.

MIKE BICKLE, International House of Prayer of Kansas City

Few people write on spiritual gifts as wisely, biblically, and helpfully as Sam Storms. This book covers all kinds of practical and theological questions about the use of the gifts, and does so with insight and clarity—so if you're looking for answers to any of them, look no further.

Andrew Wilson, Teaching Pastor at King's Church London

PRACTICING THE POWER

PRACTICING THE POWER

WELCOMING THE GIFTS OF THE SPIRIT IN YOUR LIFE

SAM STORMS

ZONDERVAN

Practicing the Power

This title is also available as a Zondervan ebook.

Requests for information should be addressed to:
Zondervan, *3900 Sparks Dr. SE, Grand Rapids, Michigan 49546*

Library of Congress Cataloging-in-Publication Data

Names: Storms, C. Samuel, 1951- author.
Title: Practicing the power : welcoming the gifts of the Holy Spirit in your life / Sam Storms.
Description: Grand Rapids, MI : Zondervan, [2017]
Identifiers: LCCN 2016039853 | ISBN 9780310533849 (softcover)
Subjects: LCSH: Gifts, Spiritual.
Classification: LCC BT767.3 .S77 2017 | DDC 234/.13--dc23 LC record available at https://lccn.loc.gov/2016039853

Art direction: Tammy Johnson
Interior design: Denise Froehlich

Printed in the United States of America

---

23 24 25 26 27 LBC 12 11 10 9 8

With deep and heartfelt gratitude,
I dedicate this volume to
Wayne Grudem.
Thank you for our long and intimate friendship,
your constant encouragement and support,
and for a lifetime of tireless and Christ-exalting ministry to the people of God.

CONTENTS

FOREWORD

It is not an exaggeration to say I have been waiting for this book for close to fifteen years.

I came to faith in a church that preached extended sermons on why the gift of tongues didn't exist and the dangers of the charismatic movement. As an eighteen-year-old Christian, this wasn't hard to believe. I could see the abuses. But God in his mercy wanted to show me some things that would stand in sharp contrast to the teaching I had heard at my home church.

God's first mercy was the gift of an eclectic group of Christian friends. These guys absorbed me into their group soon after my conversion. They were a mix of some serious Church of Christ kids and four or five guys who attended the Assembly of God. I was Baptist, so you can imagine the robust dialogue that took place as we shared what we were learning at our respective churches. Topics of discussion ranged from the right kind of worship music in a service to tongues as evidence of salvation—and everything in between! With this group I developed a deep love for the Scriptures and sought to humbly understand what others believed. I learned that being gracious to others was pleasing to God. Even though I strongly disagreed with them on many issues, I knew that they deeply loved Jesus. They were a refuge for me as an infant in Christ, and they taught me through their love for the Bible and for me.

God's second mercy to me was a gifting of the Spirit of God in a way that had place in the church I was attending at the time. Though I am primarily a preacher/teacher, I also have a strong gift of evangelism, and from time to time have had what Sam defines in this book as "prophetic words" for people. God used this gift of prophecy in powerful ways that led people to become Christians, repent of secret sin, and seek reconciliation in their broken relationships. It's a gift that seems to come and go in my life. I can preach and teach every week but the prophetic gifting seems to vanish for months at a time. Still, that experience with the gift of prophecy left me feeling like a theological orphan. I embraced a Reformed view of soteriology, I am an unapologetic complementarian and have a high view of the Scriptures as the inerrant Word of God. But as a budding continuationist (one who believes that the miraculous gifts of the Spirit continue today), I was now somewhere between the charismatics, the Reformed, and my Baptist roots. In time, God would introduce me to another group of deep friendships that would help me, push me, and challenge me through robust dialogue to grow in a healthy understanding of the Scriptures.

When I became the pastor of The Village Church, it was a seeker-sensitive (Willow Creek model) Baptist church. I didn't think it was possible for a church like this to practice the gifts of the Spirit as we see them operating in the Scriptures. I knew that I could navigate the questions and challenges of growing in the gifts myself, but I wasn't sure how to work with others or lead a church in using the gifts. That's why I started by saying that I've been waiting for the book you are holding for fifteen years. This is the help I've been waiting for!

Sam writes with biblical conviction and a practical know-how that I've come to love. If you want to grow in your understanding of the gifts of the Spirit; if you feel God calling you to walk in the gifts as a covenant community, but you aren't sure where to start; and if you want to do all of this in a way that is Christ honoring and loving to other people, I believe this book will serve you well.

Matt Chandler
Lead Pastor, The Village Church
President, Acts 29 Church Planting Network

INTRODUCTION: GOD GOING PUBLIC

I've been told on any number of occasions that what I long for most, what I pray for and labor in God's grace to develop, and what accounts for the writing of this book, is a pipe dream. It's an elusive and ultimately unattainable myth; a pie-in-the-sky-by-and-by religious fantasy that has about as much hope for success as the search for Sasquatch (that mythological, hominid-like creature more popularly known as Bigfoot)! What am I talking about? I'm talking about a local church in the twenty-first century that is committed to the centrality and functional authority of the Bible and to the effective, Christ-exalting operation of all spiritual gifts.

I'm talking about a congregation of born-again followers of Jesus who are gospel-centered, who maintain a high view of the sovereignty of God in salvation, and who are intolerant of manipulative excess and self-serving fanaticism, yet who also delight in speaking in tongues, praying for the sick, and prophesying to the edification, encouragement, and consolation of other believers.

I'm talking about individual Christian men and women who are intellectually exhilarated by complex biblical truths yet unafraid to give public expression to deep emotional delight and heart-felt affection for Jesus. I'm talking about theologically sophisticated followers of Christ who are open to and hungry for the present tense voice of the Spirit while always subject to the functional and final authority of the written text of Scripture.

Those with a slightly more charitable spirit will tell me that such a church is less comparable to the search for Sasquatch and more like unto the history of the dodo bird. That flightless bird endemic to the island of Mauritius was last sighted (if sources can be believed) in 1662. The dodo, said one author, has rightly become the "symbol of extinction and obsolescence." So, too, is the local church that can hold in biblical balance the foundational truth of God's written Word and the supernatural movements of the Holy Spirit in and through spiritual gifts. The last sighting of a church of this sort, so say the critics, was sometime in the first century AD, when capital "A" Apostles still walked the earth. With their departure from the scene, we should not waste our time thinking and praying—much less striving—to build a body of believers in which revelatory gifts such as word of knowledge can flourish alongside serious theological reflection.

I've heard it countless times: "You can't live with the expectation that the Spirit will speak directly to you apart from Scripture and at the same time build your life and ministry on the rock-solid foundation of what he has already said in and through Scripture. You can't speak in authentic New Testament tongues and at the same time preach verse-by-verse through the books of the Bible. You can't pray expectantly for miraculous healing and be devoted to the importance of Hebrew and Greek exegesis. You can't be a Calvinist and a charismatic! And you certainly can't expect anyone else to participate in a local church that purports to embrace both sides of this unbridgeable spiritual chasm."

So they say.

If you are of one mind with such critics, this book will make little sense to you. "Don't waste your time," you are thinking. "The 'power' you so passionately want to 'practice' through spiritual gifts isn't available any more. And if it is, it only comes rarely, and even then, largely through the written Word and not the miraculous charismata. We are centuries removed from the sort of church you want to see."

To be clear, I rejoice in the power of the Spirit mediated through the inspired and inerrant Word of God. And I trust that everything in this book is based on what can be found nowhere else but in that written text we call the Bible. In this, I agree with my critics. The Bible is the basis for what we believe and the norm for how we live out our faith.

But I've written this book for those of you who, like me, are of the mind that the power of the miraculous charismata is still available for those who believe, pray for, and humbly pursue it. And it is my hope that this handbook on how to implement spiritual gifts in a local church will prove to be helpful and useful.

More Power, Please!

So why should you read a book like this? Why should you care? Aren't there enough problems that Christians confront in the local church? Isn't this debate about spiritual gifts a secondary issue? Shouldn't we devote our energies to wrestling with so-called same-sex marriage or abortion or the refugee crisis? Shouldn't we spend time studying and defending doctrines like the deity of Christ, his bodily resurrection, or talking about whether baptism is necessary for the forgiveness of sins? Is this really a topic that warrants our attention, a topic that calls for my concern?

Yes, I believe it is.

Lurking beneath the surface in most of the objections to a book of this sort is a misconception about the nature of spiritual gifts. The closest thing to a definition of spiritual gifts that we find in the New Testament is found in the word the apostle Paul used in 1 Corinthians 12:7. Spiritual gifts, said Paul, are a "manifestation" (Gk., *phanerosis*) of the Holy Spirit. They are not some thing or some stuff that is separate from God, something else sent by God. *The gifts are God himself working in and through us.* They are concrete, often tangible, visible and vocal disclosures of divine power showcased through human activity. A *charisma* or gift of the Spirit is the Holy Spirit himself coming to clear and sometimes dramatic expression in the lives of God's people as they minister one to another. As I wrote years ago in my book *The Beginner's*

Guide to Spiritual Gifts, "Gifts are God going public among His people."[1]

Although the issue of spiritual gifts is of secondary importance, especially when compared with such pressing matters as the Trinity, the bodily resurrection of Jesus, and salvation by grace alone through faith alone, it is by no means of little importance. For when we affirm and welcome the operation of the *charismata* (spiritual gifts, pl.) in our lives, we are affirming and welcoming God himself.

If we honestly assess the spiritual condition of our lives and the health of our churches, many of us will be forced to concede that our lives are devoid of meaningful, transformative power. We have an urgent need for a greater infusion of God's omnipotent and limitless power in our lives individually and in the church corporately. But even assuming this need is real, why focus on spiritual gifts? What is it about the so-called charismata that makes them so essential to an experience of divine power?

One word in two texts should help to answer that question. In 1 Corinthians 12:6 Paul says this about spiritual gifts: ". . . and there are varieties of activities, but it is the same God who empowers them all in everyone." A bit later, in verse 11, he reminds us that "all these [spiritual gifts] are empowered by one and the same Spirit, who apportions to each one individually as he wills."

In both of these texts we find different forms of the same basic term, translated in slightly different ways. We can render them this way: ". . . and there are varieties of *energizings*, but it is the same God who *energizes* them all in everyone." And these gifts are "*energized* by one and the same Spirit." This is Paul's way of telling us that spiritual gifts, whether gifts of tongues or teaching, whether exhortation or evangelism, whether prophesying or pastoring, are

1 Sam Storms, *The Beginner's Guide to Spiritual Gifts* (Bloomington, Minn.: Bethany House, 2015), 13.

the effect or result of divine power. Spiritual gifts are the concrete, tangible manifestations of divine energy in and through followers of Jesus. Paul is writing that this energizing power from the Spirit is essential to the church as a whole and in the lives of individual church members to enable them to reach maturity.

God's power comes to us in a variety of forms, but spiritual gifts are the primary expression of God's work in our midst. This is why it is of the utmost urgency that pastors and believers in every church be equipped in the exercise of all the gifts "for the common good" (1 Corinthians 12:7). This is why I have written this book and why I believe it is so important for you to read it.

CHAPTER 1

WELCOME TO THE WORLD OF THE SPIRIT

The following email is typical of what I receive on an almost daily basis. The pastor's name, his church, and the city where he lives have all been changed:

> My name is David Smith and I serve as the lead pastor of a church of about 500 people here in north Texas. We planted our church five years ago and God seems to be doing much in our midst. Over the years I have received prophetic words encouraging me to explore the gifts of the Spirit and to lead others to do so as well. My aim is to dismantle the false dichotomy that suggests a church must choose between either being anchored in the Scriptures or animated by the Spirit in her worship and mission. I affirm, on exegetical grounds, the full range of spiritual gifts presented in the Scriptures, although I have not personally experienced them or seen them in practice in the life of the local church. I am writing to you because, although I desire to pursue and implement the gifts in the life of our congregation, quite honestly, I have no idea how to do it. So I guess you could say I fall into the category of those who say they are theologically continuationist but are practical or functional cessationists. We want to be faithful to Scripture but also to avoid the extremes of certain charismatic churches. Do you have any advice for me?

I'm not exaggerating when I tell you that I've received hundreds of emails, phone calls, and other queries like this over the years. How do I respond? Well, I usually encourage those asking to read two of my books: *The Beginner's Guide to Spiritual Gifts* (Bethany House), and *Convergence: Spiritual Journeys of a Charismatic Calvinist* (Enjoying God Ministries). I also direct them to a sermon series I preached at Bridgeway Church on 1 Corinthians 12–14. That series is available at my church website, www.bridgewaychurch.com, in both audio and video format together with the notes from each message.

But many of those who write to me respond by saying: "Sam, I already agree with what you've written and preached on this subject. What I *need* now is some practical guidance. How do I implement these truths in my life and in my church in a way that is not manipulative or artificial? How can I hold firmly to the centrality of biblical authority at the same time I pursue and practice spiritual gifts?"

My desire is that *every follower of Christ* will come away from this book with a better understanding of the spiritual gifts and will be energized by the power of the Spirit. But my aim is not to rewrite the books I've already published on this subject. Neither will I spend time trying to persuade you of the validity and operation of all spiritual gifts in the present day. For those who would like a brief, crash-course introduction to the debate between continuationism and cessationism, I've included an appendix that summarizes the core issues.

Instead, I'm writing this book for those like "David Smith" above who are convinced from God's Word that the Spirit is still operative in and through the charismata—but you don't have a clue what to do next! You're a bit hesitant, maybe even frightened, by what might happen if you were to move forward and pursue and practice the full range of spiritual gifts that we read about in 1 Corinthians 12–14. My guess is that your pastor, along with the staff and elders of your local church, are even more frightened about this than you! And there's no telling what the congregation as a whole might think or do if they were to discover the direction in which you're moving.

Are You Ready for This Book?

I've written this book with every believer in mind. At times, however, I'll speak more directly to issues that concern pastors and church leaders, since they will need to consider the impact of their decisions on the entire church. That said, if you are a church pastor reading this, I want to encourage you to find other men and women to pursue this journey with you. One of the greatest assets to a local church pastor seeking the exercise of spiritual gifts in his church are men and women who share his passion and are willing to bear the burden and pay the price required to make it happen.

To that end, what I've written should be of interest and benefit not only to pastors, elders, and leaders in the local church but also to all Christians who would identify with the following characteristics:

- You are male or female, young or old, and you believe in the foundational importance of an inspired and inerrant Bible. You expect on a Sunday or in a small group gathering to hear God's Word expounded, explained, and applied. You won't believe something that doesn't have biblical warrant, and your theological radar is sensitive to deviations from historic, orthodox, evangelical truth.
- You are a Christian who values the importance of the mind and the power of truth. You believe that genuine spiritual experience is almost always the fruit of heightened insight into the revelation of God in Scripture. You would agree with Jonathan Edwards who argued that spiritual affections—a "religion of the heart"—are the result of light in the mind.
- You are the sort of person who bristles at any hint of

manipulation. You value authenticity and are offended by those who use illicit or artificial tactics to create spiritual fruit like joy or to induce a forced spiritual experience.

- Related to this, you disdain some of the methods employed by certain TV evangelists to produce tears or trembling or other physical manifestations that they identify as proof of the Spirit's presence or as a sign of their own anointing and spiritual authority (as well as a reason why you should contribute a large sum of money to support their ministry).
- You are nervous about what might happen both to you and others in your church if unbridled fanaticism is unleashed. You value self-control not because you are proud or want to maintain an image of religious sophistication but because you recognize self-control as a fruit of the Holy Spirit and have witnessed many instances of people who exhibit physical signs of what they suppose is the Spirit's influence.
- You are a bit skeptical and cautious about supernatural gifts and overt demonstrations of spiritual power, because you've never actually seen a display of such that you are convinced was thoroughly biblical.
- You are passionate to see God work in life-changing ways among his people. You long to pray with success for the sick and see them healed. You are persuaded that merely knowing the truth, while essential, isn't enough, that God has made himself known in Christ to actually transform lives and to deepen our intimacy with him.
- You desperately want to prophesy, as Paul commanded in 1 Corinthians 14:1, because as he later says in 1 Corinthians 14:3, you want people to be edified, encouraged, and consoled. Your prayer life isn't what it should be, and you wonder if the gift of tongues might be a blessing that would expand your commitment to intercede for yourself and for others.

- You've encountered people you believe were seriously demonized and felt helpless to bring them deliverance and freedom. Exercising our God-given authority and power over the demonic realm is something you've always wanted but you were afraid to pursue. You've sensed the presence of God during times of exalted worship and you long to experience his nearness and actually feel his love in new and life-changing ways. Your feeble efforts to evangelize lost souls have left you frustrated. You desire not only the incentive and energy to share your faith with greater clarity and zeal but you want to see words of knowledge and physical healings accompany the proclamation of the gospel.
- You are weary of the weekly, often monotonous and traditional routine in church life that rarely challenges your daily existence and puts teenagers to sleep and offends the non-Christian who dares to visit your services. Put simply, there is no real power to speak of in what occurs on a Sunday morning, and you dread the lifeless ritual that passes for worship. You long to encounter the living God and to be energized by his love for you. And you are determined to do whatever it takes, no matter the sacrifice required (within proscribed biblical boundaries of course), to bring it to pass in the experience of your local church.

Does any of this describe you right now? If you resonated with any or all of the preceding, this book is for you. And if simply reading through these descriptions caused a measure of curiosity to arise in your heart, this book is for you.

But I need to warn you up front. There is a cost involved, a price you must pay. If you wish to pursue deeper spiritual experiences, it will require commitment and sacrifice.

Are You Willing to Pay the Price?

My working assumption is that you are reading this book because you sincerely desire to see a more robust and vibrant expression of the Holy Spirit at work in your personal life and in your church. Please know that this is a good thing! Paul's exhortation in 1 Corinthians 14:1 is that we should eagerly desire spiritual gifts, especially prophecy. To long for and humbly pursue all the spiritual gifts that are described in the NT is both pleasing to God and *biblical*. That being said, there are several other things you must consider if you wish to experience God's Spirit and see his power manifest.

First, take a moment to answer this simple question: How important is it to you that spiritual gifts operate fully? If you regard this as something optional and not worth the effort or sacrifice that must be made, you will not be willing to endure mistakes, deal with flaky folk, and push through those times of discomfort. You won't be willing to take risks or look stupid. I've spoken with countless Christians and local church leaders who, when pressed, honestly admit that while they prefer having all the gifts operating, it doesn't rank all that high on their list of priorities. If you are a church leader, this is an especially important question for you, because at the first sign of failure or push back on the part of people in the church or perhaps under threat of the loss of income, leaders are tempted to shelve the discussion and move on to other matters.

Some leaders refuse to move forward unless they have a guarantee in advance that no mistakes or errors will be made. Absent that guarantee, forget about it! Having been in ministry for more than four decades, I can say that *rarely* is anything done in the life of the local church, especially if it's new or different, that is devoid of error. Mistakes should be expected. We are by nature and choice mistake-prone people. It's a consequence of our sin. We act out of fear or selfishness or self-protection or pride and ambition.

Sometimes it's simple ignorance. Should the day come when these inclinations in the human soul are wholly eradicated, we might be able to obtain a guarantee that no goof-ups or gaffes or odd behavior will occur.

Obedience must matter more to you than success or your image. It's easy to assent to that statement—who wouldn't agree? No one openly declares that they are obsessed with what other people think and are reluctant to obey God's Word lest it diminish the size of their congregation. Instead, we figure out a way to justify our disobedience to God's Word. But in our hearts, we know that to obey the commands of Scripture in this regard comes with a price we simply aren't willing to pay. We are quite adept at rationalization when our livelihood is on the line.

I came to grips with this principle several years ago.

A televangelist (whose name you would immediately recognize, so I've left it out) was attempting to minister to the people in his audience, both those who were physically present and those, like me, who were watching on TV. He would periodically close his eyes, tilt his head slightly upward, poised to listen to what he claimed was the voice of God.

"Yes, Lord, okay, I understand. Uh huh, right." He would then turn and share the word he was hearing with his audience. Once again closing his eyes, he repeated the performance, but with a slight twist: "What was that, Lord? Hold on. Just hold on. I'll get back to you in a minute."

Needless to say, putting God on hold while he attended to what he believed was a more important matter was instantly offensive to me. What made this even worse was that he proceeded to pray for the sick and pronounce the healing of numerous people in the audience.

The entire affair was highly manipulative and irreverent, even blasphemous. I remember feeling a knot develop in my stomach. I was physically repulsed by the disgraceful manner of what this man called ministry. I quietly but decisively said to myself: "If that's what it means to operate in the gifts of the Spirit, I want no part of it."

No sooner had I silently spoken those words to myself than this question flashed in my mind: "Sam, are you justifying your disobedience to what Scripture tells you to do because someone else badly abused what he claimed was a spiritual gift?" I knew the answer to that question, and it stung my soul.

Ever since that day, I have realized that I tend to live by an unspoken eleventh commandment, one that is not found in the Bible but guides my actions and thoughts all too often. I call it the Eleventh Commandment of Bible-Believing Evangelicalism, and it goes like this: "Thou shalt not do at all what others do badly." It's the habitual response that we have to completely reject something when we see someone else doing it in a way we feel is wrong or manipulative.

Stating it this way makes it seem harsher than it typically feels when we obey it. When we see someone browbeating a non-Christian, trying to extract a confession of faith from him, few of us resolve that we will never share our faith in Christ again. When we endure a bad sermon where the preacher twists the text and makes inappropriate applications of it, we don't decide that preaching itself must be abandoned. The same could easily be said of countless other things we observe in the professing Christian church.

But for some reason it's different with the so-called miraculous gifts. The eleventh commandment comes into play, and we decide there is nothing to redeem here. Let someone speak loudly in tongues in a corporate gathering without the benefit of interpretation, and we decide that we'll *never* permit tongues. Or we see someone, like the TV evangelist I mentioned, manipulate a crowd with a word of knowledge or prayers of healing, and we make an inner vow *never* to permit anything remotely similar in the life of our church. That's what I felt as I watched the evangelist that day.

Looking back now, I know that this so-called TV evangelist

served a purpose in my life. I began to see that I could not rely upon my initial, gut-level response to these experiences. They were leading me to obey a law that is not found anywhere in Scripture. That day, I resolved in my heart that I would never justify my disobedience to God's Word because of the abusive or embarrassing practices of others.

Of course, I suspect that some of you are saying to yourselves: "That's not why I'm against spiritual gifts. It's because I don't believe the Bible warrants our thinking the Spirit still imparts them today." That's fine, if that's honestly what you believe. But I would ask that you search *both* the Scriptures and your heart and ask the Spirit to bring conviction if your motivation is wrong, as mine was.

If you sincerely do not believe that all spiritual gifts are valid today, so be it. My goal in this book is not to convince you otherwise. But if you are open to the idea that God is still working through all of the gifts today, start here. Make certain that you are not deterred from the pursuit of the gifts because you are offended by a self-serving evangelist on TV or a preacher in that church down the street who claims to be operating in the power of the Spirit.

A second reason why many choose not to press forward in practicing the power is because the effort is too time intensive. Pressing forward in the power of the Spirit isn't easy. It entails a substantial shift in your focus, your priorities, and will begin to change the spiritual culture of your church. It's one thing to talk about changing the cover design on the Sunday morning bulletin. And while a few might protest your decision to remove the American flag from the sanctuary, it's probably not going to take years of arguing to make it happen. Some changes take more work, like deciding that it is biblical and necessary to implement a formal covenant membership in your church. Or maybe you decide that it would be better to characterize your small groups as missional communities instead of life groups. As challenging as such changes may be, you are probably going to survive them.

But affirming the validity and engaging the practice of the full range of spiritual gifts is another matter altogether. When you begin to make room in your services to pray for the sick or to facilitate prophetic words, well, get ready to duck! These changes will require a significant sacrifice of time and energy. In some cases, it will be more costly than you can imagine. People who protest must be dealt with lovingly and tenderly. Some will threaten to leave. Others will simply stop showing up without bothering to let you know. Rumors will fly about your abandonment of the finality and sufficiency of Scripture. There will be hours you must devote to meetings to educate and encourage people about what is happening. If it sounds like I'm trying to discourage you from doing this, please know that I'm not.

But I want you to know what you're facing.

One thing I've learned is that a successful transition will only happen (and there is still no guarantee) if the pastor is committed to teaching and preaching on the subject of spiritual gifts consistently on Sunday mornings. He must be committed to regular and repeated teaching on the subject, and the church as a whole must be quick to respond to the direction and correctives set forth in God's Word.

Making It through the Transition

When I first made the theological changes that we're talking about, I began by teaching verse by verse through 1 Corinthians 12–14. I followed that teaching with a yearlong expositional series on the book of Acts. Then came a twelve-week series on worship and fifteen messages on spiritual warfare. Why? Because Bible-believing evangelicals will never be truly open to the pursuit of spiritual gifts unless they see them clearly taught in Scripture. Even then, not everyone will be convinced, but in my experience, this *must* happen at some point. So you've got to study Scripture. If you want to see your church change, that change must begin with the spiritual leaders, and the church must see that this is a matter of utmost urgency for the pastor and the elders in the body. They need to be assured that the church will provide a safe environment for the practice of spiritual gifts.

I would be less than honest if I did not warn you of the offense that many will take at your efforts. Often the offense is not about the biblical validity of the spiritual gifts for today, but a rejection of the association with the charismatic subculture. Some people will not be able to differentiate between the legitimate faith required for the implementation of the gifts and the presumptuous attitude of entitlement that is found in certain charismatic and Pentecostal churches. You and your church will be guilty by association. Sadly, the name-it-and-claim-it-blab-it-and-grab-it-if-you-believe-it-you'll-receive-it mentality has so muddied the waters of the modern charismatic movement that you will face a battle to communicate clearly what the Bible teaches about the power of the Spirit.

You must be willing to suffer loss to be entirely faithful to what God has commanded. For the church leaders reading this, it may mean that people leave your church or stop contributing financially. If you are an individual who wants to pursue the gifts, it may mean being misunderstood or being rejected from certain groups within the congregation. Some of your friends may leave before a healthy and biblically rooted expression of the charismata develops. Your reputation could suffer. You may be accused of going soft on doctrine and of being overly subjective and emotional or of losing confidence in the transforming power of Scripture and its total sufficiency.

What you must remember at each step along the way is that God is not as easily offended by our errors and messes as you and other people are. We tend to project onto God our fears and anxieties. We envision him wringing his hands in worry and consternation, mumbling under his breath: "Oh, my, I hope he doesn't mess things up. These humans are always the sort who take things too far. They 'believe' me for things I never promised. What will become of my reputation if someone does something silly or stupid?"

Yes, I'm being sarcastic. But my point is that God does not sit on pins and needles worrying that you might cross a line and look like a fool in the process. I'm not saying that he approves of mistakes or excess or willful sin. He delights in courage and faith and the risks we take to avail ourselves of all that he has made available. He doesn't expect perfection. He wants passionate people who are devoted to his glory. If we stumble along the way, perhaps falling flat on our faces at times, he's not disappointed, angry, or embarrassed by our failure.

Be aware of your own thoughts toward others as well, when you are tempted to look down on those who make mistakes or get it wrong and embarrass you. My friend Simon Holley pastors Kings Arms Church in Bedford, England, and during a sermon he preached at our church he mentioned how his congregation responds when people try and then fail. On one occasion a lady shared how she had stepped out in faith and spoke what she believed was a word of knowledge to another lady on the train. She turned out to be completely wrong. But instead of curling up in a fetal position in shame, she shared her mistake before the entire church. They applauded her, not with the golf applause—that restrained and virtually muffled patting of the hands. No, we're talking about a raucous clapping of the hands.

Someone attending that day was confused by the response. "I don't get it," he said. "You guys applaud failure?"

"No," said Holley. "We applaud courage."

Holley's point is that God is far more pleased with our obedience than he is with our success. Success is not something we ultimately control. I can't guarantee that my prayers for the sick will result in healing. I can't promise that my word to you will be spot-on accurate. But I *can* control whether or not I am willing to step out and take a risk. And the risk is worth it. I've never had someone to whom I made a failed attempt to minister tell me later that they wished I had kept my mouth shut. They invariably feel loved and cared for. They appreciate that someone took enough interest in them to run the risk of looking foolish. Our responsibility is to obey God's Word. God's responsibility is to act in accordance with his will and, according to his calendar, to do whatever it is that most pleases him. We please him not by always producing results but by always practicing obedience.

So get rid of the idea that God is offended by your failure or that he will bench you for the rest of the game because you missed it. If you are humble and acknowledge that you aren't perfect and that your ultimate aim is to honor God through obedience to his command, you won't give up trying and he will delight in your efforts on his behalf.

One last word about our failed attempts to walk in the power of the Spirit's gifts: when a mistake is made, seize the occasion and turn it into an opportunity for instruction and encouragement. Don't shrivel up and withdraw. Don't tell yourself that you'll never try anything so stupid again. Acknowledge that perhaps things were not done in perfect harmony with biblical guidelines, but the last thing you want is to put someone under heavy condemnation or make them feel like an outcast in the body of Christ.

Let me give you an example of how we should respond when someone makes a mistake.

Tongues and Tambourines!

Several years ago, I was attending a conference in Fort Worth, Texas. I was very new in my understanding and experience of the Spirit's power. If something I did went amiss in the course of the meeting, my natural response was to crawl under my seat and hide from shame. But Jack Hayford taught me something important at this conference. Hayford, as you may know, is a seasoned leader in the Foursquare denomination. He is a classical Pentecostal pastor and theologian, but even (perhaps especially) non-Pentecostals can learn a lot from the kindness and patience that I experienced that night.

There was a brief pause in the time of singing and a familiar transition between songs with the clanging of multiple tambourines as well. Suddenly, in the upper regions of the convention center, a lady stood up and began to pray, shouting aloud in tongues. Everyone froze. You could almost hear people holding their breath, terrified that inhaling or exhaling might bring down the rafters, or, worse, the wrath of Almighty God. Her voice brought the entire event to a sudden and shameful halt.

Jack Hayford rose from his chair and calmly walked to the podium.

Hayford wasn't scheduled to speak that night. But the leadership of the conference immediately deferred to him and allowed him to address the lady, hopefully bringing some measure of spiritual order to what felt like fleshly, self-serving chaos. He spoke, and I paraphrase:

> "Ma'am, I trust that you love the Lord Jesus with all your heart. Your zeal to express that love through tongues and to minister encouragement to the rest of us is commendable. So please don't think for a moment that what I'm about to say is a rebuke or in any way a denunciation of your desire to honor God. And the rest of you here tonight have my permission to go ahead and breathe!"

And we did! Hayford continued:

> "Spiritual gifts are a wonderful blessing, and I applaud the leaders of this conference for making room for their exercise. But the

> Bible also has clear guidelines for how they are to be employed. In 1 Corinthians 14 the apostle Paul tells us that in a corporate gathering such as this, the purpose of which is the edification of all believers, everything should be done in an intelligible manner so that we might understand and be instructed. This is why he insisted that if there is a tongue, there must be an interpretation. May I suggest that, given the size of this gathering and the virtual impossibility of knowing whether or not there would be an interpretation, all such expressions of tongues be done quietly or not at all."

Hayford sat down. The rest of us collectively sighed with joyful relief. What I learned from that experience is that *we don't have to be afraid of spiritual gifts, even if someone does it badly.*

We don't have to legislate against spiritual gifts because someone somewhere once stepped out of line by ruling that no spiritual gift will ever again be allowed to manifest itself in our church gatherings. Hayford gently, but firmly, took the opportunity to teach everyone present what the Bible said. And though I didn't speak with her, I'm confident the woman who spoke felt loved and cared for by Hayford. I can't imagine that she was humiliated, as is so often the case when others mangle the opportunity to speak truth to someone who stepped out of line.

I recall saying to myself as Hayford concluded his words, "Ok, then. That didn't hurt much. God didn't incinerate anyone. We all learned an important lesson. The lady felt loved, even though she was corrected. The leaders of the conference didn't need to panic. And the Word of God was upheld as authoritative."

My conclusion from that experience informs my advice to you: Don't freak out when someone fails. Don't panic. Give everyone time to catch their breath. Open your Bible and very gently but with clarity explore together what ought to happen in such cases. Reassure others that if they happen to be the perpetrators of an error at some time in the future that they will not be ridiculed, humiliated, or cast out to the lions. You can accomplish a great deal of good by responding as Jack Hayford did that night.

"Only God Can Make the Wind Blow"

Finally, let me encourage you to never forget the power of God. In John Piper's wonderful book *When I Don't Desire God,* John shares an illustration. He uses it to make a slightly different point in that book, but I think he'd be fine if I co-opt it here for our purposes.

Imagine that you've decided to go sailing. The problem is that you know next to nothing about sailing! So you go to the store and you purchase several books to find out what's involved. You carefully read them and then you talk to a veteran sailor who answers questions for you. The next day, you rent a sailboat. You examine it closely to make certain that everything needed for a successful sailing experience is present and in good working order. Then, you take your boat out onto the lake. Your excitement is at a fever pitch, though you're also afraid. But you follow the instructions you've read and the counsel received from the experienced sailor, and you launch your boat into the water. You carefully monitor each step and hoist the sail.

At that precise moment you learn a crucial lesson. You can study sailing. You might even be able to build a sailboat. You can seek counsel from the wisest and most veteran of sailors. You can cast your boat onto the most beautiful of lakes under a bright and inviting sun. You can successfully hoist the sail. But—and this is a big "but"—*only God can make the wind blow!*

You and I can study the Bible. We can learn everything there is to know about spiritual gifts. We can honor and submit ourselves to the Lord Jesus Christ. We can orchestrate a worship service according to biblical guidelines. We can do everything that lies in the power of a Christian man or woman. *But only the Spirit can make the wind blow!* Whether or not the sails fill with a breeze, whether or not the boat moves an inch in the water, is dependent on the will of the sovereign Spirit who blows when and where and however much he pleases. You and I cannot force him to move. Not even our obedience guarantees that the Spirit will do what we have hoped and prayed that he will do.

We cannot compel the presence of the Spirit. We cannot create the operation of a spiritual gift in accordance with biblical standards of conduct. We can obey and pray that the Spirit will be pleased to blow in and through our acts of obedience. If the Spirit chooses not to move, we cannot, indeed we must not, attempt to coerce him. And we should not give up ever trying to sail again because of a calm day when the wind wasn't blowing. Most important of all, don't try to blow into the sail yourself or forget the wind and use paddles instead. That's not sailing.

Remember that the Holy Spirit is a person with a will and with preferences. That's why I use a personal pronoun to describe him. The Holy Spirit wants to be *pursued* but refuses to be *pushed*. Never lose sight of the fact that whether or not a particular spiritual gift is manifest and to whom it may or may not be given is entirely up to the Spirit himself. Gifts are bestowed and operate at his discretion, not yours or mine.

As Paul said, "All these are empowered by one and the same Spirit, who apportions to each one individually as he wills" (1 Corinthians 12:11). So, if you find yourself lacking a specific spiritual gift, notwithstanding your persistent and passionate prayers that it might be granted to you, the time may come when you should pause and thank God for whatever gifts he has been pleased to bestow and move on in the ministry he has already granted you.

I'm saying this as a word of encouragement to those who are hungry for the Spirit's power, who carefully do everything that the Bible and practical wisdom requires, but who see little to no results.

Don't give up! Don't look for someone to blame. Don't conclude that the gifts "aren't for today." Rather, resolve in your heart to bring your boat to the lake every day until Jesus returns! Launch onto the waters and pray for wind! I'm simple-minded enough to believe that God will honor that sort of persistent obedience and propel your boat by the wind of his Spirit.

Are you hungry for more of the Spirit's presence in your life? Are you desperate to see his gifts and power operate in life-changing ways? And is it your heart's desire that this be done in a way that honors the finality, authority, and all-sufficiency of God's written, canonical Word? If so, let's look at where to begin.

CHAPTER 2

EARNESTLY DESIRE SPIRITUAL GIFTS

Earlier, I said that the Holy Spirit wants to be pursued and will not be pushed. This is just another way of saying that if we want to see and experience the full range of spiritual gifts we must relentlessly seek them. Is this idea of pursuing the gifts biblical? It certainly is! We see this encouragement to pursue the gifts, ask God for them, and pray for them in two passages in 1 Corinthians. These verses tell us that it is not only permissible to seek the spiritual gifts—it is mandatory.

The first passage we'll consider is 1 Corinthians 14:1. "Pursue love," says Paul, "and earnestly desire the spiritual gifts, especially that you may prophesy." This text says nothing about prayer, so how can I suggest that we should ask God and pray for more spiritual gifts than we already have? The answer is found by putting this passage from chapter 14 together with an earlier passage in chapter 12.

In 1 Corinthians 12:11 Paul tells us "all these [that is, all the spiritual gifts he has just enumerated in vv. 8–10] are empowered by one and the same Spirit, who apportions to each one individually as he wills." This means that the Holy Spirit is the one who decides who gets what. We don't. But we *are* told to "earnestly desire" spiritual gifts. Isn't it reasonable to think that if we are responsible for desiring spiritual gifts and the Spirit is responsible for distributing them, we should *ask* that he fulfill our desire by granting us the gifts we want to see manifest in our lives? I would suggest that the "desire" we feel for certain gifts is likely itself the fruit of the Spirit's work in our hearts. He desires (or wills) to grant us a gift (or gifts), which awakens in us a desire for the very thing he is determined to impart.

Don't forget that Paul issues this exhortation in 1 Corinthians 14:1 to Christians. These are men and women who have already been born again and already possess at least one spiritual gift. Paul is exhorting believers, in whom the Spirit already permanently dwells and to whom the Spirit has already granted at least one gift, to "earnestly desire" yet *more* gifts. This indicates that we have a responsibility to pursue their presence in our lives. And how do we do this? By asking God for their impartation.

Prayer as Earnest Desire

Another passage that connects seeking the gifts and prayer is found in 1 Corinthians 14:13. Here Paul writes, "Therefore, one who speaks in a tongue should pray that he may interpret." Paul is speaking about a believer who already has the spiritual gift of speaking in tongues, and he tells her to ask God for the spiritual gift of interpretation of tongues. Why? Paul wants everything that occurs in the corporate assembly of God's people to be intelligible. If there is no interpretation of tongues, what is said in tongues is of no value to others present. This is a key principle for exercising the gifts. If you are going to exercise your gift of speaking in tongues in a setting whose purpose is the edification or building up of other Christians, either make certain that someone with the gift of interpretation is present (see 1 Corinthians 14:27–28) or pray that God would grant you yourself the ability to interpret your own tongue.

We should also consider Paul's counsel to young Timothy. He writes to Timothy: "Do not neglect the gift you have, which was given you by prophecy when the council of elders laid their hands on you" (1 Timothy 4:14). Timothy was a born-again Christian when the elders prayed for him, and it was at that time, *subsequent to his conversion*, that the Spirit imparted a spiritual gift by means of a prophetic word spoken by one of those ministering to him. The word translated as "gift" in this text is *charismatos*, from the noun *charisma*, and it is sometimes translated with the word *spiritual* added to it ("spiritual gift") throughout 1 Corinthians 12–14.

We also find in this passage in 1 Timothy some guidelines for how we are to pray and what we might expect from those prayers. Although Paul refers to the "elders" praying for Timothy, I don't think he intends for us to see this as a prohibition against ordinary believers praying for one another. He is simply calling out a responsibility that the elders have. In our church we regularly make an appeal to people who desire a particular spiritual gift. Perhaps on this day the Lord has impressed upon us the importance of the spiritual gift of evangelism. On another day it might be the gift of mercy or giving or prophecy. In any case, we gather around the individual who "earnestly desires" the gift, lay hands on that person, wait patiently to see if the Spirit might impart some revelatory instruction regarding the believer (note that it was "by prophecy" that Timothy received his spiritual gift), speak forth whatever the Spirit discloses, and then pray something along the lines of:

> "Heavenly Father, we thank you for your gracious work of salvation in _________. We rejoice in knowing that your precious Holy Spirit now abides permanently in your child. Lord, we also know that you alone can empower your children for ministry. _________ has experienced an increasing desire for the gift of giving (or tongues, or prophecy, or serving, etc.). We hope that this desire is the work of the Spirit in his/her heart. So we ask now that you would graciously impart this gift to him/her. Grant him/her immediate opportunities to exercise this gift for the building up of others and the praise and honor of Jesus. And Lord we also ask that you would be pleased to confirm the presence of this gift through some prophetic revelation, whether by word of knowledge or dream or vision."

When you are praying in this way, don't be in a rush to finish. Several people should be given the opportunity to pray a similar or even identical prayer. We also encourage the believer to give expression to his or her own desires in prayer for this gift.

God's Sovereignty: Que Sera, Sera?

I once had a conversation with another Christian who objected both to the idea that a Christian might receive a spiritual gift subsequent to conversion (over and above whatever gift she might already have been given) and the idea that we are somehow responsible to actively and energetically pursue spiritual gifts. In his argument, he focused on the gift of tongues and he said something like this:

> "When I read the New Testament, I don't see any indication that what a person believes about the validity of spiritual gifts today has any affect whatsoever on whether or not they will operate effectively in any particular gift. Furthermore, nowhere in Acts do we read that the gift of tongues was imparted because of the spiritual posture or pursuit or prayer life of the believer. It was always and only a sovereign act of God."

I had a quick and simple response for him. I asked him if he was saying that one's theological convictions about the validity or cessation of tongues and other gifts have no practical effect on whether or not a person eventually experiences them. He affirmed that this was, indeed, what he was saying. But here is the problem with this idea. Our beliefs control and shape our zeal, our expectations, our prayer life, and especially how we respond to and interpret claims people make regarding their experience of supernatural phenomena.

Now, I have a very high view of God's sovereignty in all affairs of life and salvation. My friend seemed to be embracing what is sometimes called a "hyper-Calvinistic" point of view, one that borders on fatalism. He had excluded from his argument of God's sovereignty any notion of passionate prayer or human responsibility. But is this understanding of God's sovereignty biblical? Let's take a look at how the book of Acts portrays the manner in which the gift of tongues was imparted.

First of all, we are told that those present on the Day of Pentecost were there in obedience to the command of Jesus: "But stay in the city until you are clothed with power from on high" (Luke 24:49; cf. Acts 1:5, 8). There is no reason to believe that if those listening had disbelieved Jesus' promise or disobeyed his command, refusing to wait with the others in Jerusalem for the outpouring of the Spirit, that they would have received tongues, irrespective of their response to him.

The text doesn't tell us if they were praying to receive tongues. Maybe they were, maybe they weren't. I tend to believe that, given John's and Jesus' prophecies of the impending Spirit baptism and the coming of divine power, the disciples were just sitting silently. My guess is that they were expectant, asking Jesus to do what he had promised. So while we don't know exactly what they were doing in preparation for the coming of the Spirit, for someone to say that God gave tongues to all of them *irrespective of their obedience or belief or prayer* is simply not true. The text is silent there.

A second reason why I find my friend's argument misleading is the story of Cornelius in Acts 10. This passage is about the spread of the gospel to the Gentiles. I think most everyone acknowledges that we are dealing here with an unusual geo-ethnic expansion of the gospel that called for the same phenomenon that occurred at Pentecost in order to attest to the reality of their acceptance by faith. Peter and the others understand that the experience of Cornelius and the other Gentiles receiving the Spirit and speaking in tongues served a unique purpose in this case—corroborating the fact that "the gift of the Holy Spirit was poured out *even* on the Gentiles" (Acts 10:45, emphasis mine). This leads Peter to conclude that they were fit subjects for water baptism, similar to those among the Jews who had believed and received the Spirit. I hardly think this example from Acts 10 is sufficient warrant for drawing the conclusion that if God wants his people to speak in tongues they will do so irrespective of their own beliefs, prayers, desires, or state of mind and heart.

Another passage to consider is Acts 19. Here we are told that individuals spoke in tongues only "when Paul laid his hands on them" (19:6). In the course of Paul's explanation of the gospel and possibly hearing about the events of Pentecost, did these "disciples" of John express their own desire to experience what those did in Acts 2? Again, we don't know. The text is silent. What we do know is that Paul was dealing with a situation that is altogether unrepeatable today. These "disciples" were men who had embraced the baptism of John but had lived in the overlap of the transition from the old covenant to the new covenant. They evidently lived at a distance from Jerusalem and had no access to the news of what had happened on Pentecost. This is not a paradigmatic event for us today, as no one today lives in this sort of redemptive-historical time warp.

I believe my friend was reading assumptions into these incidents in Acts. In fact, the only other place where the gift of tongues is explicitly mentioned (outside the dubious long ending of Mark) is in 1 Corinthians. From this passage we know that not everyone in Corinth spoke in tongues, indicating that, in a time when the gift of tongues was clearly God's will for his church, some (possibly many) Christians did not receive the gift. If they all had spoken in tongues, Paul would not have had to say in 1 Corinthians 14:5 (NASB), "I wish that all of you spoke in tongues." So clearly not everyone did.

My friend's argument seems to go like this. If spiritual gifts are designed and intended by God to function in the church throughout its existence into the present day, then such gifts will consistently appear by divine fiat, irrespective of how people live, what they believe (especially regarding the continuation or cessation of said gifts), and whether or not they pray for and pursue such gifts and are committed to practicing them in accordance with Scripture.

I find this approach to the Christian life somewhat presumptuous, irresponsible, and negligent of God's ordained means to achieve his ordained ends.

If we apply this way of thinking to other areas of life, why would we bother praying at all? Why pray if God is going to do what God is going to do regardless? *Que sera, sera!* Whatever will be, will be! If the principle my friend is defending is correct, why would Jesus have rebuked his disciples for their failure to pray when attempting to cast the demon out of a young boy (Mark 9:28–29)? Why wouldn't we conclude that if God wanted the boy to be delivered he would sovereignly do it without calling for or waiting upon the prayers of others on the boy's behalf? And why should we obey Jesus who commanded us to persevere in prayer, telling us to keep on asking, keep on seeking, and keep on knocking (Luke 11:9–10) to receive the gifts and blessings of the Spirit that we so desperately need (Luke 11:13)? And why would James tell us that "you do not have, because you do not ask" (James 4:2) if God typically grants gifts and blessings as sovereignly and irrespectively of our desires and prayers as my friend suggests?

Neither my friend nor I have any idea what the Corinthians did or did not do to receive their spiritual gifts. He is suggesting that they received them apart from their desires or prayers. But the text is silent. Well, almost silent. We are left with the explicit exhortation to pray for the spiritual gift of interpretation in 1 Corinthians 14:13. But why would Paul issue such an imperative? Why bother, if God's will is to grant the gift of interpretation? It seems to me that Paul believed that the reception of a spiritual gift is dependent on one's prayer for it. Ask and you shall receive. Don't ask, and you shouldn't expect to receive.

At this point, I also find it helpful to look at the history of spiritual gifts and how they have operated in the church over the nearly 2,000 years of church history. I believe that one of the reasons why spiritual gifts are less frequent in certain seasons of church history than in others is due to the fact that people didn't seek, pursue, or passionately and incessantly *pray* for these gifts. And often the reason they didn't pray for them or ask for them is because they had a prior conviction or belief that they did not exist or were not available to them.

In other words, *they had not because they asked not, and they asked not because they believed not!* Not believing in the validity of the gifts leads to not believing that God would grant them, so they didn't ask for them. And not asking for them, they didn't receive them. So is asking irrelevant? Not at all! Throughout the Bible God most commonly works through prayer.

The hungry are those who are filled. The thirsty are those who are given drink. Those who ask and seek and knock are those to whom the door is opened. Can God set aside this principle and grant gifts, irrespective of our theological beliefs about their validity, irrespective of our disobedience in praying for them? Of course he can. And this has likely happened countless times throughout the history of the church. But these special mercies of God, working sovereignly to bless his people, do not cancel out the responsibility we have. We cannot expect God to do things for us if we ignore the commands he gives us related to their impartation! Even though we believe he *can*, we should never expect God to do for us *apart* from prayer what he has promised in his Word to do for us only *through* prayer.

CHAPTER 3

THE NON-NEGOTIABLE NECESSITY OF PRAYING

I realize that the title to this chapter sounds a bit redundant. After all, if something is necessary then it is by definition not up for negotiation. So why did I choose it? To reinforce that there is little, if any, hope for the proper use of spiritual gifts apart from a focused and consistent commitment to praying. Notice that I did *not* say a focused and consistent commitment to "prayer" but to "praying." There is a difference.

Many Christians will say they are committed to prayer. But how many actually pray? Believing in the value of prayer and writing it into the mission statement of your church is one thing. Actually praying is something else. If you want your life to experience divine power, it needs to be a praying life. If you want your church to operate in the full gifts of God's Spirit, it needs to be a praying church.

From the first day that I was awakened to the importance of spiritual gifts in the life of the church, prayer has had an irreplaceable role. What I have in mind here is not praying for individual gifts for people but experiencing corporate prayer, everyone in the local church interceding on behalf of everyone else.

The year was 1989, and I had approached the elders of our church to ask that we conclude each Sunday service with an opportunity for people to receive prayer from trained intercessors. At the time, we were a typical Bible church. I would conclude my message with a closing benediction and then simply dismiss the congregation. But I had come to believe that if we ever hoped to see people healed physically or hear from the Spirit in words of knowledge and prophecy that we needed to provide opportunities for this to occur. Something needed to change.

The elders were initially reluctant, largely because their only experience with what I was asking was related to an extremely charismatic church in the community. Through its fanaticism, it had given a bad name to everything "spiritual" or remotely charismatic. The elders were understandably concerned that my suggestion might lead us down a slippery slope and open the door to excess.

I asked if they would grant me the freedom to handpick a half dozen or so couples whom I trusted to personally train in the practice of intercessory prayer. I asked for a year in which to do this, and after that time they could reconsider my proposal. So we went forward with that plan.

After training these couples for a year, the elders were happy to approve a time of prayer ministry at the close of each service. There wasn't anything particularly fancy or unusual about what we did. I utilized a prayer model I had learned from John Wimber, founder of the Association of Vineyard Churches. I made some slight changes to it, but by and large it was the model that Wimber popularized. We invited anyone of any age to come to the front of the auditorium and receive prayer for physical healing, emotional encouragement, relational struggles, or whatever other issues they were facing at the time.

So did we experience radical healings and powerful moves of the Holy Spirit? Things didn't change much at first. But change came; slowly and unmistakably we began to see things happen. At the heart of our ministry were the words of James chapter 4, verse 2: "You do not have, because you do not ask." I understand this to mean that *God loves to be pursued*! God loves to be asked, repeatedly, over and over, without fear on our part that we are nagging him or laboring in unbelief. God is pleased to draw near and pour out his power and do wonderful, even miraculous, things when his people persevere in prayer, asking again and again that the Spirit work in people's hearts, bodies, souls, and minds.

I'm not saying that you will never experience the supernatural operations of the Spirit unless you embrace and utilize the prayer model that I'm articulating in this chapter. But I don't think it likely that you will. I believe that when people pause and pray, when they linger over one another with intercessory cries, the Spirit is more inclined to speak to them than if they simply pat each other on the back with the standard Christian cliché: "I'll be praying for you." Don't promise to pray for people. *Practice* praying for them. Just do it!

Someone once said that all theological error begins with truth. We start out with something altogether biblical and then take it to such an extreme or fail to put proper parameters around it and end up in something false and misleading. This is certainly the case when it comes to prayer. We begin with the glorious truth that God is generous and abundant and loves to enrich his people spiritually with all the blessings secured for us in heavenly places in Christ Jesus (see Ephesians 1:3).

We then fall into the presumptuous error of thinking that God will bestow all those blessings irrespective of our asking for them. We assume, falsely, that God will give us apart from prayer what he has promised to give us only in response to prayer. We say to ourselves: "God is a good God. He is generous and kind and effusive with his blessings. He loves his children, and I'm one of them! So although I know I should pray and continually seek his face, if I don't I can count on God to come through for me anyway. After all, that's what being God is all about, isn't it?"

Well, no, it isn't. Although Isaiah here is speaking of God's relationship to Israel, I believe the principle he articulates is true of God at any time in redemptive history:

> *Therefore the Lord waits to be gracious to you,*
> *and therefore he exalts himself to show mercy to you.*
> *For the Lord is a God of justice;*
> *blessed are those who wait for him.*

> For a people shall dwell in Zion, in Jerusalem; you shall weep no more. He will surely be gracious to you at the sound of your cry. As soon as he hears it, he answers you. (Isaiah 30:18–19)

This is stunning, to say the least. If God is gracious and loves to show his mercy to his people, then why doesn't he just do it? Why does he wait to be gracious? Why does he first require that he hear "the sound of your cry"? For heaven's sake, Lord, or perhaps we should say, for our sake here on earth, just do it. Just give it. Just pour out your mercy and whatever other blessings or help or provision we need. Why do you insist that we first "wait" on you in prayer?

It's important to God that we ask him for things he knows we need.

From a human perspective, it might seem quicker and far more efficient if God were simply to bypass prayer and get on with the giving! But that is not his way. He finds particular honor and glory in being the One to whom we must humbly come to receive that which we need.

But this doesn't mean that we repeat our requests mindlessly before God. Just before Jesus gave us what has come to be known as the Lord's Prayer, he said this to his disciples:

> "And when you pray, do not heap up empty phrases as the Gentiles do, for they think that they will be heard for their many words. Do not be like them, for your Father knows what you need before you ask him." (Matthew 6:7–8)

Here we are told that we should not babble on with meaningless and repetitious phrases, as if God were impressed by mindless verbosity. Never fall into the trap of thinking that God is impressed by the same things that impress us. You and I may be overwhelmed and duped by loquacious people whose verbal skills far exceed our own. But God isn't.

The reason we should be succinct in prayer is that *God knows what we need before we ask him*. But if God knows all our problems and needs *before* we ask, why ask at all? We must remember that, generally speaking, God has determined not to fulfill our needs unless we ask him to. Our petitions are the *means* by which God has purposed to give us what he already knows we need.

In addition, the doctrine of divine omniscience compels us to be totally honest with God in prayer. When dealing with someone whose knowledge of you is limited, you can pretend, manipulate, deceive, and even lie to them. But omniscience demands honesty. You cannot pretend or playact with someone who can read your heart and mind, who knows your motivation. I believe it was Augustine who once said, "God does not ask us to tell him our needs that he may learn about them, but in order that we may be capable of receiving what he is preparing to give."

Of course on occasion, God does bestow great and glorious gifts even in the absence of our asking for them. But it is sinfully presumptuous and downright disobedient on our part to assume that he will bestow those gifts and then neglect or refuse to pray based on that assumption. Again, we must never assume that God will give us apart from prayer what he has promised in Scripture to give us only in response to prayer. The reason God instituted prayer is so we have a predictable channel of communication with him *through which we can express our desire*. Just having the desire for something doesn't mean you've asked God for it. God has given us prayer as a means through which we can earnestly seek him and his gifts.

The Purpose of Prayer Training

Prayer is a skill that takes time and training to learn. Just like getting to know a person through communication, getting to know God through prayer takes time and learning. Jesus says, "Everyone who has heard and learned from the Father comes to me" (John

6:45). The Spirit is a solid teacher, not just a spontaneous voice in the wind. I say "training" because the time you spend in prayer is not simply casual (although there's a spirit of freedom in it). Prayer is hard work, like it is building any other relationship through consistent and healthy communication. Therefore the best way to think of growing in the power of the Spirit through prayer is training. Whether you start your training privately or you are ready to train your church as a whole, I offer a model that our church has used. We offer this content at our church no fewer than four times a year. If you are a leader or teacher thinking of teaching on prayer, I recommend making it your goal through the teaching to increase the level of *expectancy* in the hearts of your people when they pray for themselves or for others. That word—expectancy—is rather explosive.

Many in the church today will say they believe that God still heals, but rarely if ever do they actually lay hands on the sick and pray with any degree of expectancy that he will. One reason is that they often confuse praying *expectantly* with praying *presumptuously.* Prayer is presumptuous when the person *claims* healing without revelatory warrant or on the unbiblical assumption that God *always* wills to heal then and there. They then feel required to account for the absence of healing by appealing either to moral failure or deficiency of faith (usually in the one for whom prayer is offered). Sometimes they shift the blame for the lack of healing to a demon. But I digress.

I want nothing to do with the name-it-and-claim-it approach, which insists that you must believe in advance that what you ask will always be yours. Having said that, there is a place for believing that God will move powerfully and having hope that what we are asking is according to his will and something he is pleased to perform. But that happens on rare occasions and is itself a manifestation of the spiritual gift of faith.

Instead, we should pray expectantly, offering a humble petition to our merciful God for something we don't deserve but that he delights to give (Luke 11:9–13; cf. Matthew 9:27–31; 20:29–34; Luke 17:12–14). Expectant prayer flows from the recognition that Jesus healed people because he loved them and felt compassion for them (Matthew 14:13–14; 20:34; Mark 1:41–42; Luke 7:11–17), a disposition in the heart of God that nothing in Scripture indicates has changed.

In our teaching, we need to try to demystify healing prayer. People often elevate prayer ministry to a level beyond what is accessible to the average believer. They mistakenly think that only ordained clergy can pray with power or that one must speak a certain spiritual lingo to sway God's heart to say yes to our requests. Prayer, so they think, is for supersaints, not average lay folk. My goal in the teaching we do is to help them embrace their responsibility as believers to incorporate healing prayer as a regular, normal, aspect of what it is to be a Christian.

Finally, this teaching seeks to provide people with biblical principles to guide their thinking as they pray for the sick and wounded, as well as practical guidelines on how to actually pray for people in a way that honors God and blesses them. There are also two extremes that we must avoid here. One is a *functional deism.* Deists are those who believe in a Creator God but put little to no confidence in the possibility that he will intervene and act supernaturally in response to our prayers for him to do so. God is there, and he is good, but he prefers to let the world operate under those natural laws that he instituted when he first called the material creation into existence out of nothing. Many evangelicals act as if they believe this, living as if God won't intervene in response to our prayers.

The other extreme I encounter is an odd combination of magic and manipulation. In this understanding of healing prayer, people believe that we can somehow coerce God to respond if we just speak the right words in just the right tone of voice. In this view, God is reduced to a genie in a bottle that pops out to perform magical tricks so long as we utter the right words at the right time.

Instead of being functional deists or magicians, we should strive to hold two biblical truths about God in tension: God's goodness and his sovereignty. God is good and loves to give gifts to his children when they ask (Luke 11:11–13). But he is also sovereign and cannot be bullied to act in a way that is inconsistent with his eternal purposes (James 5:13–18). We must allow room in our theological framework for a redemptive purpose in suffering as well. Though some of the more extreme representatives of the charismatic world deny this, the truth is that God can and often does use our physical maladies to achieve our spiritual and moral refinement. My goal here is not to defend a theology of healing and suffering, so I won't take time to unpack that truth. If you want to learn more about this, you can start by reading the chapter on healing in my book *The Beginner's Guide to Spiritual Gifts*.[1]

The Role of Faith

Another persistent obstacle in motivating people to pray is the misconceptions people have about the role of faith and how it relates to prayer. Some believe that if they don't pray with absolute and unyielding confidence that God will respond right then and there, they might as well not pray at all. They want to avoid the feelings of guilt and inadequacy they experience when they attempt to pray and discover that nothing happens. I've addressed the nature of faith in healing prayer elsewhere, so let me simply summarize the primary concepts here as they apply broadly to prayer for God's miraculous works of mercy.[2]

When we talk about the sort of "faith" that God honors with healing or miracles, we do not mean the faith you exercised when you first trusted Christ for salvation, what might be called *converting*

1 *The Beginner's Guide to Spiritual Gifts*, 55–79.
2 Ibid., 59–68.

faith. This is the faith present in every born-again heart. Neither do I have in mind the faith that you are exercising right now as you read this book. This is a *continuing* faith, a daily confidence that God is present with us and will never leave us or forsake us, faith in his goodness and the surety of his promises that sustains us moment by moment through the difficulties and challenges of life.

There is also what we might call *charismatic* faith, which I believe is what Paul had in mind when he spoke of the spiritual gift of faith in 1 Corinthians 12:9. How is it different? While all faith is an expression of trust and humble dependence upon a person or promise, this is the experience of faith that arises somewhat spontaneously and unexpectedly in our hearts. It is that sudden, supernatural surge of confident assurance that God is going to do something right now, right here. Look closely at Mark 11:22–24 (cf. Matthew 17:20–21; 21:21–22); 1 Corinthians 13:2; and James 5:15 for some biblical examples of this. This expression of faith is a unique gift that is not universal for all believers, but given sovereignly by the Lord to specific individuals on particular occasions. Of course, any believer is a candidate for this experience, and on two or three occasions God has been pleased to bless me with this remarkable ability to believe what on any other occasion I likely would not be able to believe.

To summarize, I can believe God at any and all times that nothing will ever separate me from the love of God in Christ. I can believe God at any and all times that he is able to work all things, even painful and tragic things, for my good and his glory. But I cannot believe at will, that is to say, at *my* will, that God is going to heal someone for whom I pray or perform a miracle on the spot. This confident prayer is a prayer that I can only pray when *God* wills it and enables me to overcome all hesitation and doubt to believe it.

At this point people often bring up the words of Jesus in Mark 11:22–24. In response to a question Jesus asked his disciples about the withering of the fig tree (vv. 20–21), he answered the question for them with these words:

> "Have faith in God. Truly, I say to you, whoever says to this mountain, 'Be taken up and thrown into the sea,' and does not doubt in his heart, but believes that what he says will come to pass, it will be done for him. Therefore I tell you, whatever you ask in prayer, believe that you have received it, and it will be yours." (Mark 11:22–24)

The first thing I look for to understand a statement like this is some cultural background to help me understand the context. In the time of Jesus, phrases like "moving" or "casting" a mountain into the sea were proverbial references to the miraculous. Why would anyone want to literally make a mountain fall into the sea? The point of these expressions is to highlight the fact that otherwise humanly impossible feats, events that require supernatural and miraculous power, can occur when prayer is filled with faith.

The instantaneous and miraculous destruction of the fig tree (see Mark 11:12–14) served as an object lesson to the disciples of what can be achieved by faith in God's power. It is as if Jesus was saying to Peter: "Pete, your comment tells me that you are amazed by the sudden and supernatural withering of the fig tree. But if you have faith in God, all things are possible through prayer." So we must recognize that the belief or faith here is not a case of a Christian forcing himself to believe what he does not really believe. It is not a wrenching of one's brain, a coercing of one's will, a contorting of one's expectations to embrace as real and true something that one's heartfelt conviction says otherwise. Jesus is not telling us that when doubts start to creep in you should put your hands over your ears, close your eyes, and say to those doubts, over and over again: "Lalalalala, I can't hear you. Lalalalala I can't hear you!" That's not faith. That's make-believe. That's spiritual pretending.

On the other hand, we are responsible to take steps that will facilitate the deepening of faith in our hearts. We can do things by God's grace which will expand our confidence in God's goodness and his greatness and help diminish, if not drive out, our doubts. As I read and study and meditate on the character of God, my confidence in what he can do increases. As I reflect and ponder the grace and kindness of God, my confidence in his goodness grows and intensifies.

Clearly there are other factors that have to be taken into consideration when we ask God for things in prayer. Faith is not the sole condition for answered prayer. We have to ask him with the right motives (James 4:1–3). I say to the men reading this book, we have to be treating our wives with gentleness and kindness and understanding (1 Peter 3:7). We have to clean the slate, so to speak, in our relationships with others. This is why Jesus continued in his explanation of faith and prayer, "And whenever you stand praying, forgive, if you have anything against anyone, so that your Father also who is in heaven may forgive you your trespasses" (Mark 11:25).

His point is that if you harbor unforgiveness in your heart toward others, it isn't likely that God will answer your prayer, no matter how much alleged faith you think you have (see Matthew 6:14–15).

And we have to ask in accordance with God's will. It doesn't matter if I am somehow able to banish all doubt from my mind and convince myself that I've already received what I asked for. If what I'm asking isn't consistent with the will and character of God, the answer will be no.

No amount of faith will force God's hand to do something that is contrary to our welfare. It doesn't matter how persuaded you are or how much faith you have, you simply don't want God to answer every prayer you pray! Look with the benefit of hindsight on some of the things you once believed you needed and were convinced that God would give you. Yikes! "Thank you, Lord, for saying no to many of these prayers. It would have been devastating had you said yes." Sometimes God says no to prayers that are offered up in faith because he has something even better in store for us, something he plans on giving to us at a more appropriate time.

So it is irresponsible and insensitive to suggest on the basis of Mark 11 that if someone doesn't receive from God what they asked for it is because they are at fault in failing to have enough faith. The absence of faith *may* be a factor, but it is not the only factor. There are other things that can also account for unanswered prayer.

The only way anyone can fulfill the condition set forth by Jesus is if God himself chooses to impart to us the faith he requires. Faith, ultimately, is a gift from God. When God wants to bless us with a miraculous answer to our prayer, he will take the initiative to cultivate and build into our hearts the fulfillment of the condition he requires. Therefore, each time as we pray, each time as we seek God for what only God can do, let us begin by asking God for an extraordinary, powerful faith. Let us ask God that he work in us to produce and sustain the confidence that he is pleased to bless.

CHAPTER 4

FASTING FOR POWER

Fasting? What's not eating got to do with spiritual gifts? Believe it or not, *everything*. Fasting is consistently portrayed in Scripture as one of the primary ways that we seek God and those blessings that he has promised to us if only we would ask. So, when someone asks about the relationship between fasting and spiritual gifts, I direct their attention to Paul's exhortation in 1 Corinthians 14:1 that we seek or pursue spiritual gifts, especially prophecy. Fasting is pursuit. Fasting is spiritual seeking. Fasting is asking with an extraordinary intensity and passion.[1]

But first let me set the record straight about fasting. Fasting is not primarily about not eating. In fact, fasting is *all about* eating, of a sort. Fasting is feasting on God, drawing deeply upon his presence, depending wholly on his power, enjoying his goodness, gazing on his beauty, and trusting him to do for us what we could never remotely expect to do on our own. The reason we don't eat is to help us focus on the energy that comes from God. As Dallas Willard says, "Fasting is, indeed, feasting. When we have learned well to fast, we will not suffer from it. It will bring strength and joy." We gain real power from fasting.

Needless to say, this calls for some explanation. My reason for saying that fasting is crucial to the presence and exercise of spiritual power is found in what the Bible as a whole has to say about it. I have in mind specifically the way in which fasting is portrayed as the

---

1 I've written more extensively on fasting in my book *Pleasures Evermore: The Life-Changing Power of Enjoying God* (Colorado Springs: NavPress, 2000), 165–84. I also highly recommend John Piper's book *A Hunger for God: Desiring God through Fasting and Prayer* (Wheaton, Ill.: Crossway, 2013), on which I'm greatly dependent for what follows.

expression of God's people who are desperate and needy. Fasting is not about denying yourself; it's about satisfying yourself . . . in God. Fasting is not about physical pain, but spiritual pleasure. Fasting is the first cousin to prayer in the sense that together they are the ordained means by which God is pleased to give us what we need.

I realize that nothing seems as silly to our natural minds or as repulsive to our bodies as fasting, especially in light of the instant self-gratification of our consumer-oriented world where life is all about seeking and obtaining whatever suits our fancy. "You deserve the best," they tell us. "You can have it now!" "Grab for all the gusto you can!" To our world, fasting makes absolutely no sense at all.

Even from a Christian point of view, it seems a little odd. If God has generously created food "to be gratefully shared in by those who believe and know the truth" (1 Timothy 4:3 NASB), what possible reason could there be for abstinence? It seems like something reserved for weird people, odd people, or, at worst, the masochist who somehow enjoys inflicting pain upon himself!

The reputation of fasting has also suffered because of its association in the minds of many with the ascetic abuses of medieval monks and hermits. In centuries past, fasting was often subjected to rigid regulations and was combined with extreme forms of self-mortification and self-denial. Little wonder, then, that fasting seems so often to contribute to that "holier-than-thou" mentality we all want to avoid. In the minds of many, fasting is inseparable from showy and ostentatious self-righteousness.

One thing that will help us in our attitude toward fasting is to distinguish it from other reasons why people don't eat. For example, fasting is not a *hunger strike*, the purpose of which is to gain political power or to draw attention to some social cause. Fasting is not *health dieting*, which insists on abstaining from certain foods for physical reasons. Saying no to burgers and shakes so you can look better in this summer's swimsuit is not biblical fasting. Biblical fasting has nothing to do with *anorexia nervosa*, an eating disorder in which a person starves herself to lose weight, either out of self-contempt or in hope of becoming fashionably and loveably thin (or for any number of other reasons). And fasting must be distinguished from how it is practiced in numerous *pagan religions*: to control or appease the gods, or perhaps to make contact with spirits in order to manipulate their power.

So what does the Bible say about fasting? Let me highlight six fundamental truths about fasting for you.

(1) Remember that fasting is always motivated by deep desire. There is certainly a measure of physical pain or inconvenience that comes with fasting, but contrary to popular opinion, fasting is *not* the *suppression* of desire but the intense *pursuit* of it. We fast because we *want something more* than food or the activity from which we abstain. We say no to food or certain conveniences for a season only to fill ourselves with something far more tasty, far more filling, far more satisfying. If one suppresses the desire for food, it is only because he or she has a greater and more intense desire for something more precious. Something of *eternal* value.

That is why I say without apology that *fasting is feasting! It's about feeding on the fullness of every divine blessing secured for us in Christ.* Fasting tenderizes our hearts to experience the presence of God. It expands the capacity of our souls to hear his voice and be assured of his love and be filled with the fullness of his joy.

Let me say it again: Fasting is *not* primarily about *not* eating food. *It is primarily about feasting on God.* In other words, *what* you don't eat or *how long* you don't eat or whatever activity you deny yourself isn't paramount. What you *do* eat, spiritually speaking, is critical. Feed on God. Don't simply taste; don't nibble; don't snack. Feast on him! Seek him. Part of this is a time issue: If you take something like eating out, that frees up more of your time to cry out to him, focus on him, and worship him. Invite him to fill you up "to all the fullness of God" (Ephesians 3:19 NASB). Entreat him to sustain you and supply you and succor you. Lay your heart open before the Lord and ask for him to search and stretch you (cf. Psalm 139:23–24). Repent often! Then, when your fast is finished, rejoice in the food or the fun he has provided and give him thanks for all good things.

Consider Jesus' words to his disciples in John 4:31–38. I'm sure Jesus appreciated their concern for his welfare, but he wanted to make a point. So when they insisted that he eat something, his response was startling: "I have food to eat that you do not know about" (4:32). No, Jesus didn't have a double-patty Big Mac or an extra-large meat-lovers pizza hidden inside his robe. Nor were his words a clever turn of phrase. Jesus is telling them (and us) that he is strengthened and sustained by the presence of his heavenly Father.

Fasting is about ingesting the Word of God, the beauty of God, the presence of God, the blessings of God. Fasting is about *spiritual indulgence*! It is not a giving up of food (or some activity) for its own sake. It is about giving up food *for Christ's sake.*

We are always driven to fast because we hunger for something more than food. This means that fasting is motivated by the prospect of pleasure. The heart that fasts cries out, "This I want more than the pleasure of food!" Some (wrongly) fast for the admiration that people give to those with amazing willpower. But we rightly fast for the reward from God alone, given without regard for the praise of men. We don't fast because we hate our bodies and look to punish them. Whatever immediate discomfort we may experience, it is a sacrifice that pays immeasurable long-term benefits. We do not fast for pain, but for the pleasure of experiencing still more of Christ Jesus and the revelation of his powerful presence.

(2) Fasting is not something you do for God but an appeal for God in grace and power to do everything for you. Fasting is not an act of impressive willpower—it is a declaration of our weakness, a confession of our utter dependency on God and his grace. Our desire for spiritual gifts must always be driven by the urgency to help others in ways that we could never achieve in our own strength or ingenuity.

(3) ***Fasting is not a statement that food or other things are bad but that God is better!*** In other words, fasting is not a rejection of the many blessings God has given to us but an affirmation that in the ultimate sense we prefer the Giver to his gifts. Fasting is a declaration that God is enough.

(4) ***Fasting should be motivated by the desire to glorify God.*** It is crucial to understand the difference between being seen fasting and fasting to be seen.[2] In Acts 13:1–3, the believers in Antioch fasted together as a group. Clearly they did not believe that Jesus' warning about fasting to be seen by men in Matthew 6:17–18 precluded corporate fasting. When you fast as a group others obviously know, but this is evidently not a violation of Christ's instruction. The church leaders at Antioch did not take Jesus to mean that we sin if someone knows that we are fasting but that we sin if our motive is to be known for our fasting so that men applaud us.

What, then, is the "reward" that God promises to give if our motive is only to be seen by him in secret (Matthew 6:18)? God sees us fasting and knows that we are motivated by a deep longing in our hearts for him and for his purposes to be fulfilled in the earth. He knows that we are not fasting to obtain the applause of people. "He sees that we are acting not out of strength to impress others with our discipline, or even out of a desire to influence others to imitate our devotion. But we have come to God out of weakness to express to him our need and our great longing that he would manifest himself more fully in our lives for the joy of our soul and the glory of his name."[3]

And when he sees this, he responds. He responds by giving to us more of himself and the blessings secured for us in Christ. He

---

2 I owe this insight to John Piper, *A Hunger for God*, 65–76.

3 Ibid., 74.

"rewards" us by answering the prayers we pray in accordance with his instruction in Matthew 6:9–13 that his name be hallowed, that his kingdom come, that his will be done on earth. Surely God can and does give us other things that we seek through fasting (whether a spiritual gift, physical healing, guidance, etc.). But chief among the results of fasting is the exaltation of God's name and the expansion of God's kingdom.

(5) Fasting opens our spiritual ears to discern God's voice and sensitizes our hearts to enjoy God's presence. The gentle words of the Spirit are more readily heard during times of fasting. God often grants insights and understanding into his will and purpose, or perhaps new applications of his Word to our lives as we fast.

In Acts 13:1–3 we see Saul (Paul) and Barnabas, together with leaders of the church in Antioch, seeking direction from the Lord as to where they should go as a church in terms of ministry. Their desperation to hear God's voice and follow God's will could find no more appropriate expression than through bodily denial. As they turned away from physical dependence on food, they cast themselves in spiritual dependence on God.

"Yes, Lord, we love food. We thank you for it. We enjoy it as you want us to. But now, O Lord, there is something before us more important than filling our mouths and quenching our thirst. Where would you have us go? Whom shall we send? How shall it be financed? Lord, we *hunger* to know your will. Lord, we *thirst* for your direction. *Feed* us, O God!"

Their fasting became the occasion for the Spirit's guidance to be communicated to them. Don't miss the obvious causal link that Luke draws. It was *while* or *when* or even *because* they were ministering to the Lord and fasting that the Holy Spirit spoke. I'm not suggesting that fasting puts God in our debt, as if it compels him to respond to us. But God *does* promise to be found by those who diligently seek him with their whole heart (Jeremiah 29:12–13). People who are merely "open" to God rarely find him. God postures himself to be found by those who wholeheartedly seek him, and fasting is a single-minded pursuit to know, hear, and experience God.

What God said to them in the course of their fasting changed history. This revelatory word was spoken in a moment of spiritual hunger for God's voice to fill the void left by mere human wisdom. The results, both immediate and long-term, are stunning, for prior to this incident the church had progressed little, if at all, beyond the eastern seacoast of the Mediterranean. Paul had as yet not taken missionary journeys westward to Asia Minor, Greece, Rome, or Spain. Neither had he written any of his epistles. All his letters were the result of the missionary journeys he was to take and the churches he was to plant. This occasion of prayer and fasting birthed Paul's missionary journeys and led to the writing of 13 of our NT books![4]

(6) ***Fasting is a powerful weapon in spiritual warfare.*** (See Matthew 4:1–11.) Jesus fasted to prepare for resisting the temptations of Satan. Fasting heightens our complete dependence upon God and forces us to draw on him and his power and to believe fully in his strength. This explains why Jesus fasted at the beginning of his ministry.

It is important to note that as Jesus was standing on the brink of the most important public ministry the world had ever seen, he chose to *fast*! Have you ever paused to reflect on the eternal consequences of what transpired in the wilderness of Judea those forty days? Heaven and hell hung in the balance. Had Jesus wavered, had he faltered, had he balked, all hope of heaven would have been dashed on the very rocks with which the Enemy tempted him. Of the dozens of things Jesus might have done to withstand this temptation, he is led by the Spirit to fast. Hence, if you are even slightly inclined to dismiss the importance of fasting, you would do well to

4 Ibid., 93–112.

remember this incident and that in a very real sense your salvation is due to the fasting of Jesus.

You may be wondering: "Are we commanded to fast? Am I in sin if I choose not to?" No. But the Bible assumes we will fast. According to Matthew 6:16–18, Jesus simply takes it for granted, twice saying, "*when* you fast." Therefore, although Jesus does not say "*if* you fast," neither does he say "you *must* fast." He says, simply: "*When* you fast . . ."

In Mark 2 we see the same emphasis. When the Pharisees queried why Jesus' disciples didn't fast, he explained it in terms of his own physical presence on earth. "The days will come," he said, "when the bridegroom is taken away from them, and then they will fast in that day" (Mark 2:20).

The point here is that the Messiah has come like a bridegroom to a wedding feast. Such a moment is too joyful and stunning and exciting to mingle with fasting. Groomsmen don't fast at the bachelor party! The rehearsal dinner is no place to be sad. Jesus is present. The time for celebration is upon us. When the wedding feast is over and the bridegroom has departed, then it is appropriate to fast.

Practical Guidelines for Fasting

I would be remiss if I didn't say something about the variety of ways in which one might fast. Contrary to what many think, one need not always fast from food or drink to achieve the desired goal. Do not feel pressure from others to fast in precisely the same way they do. Nor should you impose your choice in regard to fasting on someone else or judge anyone for the decision they make in this regard. Fasting is always susceptible to legalism, so beware! Follow the leading of the Holy Spirit and your *own* conscience (not someone else's). So let's note some ways in which you might choose to approach a corporate fast.

Food and Drink

This, of course, is the most popular and explicitly biblical expression of fasting. It too, however, comes in a variety of forms.[5] You may choose to fast from caffeine or soda or wine or other special liquids that you regularly imbibe. But you need not go "cold turkey"! If you are fasting from caffeine, wean yourself from coffee or sodas gradually, reducing your intake over a span of days before you stop drinking them entirely.

You may choose to fast from sugar or from some sort of food that is a regular, even daily, part of your diet. Perhaps you choose only to eat fruits or vegetables for the length of the fast, refraining from all meat (or vice versa). In the case of both of the former two forms of fasting, you would continue to eat and drink other items to maintain your strength and health.

If you should choose to go on a liquid fast, you would refrain from eating all solid foods for a time. You might still drink Gatorade or fruit juices or perhaps eat only soups. If you choose this approach there are several things to keep in mind.

First of all, a *progression* should be observed in your fasting, especially if this discipline is new to you and you are unfamiliar with its physical effects. Don't start out with a weeklong water fast! Begin by skipping one meal each day for two to three days and setting aside the money it would have cost to give to the poor. Spend the time *praying* that you would have used for eating.

Second, remember also that there are *degrees* of fasting. There is a *regular* fast which consists of abstaining from all food and drink except for water (Matthew 4:2–3; Luke 4:2). Apart

5 It is important to remember that some people simply cannot refrain from eating and drinking in any degree at any time. This is usually due to certain medications that they cannot cease taking and often have to ingest only after eating. If you have unique physical problems that would make fasting dangerous or unhealthy, please do not alter your prescribed regimen of medication or of eating and drinking without first consulting with your physician. There is nothing to be ashamed of if you cannot fast in regard to food and drink. Simply choose another way to fast, such as those noted above.

from supernatural enablement, the body can function only three days without water. A *partial* fast is when one abstains from some particular kind of food as in the case of Daniel while in Babylon (Daniel 10:3; cf. 1:8, 12). As noted above, a *liquid* fast means that you abstain only from solid foods. Again, most who choose this path are sustained by fruit juices and the like. A complete or *absolute* fast that entails no food or liquid of any kind (Ezra 10:6; Esther 4:16; Acts 9:9) should only be for a very short period of time. For anything longer than three to five days, seek medical advice. There is also what can only be called a *supernatural* fast, as in the case of Moses (Deuteronomy 9:9), who abstained from both food and water for forty days (enabled to do so only by a miraculous enabling from God).

You may also wish to fast from all food *for only a particular meal* each day. In other words, you may choose to skip lunch for a day or two or a week, or dinner, or even breakfast. All such forms of partial fasting are entirely appropriate.

If you've never fasted before, be aware that in the early stages you may get dizzy and have headaches. This is part of the body's cleansing process and will pass with time. Be sure that you break the fast gradually with fresh fruit and vegetables. Do not overeat after the fast. Chili and pizza may sound good after several days of not eating, but please, exercise a little restraint and say no!

How long you fast is entirely up to you and the leadership of the Holy Spirit. The Bible gives examples of fasts that lasted one day or part of a day (Judges 20:26; 1 Samuel 7:6; 2 Samuel 1:12; 3:35; Nehemiah 9:1; Jeremiah 36:6), a one-night fast (Daniel 6:18–24), three-day fasts (Esther 4:16; Acts 9:9), seven-day fasts (1 Samuel 31:13; 2 Samuel 12:16–23), a fourteen-day fast (Acts 27:33–34), a twenty-one day fast (Daniel 10:3–13), forty-day fasts (Deuteronomy 9:9; 1 Kings 19:8; Matthew 4:2), and fasts of unspecified lengths (Matthew 9:14; Luke 2:37; Acts 13:2; 14:23).

Technology

Many choose to fast from some form of technology: TV, the Internet, Facebook, Twitter, email, Instagram, etc. This can be a total fast from all participation or a partial fast from just one form. The choice is yours. The length of your fast may also differ: from one day to one week, etc.

Activities

Some choose to withdraw from a certain activity that has become a regular part of their rhythm of life, such as participation in some athletic event or some routine social gathering (other than a local church small group). What is of critical importance in regard to both of these sorts of fasting is that you not simply refrain from these things but that you fill the time and energy otherwise devoted to them with prayer, Bible study, worship, witnessing, or some other spiritual endeavor.

Our Experience at Bridgeway Church

Not long ago we were facing a crossroads at Bridgeway where I serve as pastor. A significant and far-reaching decision, both spiritually and financially speaking, was pressing upon us. So I called for a church-wide, corporate time of fasting and prayer and praise. Not everyone participated in the same way or to the same degree, but many joined in wholeheartedly.

You don't need to follow our example. There are countless ways that you can do this that may be more suitable to your church and the rhythms of life among your people. In our case, we decided to set apart every day Monday through Friday from 9 a.m. to 5 p.m. for prayer, meditation, and worship. We arranged for worship music to be continuously channeled through our sound system in the auditorium. No other events were scheduled for that space. People were encouraged to come for five minutes or five hours, depending on their other responsibilities. Some came for half an hour; others dropped in during their lunch break. A few of us spent most of every hour of every day during that week in prayer and passionate seeking of God's will for our body.

It was a truly remarkable time in the history of our church. God answered our prayers and made provision for our need in a way that can only be deemed supernatural.

You may choose to follow a different path in the pursuit of spiritual gifts. But I encourage you to consider adopting some version of the practice we embraced. I say this because I am altogether persuaded that if you truly long for the manifestation of spiritual gifts, one of if not "the" prescribed means for obtaining what I believe God wants to give is by prayer and fasting. Of course, in the final analysis, it is the Spirit "who apportions to each one individually as he wills" (1 Corinthians 12:11). We cannot coerce him or contrive ways to induce him to act contrary to what he knows to be the best and most beneficial distribution of his gifts.

CHAPTER 5

PRACTICING THE POWER OF HEALING

One of the more important ways to encourage the practice of the miraculous gifts in your life and in the church is by cultivating a culture of prayer. In this chapter, we'll take a closer look at the relationship between prayer and healing, and I'll share some practical advice on how you might pray for healing with an individual. First, let's return to the question of faith. What role does our faith or the faith of the person we are praying for have as we pray for healing?

There are a number of ways in which faith is manifest in our prayers for healing. On occasion the faith of the person needing healing is instrumental (Matthew 9:22), while at other times it is the faith of a friend or family member (Matthew 15:28; Mark 2:5, 11). Sometimes the focus is on the faith of the person praying for the one who needs healing (Mark 9:17–24). At other times, faith apparently plays no part at all in the healing (John 5:1–9). Indeed, in the gospel of John, faith is *never* mentioned as a condition for healing (see also Matthew 8:14–15). The point is that on some occasions, God simply heals by a sovereign act of his will unrelated to anything in us. However, in the vast majority of cases, Jesus healed people because of *someone's* faith.

In the case of both Jairus and the woman with the discharge of blood (Mark 5:21–29), faith is directed toward Jesus as an expression of need. In Luke 17:11–19 Jesus healed ten lepers, and when one returned to say "thanks," Jesus said: "Your *faith* has made you well" (v. 19). When Bartimaeus asked Jesus to heal him of his blindness, Jesus said: "Go, your faith has healed you" (Mark 10:46–52). And in Mark 2 and the famous story of the paralytic being lowered through the roof, Jesus healed when he saw that the man's friends had faith (vv. 5, 11).

The Variety of Ways of Faith in God

Faith is never monolithic. As I shared earlier in differentiating between converting, continuing, and charismatic faith, there are different expressions and degrees of faith depending on the object of our trust or the focus of our belief. All of us have faith that God is our sole source for blessing, that he is our hope for eternal life and the fulfillment of all the promises we read in Scripture (see Psalms 33:18–22; 147:10–11).

Why was faith so important to Jesus? The simple answer is that faith magnifies the mercy and power of God. By its very nature, faith leads us to look away from ourselves and any notion of self-reliance and confidently trust God for every provision. Faith is a confession of our personal inability and of God's limitless power. When we relate to God with genuine faith, the focus is not on the person who believes but on God to whom we look and in whose promises and power we place our confident trust. Faith is an act of self-denial, a renunciation of one's ability to do anything. Faith itself carries no power; but it is instrumental, deriving its significance from the role it plays in relating us to the God who answers our prayers.

In the gospels we see that faith in Christ's ability to heal often affects the outcome. Jesus took special delight in healing those who trusted in his power, people who were open and receptive to his ability to perform a mighty work.

In Matthew 9:28–29 Jesus asks the two blind men one question—"Do you believe I am *able* to heal you?" Jesus wants to draw out what they think about him, whether or not they trusted him and his ability to heal.

"Yes, Lord," came their response.

"According to your faith be it done to you," said Jesus, and they were instantly healed. Jesus regarded their confidence in his power to help them as "faith" and dealt mercifully with them on that basis.

Although you and I may think that our confidence in divine omnipotence is too obvious to play a role in whether or not someone is healed, Jesus treats it as something of critical importance. The leper in Matthew 8 said to Jesus, "Lord, if you are willing, you can make me clean" (v. 2). The leper had no reservations when it came to Christ's ability. But he was reluctant to presume upon Christ's will. Notice that Jesus doesn't rebuke him for his doubts, as if it were a shortcoming in his faith that might jeopardize his healing. He healed him because of his confidence that he *could* do it. When I pray for people to be healed, I typically ask them to confess out loud their belief that God is able to heal them. I suggest you do the same.

Yet another expression of faith is our confidence in God's character, specifically, his disposition or heart for healing. This relates primarily to our trust in God's goodness and his commitment to build up and to restore. God is overflowing in compassion, and healing is a window into his heart for the welfare and blessing of his people (see Luke 11:11–13). It's also important that we have faith that God actually does heal in our day and time. To say "God, I don't know if this is something you still do today, but just in case it is, I'm going to ask you to heal me" is not an expression of the sort of faith that God delights to honor with the impartation of his power. If you are a cessationist of some degree or if you question the presence of the miraculous in the present church age, it is unlikely you will pray with much expectancy or anticipation of God saying yes to your request.

Prayer and Confession of Sin

Another aspect of healing prayer we need to briefly consider is the relationship between healing and the confession of sin. There is an important word for us on this subject in James 5:16. James writes: "Confess your sins to one another and pray for one another, that you may be healed. The prayer of a righteous person has great power as it is working." James likely has in mind sins of bitterness, resentment, jealousy, anger, or unforgiveness in our relationships with one another, though he may be thinking of other sins we have committed against God. He probably has in mind the act of confessing to the person against whom you have sinned or confessing to another believer your more general transgressions or violations of biblical laws. What this tells us is that *God has chosen to suspend healing mercy, making it dependent on the repentance of his people.* If the hurting doesn't get healed, that doesn't mean that God doesn't heal today. The presence of sin and the lack of repentance may also be a factor. The stubbornness and spiritual insensitivity of people can affect God's willingness to heal.

We should also take careful note of the example of Elijah to which James appeals in verses 17–18. The argument has been made by some that biblical miracles were clustered or concentrated in only three major periods of history: the days of Moses and Joshua, the time of Elijah and Elisha, and the time of Christ and the apostles. The point of this argument is that Elijah and Elisha, for example, were special, extraordinary, unique individuals who cannot serve as models for us when we pray.

But here James says precisely the opposite! The point of James 5:17–18 is to counter the argument that Elijah was somehow unique or that because of the period in which he lived he could pray with miraculous success but we cannot. James wants us to know that *Elijah was just like you and me.* He was a human being with weaknesses, fears, doubts, and failures, just as we are. In other words, James is saying: "Don't let anyone tell you Elijah was in a class by himself. He wasn't. He's just like you. You are just like him. Therefore, pray like he did!" And we must not forget the context: *James appeals to the example of Elijah to encourage us when we pray for the sick!* The point is that we should pray for miraculous healing with the same faith and expectation with which Elijah prayed for the end of a three-year drought.

Faith and Gifts of Healing

One of the more common obstacles that blocks people from praying for the sick is their misguided belief about what has sometimes been called "the spiritual gift of healing." The only place where a "gift" of healing is explicitly mentioned is in 1 Corinthians 12:9 and 28. In our English translations both of the words "gift" and "healing" are plural and lack the definite article, hence the translation: "*gifts of healings*." Why is this significant? It suggests that Paul did not envision a person being endowed with one healing gift that is operative at all times for all diseases. His language suggests many different gifts or powers of healing, each appropriate to and effective for its related illness, or it may suggest that each occurrence of healing constitutes a distinct gift in its own right. I've had the opportunity on numerous occasions to meet people who have what appears to be a healing anointing for one particular affliction. Some are able to pray more effectively for those with back problems while others see more success when praying for migraine headaches. This may also be what Paul had in mind when he spoke of "gifts" of "healings."

So don't accept the erroneous idea that if anyone could *ever* heal, he could *always* heal. In view of the lingering illness of Epaphroditus (Philippians 2:25–30), Timothy (1 Timothy 5:23), Trophimus (2 Timothy 4:20), and perhaps Paul himself (2 Corinthians 12:7–10; Galatians 4:13), it is better to view this gift as subject to the will of God, not the will of people. A person may be gifted to heal many people, but not all. Another may be gifted to heal only one person at one particular time of one particular disease.

I raise this because I've been in situations where a person has been asked to pray for the sick and they've said: "I can't. I don't have the gift of healing." If my reading of Paul is correct, there is no such thing as *the* gift of healing, if by that one means the God-given ability to heal everyone of every disease on every occasion. Rather, the Spirit sovereignly distributes a *charisma* of healing for a particular occasion, even though previous prayers for physical restoration under similar circumstances may not have been answered, and even though subsequent prayers for the same affliction may not be answered. In other words, "gifts of healings" are occasional and subject to the sovereign purposes of God.

Few doubt that Paul had a "gift" for healing. But his prayers for Epaphroditus weren't answered, at least not at first (see Philippians 2:25–30). Clearly, Paul could not heal at will. And aside from Jesus, no one else could either! Even Jesus had limitations from the Father on how and when he could heal (read John 5:19; Mark 6:5–6). Some might conclude from Paul's failure to heal his friend that "the gift of healing" was "dying out" at this juncture in the life of the church (in spite of the fact that late in his ministry in Acts 28:9, Paul apparently healed everyone on the island of Malta who came to him). But I think it better to conclude that healing, whenever and wherever it occurred, was subject not to the will of man but to the will of God. No one, not even Paul, could always heal all diseases. If Paul was distressed that Epaphroditus was ill, almost unto death, and that initially his prayers for him were ineffective, I doubt seriously if the apostle would have drawn the same conclusions that modern cessationists do. Paul understood the occasional nature of gifts of healings.

The fact that healing is an expression of divine mercy (Philippians 2:27) means that it should never be viewed as a right. Healing is not the payment of a debt. God does not *owe* us healing. We don't deserve healing. I believe we should have faith for healing, but there is a vast difference between faith in divine mercy and presumption based on an alleged right.

The word "mercy" is the same one used in the gospels to describe why Jesus healed people while he was on the earth. God's motive for healing hasn't changed! The primary reason God healed through Jesus prior to Pentecost was because he is a merciful, compassionate God. And the primary reason God continues to heal after Pentecost is because he is a merciful, compassionate God. God is no less merciful, no less compassionate, no less caring when it comes to the physical condition of his people after Pentecost than he was before Pentecost.

The Practice of Healing Prayer[1]

We now turn to the actual practice of healing prayer. What I suggest here is fairly simple, perhaps so much so that you may wonder if something else, something more mysterious, is called for. I don't believe so.

The first step in healing prayer is the *interview*. When someone comes to you for prayer, don't be quick to speak. Listen. Ask questions. Ask the person: "Where does it hurt? How long have you struggled with this affliction? What did the doctor say? How can I help? Is your problem primarily physical or emotional or spiritual? Are you under attack from Satan?" Gaining clear answers to these questions will help you when it comes time to pray.

But the person for whom you are praying isn't the only one you should ask. Ask the Holy Spirit as well. And ask the person in need of healing to ask the Spirit, too. Don't be in a hurry. Give yourself time to listen. Be especially careful how you use whatever prompting or insights you believe the Spirit has given. As we'll see later when dealing with the prophetic, avoid such highly charged language as, "Well, God told me just now to tell you . . ."

The second step in this process is what I call the *diagnosis*.

---

1 A shorter, somewhat abbreviated version of what follows first appeared in my book *The Beginner's Guide to Spiritual Gifts*, 205–210.

The focus is to determine, if possible, what is the cause or source of the condition. Often, the causes could be a combination of several factors. Merely living in a fallen world in which we are regularly exposed to viruses, bacteria, as well as accidents of a variety of sorts could be responsible. There is also the ever-present reality of personal sin (cf. James 5 and John 9). But be careful in pinpointing sin as the sole cause or overemphasizing it. You don't want to compound their problem with accusations that might put unwarranted guilt on their hearts. In James 5:15 the brother of our Lord says, regarding the person for whom prayer is offered, "and *if* he has committed sins," sins most likely that are responsible for his affliction, he will be forgiven. James doesn't presume to know if this is the cause, but it may be.

On occasion the problem will be emotional, deriving from the stress and pressures of daily life. Anxiety and unforgiveness may combine to contribute to physical weakness and other diseases. The cause of the sickness may be traced to their family history, which is to say that genetic factors may have contributed to the affliction. Then there are dysfunctional habits and relational sins to which they were exposed during the course of their upbringing.

Sometimes the cause of the affliction may be demonic. Jesus ministered to a woman who for eighteen years was afflicted by a "disabling spirit." "She was bent over and could not fully straighten herself" (Luke 13:11). When the Pharisees objected to his healing her on the Sabbath, he rebuked them with a question: "Ought not this woman, a daughter of Abraham whom Satan bound for eighteen years, be loosed from this bond on the Sabbath day?" (Luke 13:16).

Of course, there will be numerous instances when we simply don't know the cause of the affliction. We must be careful about drawing direct cause and effect conclusions about why a particular person suffers from a particular disease. There's no benefit to be gained in trying to be smarter than the Holy Spirit! And there's no reason to think that God would be disinclined to heal someone simply because we are ignorant of the cause or source of the disease.

There is one other situation that I want to bring to your attention. I was once asked by an extremely overweight lady to pray for pain in both her lower back and knees. When I asked if she had visited a doctor, she said yes. "He told me that it was almost certain that my excessive weight was the precipitating cause of both the pain in my back and in my knees." When I asked her about her struggle with weight, she confessed that it was due to gluttony. There didn't appear to be any other physiological or bio-chemical factors that made weight gain unavoidable.

So what ought one to do in a case like this? I certainly did not want to intensify her feelings of guilt, but the clear fact was that her lack of self-control had contributed directly to her physical discomfort. Should we pray for God to heal a physical affliction that is likely the immediate effect of a willful pattern of sinful choices? What about the person with emphysema who cannot quit a smoking habit? There is no easy answer to this conundrum. My best counsel is that one should begin with an attempt to get at the underlying root of sin or addiction in a person's life, followed by a call to repentance and encouragement to make certain alterations in one's habits of life and choices. My initial prayer for this woman was for the strength of the Holy Spirit to enable her to make substantive changes in her eating habits. Following this, I proceeded to pray for relief from the pain in both her back and her knees.

After the interview and the diagnosis, it's time to *pray*, the third step. Your prayer may take one of several different forms. The most common prayer is petition directed toward God: "Heavenly Father, in the name of your Son and our Savior, Jesus Christ, we ask that you heal your child of this affliction." I would also recommend that you be as specific as possible. Name the affliction. Ask the Holy Spirit to impart his healing power directly into or on that portion of the person's body.

There is not only prayer to God but also prayer *from* God as well. What I have in mind is the confident, Spirit-empowered command of faith in which you are led to declare: "In the name of Jesus, be healed!" Notice that I did not say, and neither should you, "In the name of Jesus, I declare that you *are* healed." If it has been determined, so far as one is able, that the cause of the affliction is demonic, one is fully justified in issuing the command: "In the name of Jesus, I command every demonic spirit to leave this child of God. Be gone and never return!" (See Luke 10:17–20). In all this, avoid thinking that God will not heal unless you say it just right or with perfect grammar or in a theologically sophisticated way. God is primarily concerned with the attitude of your heart and your compassion for the hurting and your dependence on him, not the style or sophistication with which you pray.

There are also some specific, concrete practices that I suggest you employ. For example, if possible, ask the person to close her eyes, but keep yours open. There may be physiological responses that you need to observe that will inform and guide the way you continue to pray (trembling, deep breathing, weeping, etc.). Don't rush. Spend time with them. Linger long in prayer. Be patient. If you sense or see God doing something, bless it! Be aware of possible (though not necessary) physical manifestations, as people will often report things such as tingling, spasms, warmth in the area where the affliction is located, perhaps even the alleviation of pain, which often comes gradually, in stages, rather than instantaneously. You may observe ever-so-slight trembling or deep breathing. On occasion the person will begin to weep.

When such phenomena begin to occur, it proves helpful to ask questions of the person for whom you are praying, such as: "How do you feel?" "Do you sense God is doing something?" "Are you experiencing an increase in your faith, or are you struggling with doubt or fear?" Depending on their answer, adjust your prayers appropriately. Don't be frustrated if they aren't feeling anything.

Finally, an important element is the laying on of hands. If a man is praying for a woman, or vice versa (it is always good if more than one is present if this is the case), never touch them between the knees and the neck (unless they suffer from back pain and they consent to have you place your hand there). Always ask them first before you lay hands on them ("Is it ok with you?"). I would also recommend that you consider anointing them with oil.

One of the reasons people in the church today disregard healing is because they disregard the body. They believe that to focus on the health and wellbeing of the body (at least to the degree that you would regularly pray for its healing) is misguided. Our attention is to be more "spiritual" as we focus on the condition of our souls. This is little more than a modern version of the ancient heresy of *gnosticism*.

The biblical view of the body, on the other hand, is quite positive. God created us as physical beings. We are both material and immaterial (see Genesis 2:7). The importance of the body is extensively illustrated in 1 Corinthians chapter 6. Our *bodies* were redeemed by the blood of Christ, no less than our souls (v. 20). Our *bodies* are the temples of the Holy Spirit (v. 19). Our *bodies* are designed "for the Lord" (v. 13). Our *bodies* are members of Christ himself (v. 15). Our *bodies* are capable of being sinned against (v. 18). Our *bodies* are to be used to honor God (v. 20). Finally, our bodies will be resurrected and glorified. In other words, we will spend eternity as *physically* glorified beings (see Romans 8:11, 23; 1 Corinthians 15:35–49). At the judgment seat of Christ, we will have to give an account for what we have done *in our bodies*.

There is no escaping the fact that *spirituality is physical*. Although God is spirit, he created the physical, material world and pronounced it *good* (Genesis 1:4, 12, 18, 21, 25). When God created us in his image, he gave us bodies.

On several occasions Jesus healed people with the spoken word alone. But in most instances he did so by laying his hands on them or making physical contact.[2] Perhaps the most amazing text of all is Luke 4:40, where it is said that Jesus laid hands on "every one" of those in a vast multitude who had come to him for aid. It must have been physically exhausting and time intensive for him to do so, but Jesus took the opportunity to lay his hands on every person who came to him for prayer.

You may conclude with what we might call *post-prayer directions*. Emphasize that healing is a process. If nothing happens instantaneously, the person may feel discouraged. They may blame themselves. So encourage them with the fact that God often moves slowly to test our faith and to call us to persevere in prayer. If you are wondering if there is ever a point at which you should cease praying for someone to be healed, I can only respond with the words of my friend Jack Taylor: "Never stop praying unless shown otherwise by divine revelation or death!" We all know what he meant by the word "death." As for divine revelation, he was reminding us of Paul's experience in 2 Corinthians 12. After what were most likely three extended seasons of intercession, the Lord finally told Paul as definitively as possible: "No. I'm not going to remove your thorn in the flesh. My grace is sufficient for you." Short of that sort of unmistakable instruction or the death of the one for whom you are praying, never stop praying!

Never suggest the problem or the reason they were not healed is their lack of faith. It *may* be that, but it is not for you to say. It could just as easily be *your* lack of faith that accounts for why nothing has happened. Or, as we've seen, it may not be related to anyone's faith at all.

Let the individual talk about how they feel. Ask them if they

2 See Matthew 8:15; 9:18–25, 27–31; 14:36; 17:7; 19:13–15; Mark 1:40–42; 5:21–24; 6:1–6, 56; 7:31–35; 8:22–25; 9:27; 16:18; Luke 13:10–13; 22:51; 24:50. Also note the practice of the early church in Acts 3:7; 5:12; 6:6; 8:17–19; 9:10–17, 41; 11:30; 13:1–3; 14:3; 19:11; 28:7–8. This emphasis is also found in 1 Timothy 4:14; 5:22; 2 Timothy 1:6 (cf. Numbers 27:15–23; Deuteronomy 34:9).

are encouraged, discouraged, filled with doubt or with faith. Do they feel the love of God or a sense of condemnation and failure? Address their response in a loving and biblical way, and then pray yet again for their healing! It may be necessary for you to direct them to follow through on any necessary confession of sin or reconciliation with someone else. As noted earlier, lingering unforgiveness and deep bitterness or resentment toward another can contribute to physiological ailments. Encourage them to come again and seek prayer from you (or others) as often as they wish. Make sure they know that they can come to you more than once. Asking for prayer again (and again and again) is not a sign of a lack of faith. Neither is it nagging God! Regardless of the outcome, don't ever think you have failed! The degree of healing or relief is not the measure of success: obedience is.

CHAPTER 6

IDENTIFYING PROPHECY IN THE LOCAL CHURCH

The most important (and most challenging) spiritual gift to practice and employ in the local church today for the edification of all in the body is prophecy. So I want to begin with some clarification that goes beyond what I've written elsewhere (see the *Beginner's Guide to Spiritual Gifts*). Following this I will articulate some practical guidelines for how prophecy and other revelatory gifts can be implemented in both the corporate gathering of the church and in small group settings.

Is It Prophecy?

One of the more important aspects in prophetic ministry in the local church is bringing understanding to people concerning the nature of the prophetic itself. That is to say, one must devote substantial energy to helping people discern the difference between a "prophetic" word, on the one hand, and a spoken word of exhortation or encouragement, on the other.

What is prophecy? I define prophecy as *the human report of a divine revelation*. Prophecy is the speaking forth in merely human words of something God has spontaneously brought to mind. Now, make no mistake, a word of exhortation or encouragement *may* be an instance of prophetic revelation. In 1 Corinthians 14:30 Paul describes what appears to be an "ordinary" church service where prophetic ministry is encouraged and facilitated. If one person is sharing a prophetic word and a "revelation" comes to another who is seated and silent, the person currently speaking should cease and "yield the floor" to the one to whom the revelation just came. Without getting into the specifics of how this works yet, my point is that Paul speaks of prophecy as *revelation*. All genuine prophetic ministry is based upon or flows from a "revelation" from God. But what does that mean? I find it helpful to contrast the experience of receiving a "revelation" with that of normal, routine experiences of moral conviction and illumination.

In 1 Corinthians 14:3 Paul says that prophecy is given to the church so that people might experience "upbuilding" (or edification), "encouragement," and "consolation." The problem we encounter is that virtually any time a person is instructed or built up in their faith by something a person shares with them, they are both inclined to identify what was said as prophetic. Or again, there are countless ways in which a believer can encourage another believer or can bring consolation to bear on their hearts. A simple prayer on behalf of someone who is hurting can bring consolation. Hearing a sermon in which a particular biblical text is explained and artfully applied can encourage people in their relationship with Christ. But that doesn't mean the prayer or the sermon are, properly speaking, a prophecy.

The bottom line is that *we must not draw conclusions about the cause based solely on the effect*. Many activities in the local church produce the same effect. But that does not necessarily mean they were the fruit of the same cause. Prophecy will always build up, encourage, and console, but not everything that builds up, encourages, and consoles is prophetic.

This may come as a surprise to some people, and I hope they do not find it discouraging. I have in mind those who may have been used by God to speak a word that engendered hope in the life of another Christian who had fallen into despair. Or perhaps a brother or sister in Christ is set free from the enslaving power of unforgiveness because of the timely reminder from another of how God has forgiven us in Christ. Or a worship leader may pause in the middle of a song and drive home in an especially powerful way the truth of a particular line that he has just sung. All of these are wonderful ways in which God uses believers to build up and encourage other believers, which should be embraced and encouraged.

But they should not all be considered prophetic.

Of course, all of this is wonderful. It happens countless times every week at my church, Bridgeway, here in Oklahoma City. Not long ago a prophetically gifted man came to me following my sermon on James 2:1–13 with a word about how we should conduct our post-service prayer ministry.

He had the wisdom not to start by saying, "Sam, I believe I have a prophetic word from the Lord." If he had, others might have concluded that his advice was prophetic. But I sensed that it wasn't. The text we were discussing focused on the subject of prejudice and the resultant partiality with which the early church treated people who were financially successful. I applied the principle of the passage to the subject of racial prejudice, and the man who approached me said, "Sam, I sense that it would be good if we could pray for people who've been the object of racial violence or prejudice." I agreed with him completely. In fact, at the earlier service that morning I had led our post-sermon prayer time by focusing on precisely that point of application.

So what happened here? The man who approached me during the second service felt moved by the Spirit to focus our prayer on behalf of people who had suffered in this way. It's a natural response to have these thoughts and feelings to this particular biblical text. But should we have concluded that this was a divine revelation and that our subsequent exhortation and appeal to people was of the nature of a prophetic word? No, I don't think so. I believe God honored our obedience and that several people were blessed and helped by the prayers they received from our intercessory ministry team. The effect or fruit of what happened in our hearts was the encouragement and consolation of others, in particular those who may have been the target of racial hatred. But that doesn't lead me to conclude that this was a spontaneous revelation from the Spirit.

Sometimes pastors or leaders call these instances prophetic because they want to encourage people to speak up and share what they are thinking or feeling. They don't want to discourage people who are excited that they finally heard from God in this way. So they put the word "prophetic" on an encouraging or instructive word or idea, and it seems to elevate the significance of what occurred beyond an ordinary encouragement or consolation. To be clear, I'm not suggesting that we didn't hear or sense the prompting of the Spirit. I'm simply saying that the mere fact that it was the Spirit who prompted us does not shift the nature of such activity out of the realm of what we might call natural and into the supernatural sphere of prophetic ministry.

Related to this is another common activity in our church. Many times during a service or at the close of a service a man or woman will approach me and say something along the lines of: "I have a real burden from the Lord that . . ." Or, "I'm sensing that the Spirit is saying that we should . . ." Or, "Your sermon prompted a deep conviction in my heart that I think I'm supposed to share with the entire church."

Perhaps you've experienced this as well. Are any of these an instance of what the New Testament refers to as "prophetic"? Perhaps. I don't want to rule out the possibility that what a person has "sensed" or claims to have "heard" came from a spontaneous revelation of the Spirit of God. But more often than not, I suspect that what has happened should be categorized or described in different, but not any less spiritual, terms. Most, if not all, of us have experienced deep conviction of the truth of something the preacher proclaims. It may be a promise in God's Word that the Spirit drives home to our hearts, delivering us from feelings of hopelessness. Or it may be a command in God's Word that suddenly awakens us to the fact that we've been living in disobedience to the Lord. Or there are moments when the exegesis of a text and its vivid application serve to remind us of what God has done, and we feel overwhelmed with gratitude. Perhaps our feeling of gratitude is so stunning and heartfelt that we draw the conclusion that everyone present needs to hear again the truth that first evoked it in our hearts.

But simply because the Holy Spirit is the instigator or initial cause of such mental and emotional reactions does not mean we are dealing with prophetic revelation. So what, then, should we call such experiences? There are several possible answers. In Ephesians 1:15–22 Paul prays for the Ephesian church and asks that "the God of our Lord Jesus Christ, the Father of glory," might "give" them "the Spirit of wisdom and of revelation in the knowledge of him." By this he means that "the eyes" of their "hearts" would be "enlightened" so that they might understand with greater force and clarity the "hope" to which he has called them (and us!).

I don't believe Paul is praying for the gift of prophecy in this passage, although prayers for prophetic gifts or insight are perfectly legitimate. He is simply praying that the Spirit would bring wisdom and insight into the immense blessings that we have in Jesus Christ, as well as the hope that his life, death, and resurrection have brought us. Don't be misled by Paul's use of the word "revelation." Not all revelation is the sort of spontaneous disclosure that he has in view in 1 Corinthians 14:30 or the sort of revelation that was accompanied with the inspiration and eventual canonization of biblical texts.

The Holy Spirit can reveal something to a Christian in the sense that he can enlighten or illumine the mind so that we understand more clearly some truth that before was obscure or remote. It is almost as if the Spirit turns on a light in a dark room, so that we might vividly see and appreciate the furniture that was always present, or at least enable us to enjoy and take advantage of the furniture that we always knew was there. Paul uses the word "revelation" in this way in Philippians 3:15. There he is describing people in the church at Philippi who embraced an opinion different from that of the apostle. He doesn't appear to limit it to any one particular doctrine or truth but says, "and if in anything you think otherwise, God will reveal that also to you."

Here the verb "to reveal" does not describe what God does when he makes known to apostles that Word which would later become inspired and inerrant Scripture. We know this because he's addressing average, ordinary believers in the body of Christ in first-century Philippi. I dare say that none of them ever became the author of a book of the Bible. The revelation that Paul has in view is neither canonical nor the sort that forms the basis of a prophetic word. It is simply Paul's way of assuring them (and us) that God will enable believers to understand and properly respond to the inspired instruction that Paul is giving in the letter.

We see a similar idea in 2 Timothy 2:7. There Paul doesn't use the word "reveal" or "revelation" but says this: "Think over what I say, for the Lord will give you understanding in everything." Now, what is involved in this giving of understanding? We don't know, but I think a good guess can be made. I believe Paul is saying much the same thing he said in Ephesians 1 and in Philippians 3, namely, that the Holy Spirit works mysteriously in our minds to shed light on or illumine the meaning of some truth.

Now, let's return to the example I mentioned earlier of the individuals who come to me after a service feeling impressed or moved or touched by a song or biblical text or event in the church service. Could it be that they have been the recipients of revelation that is the basis for a prophetic utterance? Yes, it's possible. But more times than not, I suspect that what they've experienced is the Spirit working to enlighten or illumine them concerning some truth or ethical principle in Scripture. It may be that the Spirit has brought conviction to their hearts as to how they might be falling short in their responsibilities. It might be as simple as a Christian man or woman reflecting on a biblical truth or remembering some great work of God in their own life or the life of someone they know.

So how do we recognize the difference between the two? There's no simple answer to that question. What we are seeking for are criteria or means by which we can know the difference between a spontaneous revelation from the Spirit that forms the basis of a subsequent prophetic word and the normal, routine, and quite common work of the Spirit in enlightening and convicting and reassuring Christians of various truths and promises in God's Word.

However, before we identify the criteria to differentiate spontaneous revelation from the normal, routine work of illumination, let me provide several typical scenarios.

A woman listens attentively to a message on Isaiah 6 and is deeply moved by the revelation of God's holiness. She feels intensely in her heart the same reverence for God's transcendent beauty, she is deeply convicted of her own sinful ways, and she cries out much as the prophet did in desperation for forgiveness. She begins to sense that all God's people should be alerted to this same truth. And of course, they should. So she approaches the designated point person in a corporate assembly and says: "I've never been so powerfully touched by the biblical portrayal of God's holiness and our sinful distance from him. The Lord has brought me to tearful confession and repentance for my sin, and I sense that all God's people need to be made aware of precisely what has so powerfully affected me."

What are we to make of this? At one level, what she has experienced is perfectly biblical, indeed, admirable. And yes, it is something that all Christians should likewise feel as they reflect on the majesty of God's utter otherness, his holiness, his moral majesty. But on another level we must ask, is this conviction of sin and this recognition of the need for God's gracious forgiveness a revelation that calls for prophetic utterance? Possibly, but not likely.

Or consider another example. A teenaged boy is pierced to the heart by the words of Paul in 1 Thessalonians 4:3 that we should "abstain from sexual immorality." He himself is not guilty of such sin, but he knows many of his friends who freely indulge in fornication. His heart is broken and he longs for them to repent and be put right in their relationship with the Lord. The burden becomes almost more than he can bear, until he shares it with his youth pastor. The latter believes this is a word for the entire church, the youth group especially. The response that follows this teenager's urgent plea for purity of life is remarkable, and something of a revival breaks out among the church's youth.

So what just happened? There is nothing in the least inappropriate with what the young man felt or in what he subsequently shared when given the platform. Many were rightly convicted of their sin. Many gloriously repented and renewed their commitment to Christ. They were exhorted. They were rebuked. They were encouraged. They regained their hope and were set on the path to renewed intimacy with Jesus. But were they the beneficiaries of a prophetic word? Perhaps. But the greater likelihood is that from one young man's conviction and zeal they were alerted and awakened to a foundational biblical truth. There was no revelation in the technical sense of the term. It wasn't that God had disclosed something heretofore unknown to the young man, or to any other believer who carefully might read the text in 1 Thessalonians 4. Certainly the Spirit enlightened his mind and convicted his conscience and energized him with courage to speak truth to his friends. But that doesn't make it a prophecy.

One more thing is essential to keep in mind. The fact that the previous instances may not have been examples of biblical prophecy does not in any way mean that it was inappropriate for them to be given a microphone and a platform from which to speak their concerns. This is a perfectly legitimate means to encourage and appeal to the body of Christ. But the personal conviction of the teenaged boy, for example, did not suddenly turn into a prophecy simply because he took what was initially an internal sense and made it a public declaration. All prophecy is indeed public declaration (although it can be one-on-one as well). But it is only prophecy if it is based on a spontaneous revelation from God.

In one particular case, I was approached by a lady who had been meditating on 1 Peter 1:8 and was overcome with the very "inexpressible" joy of which Peter speaks. She desperately wanted others to experience what God had wrought in her, and understandably and rightly so. When she was given the microphone she said: "I believe I have a prophetic word for all of you. God wants you to be filled with inexpressible and ineffable joy and to know more deeply both how much God loves you and also to feel even greater love for God in your own heart."

Does the fact that she felt she was prophesying and that this is indeed something God wants for all his children make this a prophecy? No. It is more likely an illustration of what we've been talking about in this chapter: a Christian who has been profoundly moved by the truth of God's Word and his love for his people that is so intense and life-changing that she can't help but do everything in her power to share it with others. And that's good! Would that there were more instances of such experiences. But nothing in this experience necessarily requires that we refer to what happened as revelation or her public delivery of it as prophecy.

It's not uncommon for people who've been touched in this way by a biblical text or truth or through the convicting ministry of the Spirit to feel that not to share the word on their heart would be sin. "I would be disobedient if I didn't share what God has shown me," said one young lady. "I'm not the sort who enjoys being in the public eye and I'm not a good speaker, but this is so real to me right now that I can't back down from what I believe God is calling me to do. It would be an injustice to the people for them to be deprived of what I honestly believe God is saying to all of us right now."

That scenario makes it especially difficult for the person who is leading the meeting, whether a corporate gathering on Sunday morning or a small group in someone's home. How do you say in response: "I'm sure you've sensed the truth today, and I know it weighs heavily on your heart. But that alone does not mean you've been the recipient of a prophetic revelation. The intensity of the experience is to be expected, but nowhere in the Bible are we told that the degree in which we feel the truth or the extent to which we are moved, perhaps even to tears, is a criterion for determining if it is supernatural and revelatory."

We need to understand that what I have described thus far is the normal, routine work of the Spirit in which he enlightens us to the meaning of Scripture and convicts us of some shortcoming in our lives or awakens us to the urgent need to pay close attention to some pressing issue in the church. Such experiences have been confused with the more overtly supernatural revelatory ministry in which heretofore unknown ideas or facts about a person, persons, or a situation is disclosed to an individual in such a way that it clearly is designed for public proclamation. The problem is that many Christians have collapsed the two into one. Thus, when the former occurs they instinctively assume it is the latter.

What, Then, Is Prophecy?

Prophecy is difficult to define because the New Testament never gives us a straightforward definition. Paul speaks of the gift as if everyone reading his epistles already knows what he has in mind. This problem is compounded when we realize that other revelatory gifts such as word of knowledge, word of wisdom, and perhaps discerning of spirits are not defined either. We are left to draw our conclusions based on those instances where the gift seems to be in operation. So the definition I offer is based on my synthesis and interpretation of various New Testament texts.

I will add that I don't think it is especially important to differentiate among the revelatory gifts, the distinctions between prophecy and word of knowledge, for example. Any nuance here is unknown to us and probably of secondary significance. If the New Testament authors thought these distinctions were important to know, I'm sure we'd have a more precise account of what they are. But I do think it is important that we define prophecy as I've stated here, as *the human report of a divine revelation*. Again, prophecy is the speaking forth in merely human words of something God has spontaneously brought to mind.[1]

This definition is found in several places in the New Testament. Recall Jesus' encounter with the Samaritan woman in John 4. She was to Jesus a complete stranger, yet he speaks to her of past indiscretions and the fact that she is currently living with a man who is not her husband. Her response is to say: "Sir, I perceive that you are a prophet" (John 4:19). Although we should not simply equate what Jesus did here with what Paul will later call the spiritual gift of prophecy (after all, spiritual gifts were not imparted to the church until the day of Pentecost), this seems analogous to what Paul had in mind. It also tells us that prophecy was perceived as the disclosure to a person of facts that could not be otherwise known from natural causes or sources. I suspect that what happened here is that the Holy Spirit revealed to Jesus this information about the woman. Contrary to what many have said, Jesus didn't know these things about her because he was God (though he is, of course) but because the Spirit revealed them to him.[2]

Or consider a passage from Paul's first letter to the Corinthians that confirms this understanding of the prophetic. Here Paul describes a typical gathering of the local church and says:

---

1 I first heard this definition of prophecy from my friend Wayne Grudem. See his book *The Gift of Prophecy in the New Testament and Today* (Wheaton, Ill.: Crossway, 2000).

2 I address this subject at length in my book *Tough Topics 2: Biblical Answers to 25 Challenging Questions* (Ross-shire, Scotland: Christian Focus Publications, 2015). See the chapter, "How Did Jesus Perform His Miracles?" pp. 47–62.

> But if all prophesy, and an unbeliever or outsider enters, he is convicted by all, he is called to account by all, the secrets of his heart are disclosed, and so, falling on his face, he will worship God and declare that God is really among you. (1 Corinthians 14:24–25)

Inasmuch as Paul says that "*all* prophesy," it is likely that the "all" by whom this unbeliever is convicted as well as the "all" by whom he is called to account are the people in the church at Corinth who prophesy. The "unbeliever" or "outsider" who is not known to the congregation has secret sins that are in some way revealed to the believers present, who in turn speak what God has made known and bring this man to saving faith.

A few verses later in the same chapter of 1 Corinthians, Paul gives guidelines for the exercise of both tongues and prophecy. With regard to prophecy he says:

> If a revelation is made to another sitting there, let the first be silent. For you all prophesy one by one, so that all may learn and all be encouraged, and the spirits of prophets are subject to prophets. (1 Corinthians 14:30–32)

What this text clearly indicates is that prophecy is based on or flows out of a spontaneous revelation from God to the believer. The difference is that *teaching* is based on a written text. Prophecy is based on the revelatory activity of the Spirit that coincides with Scripture but goes beyond scripture with specific application to an individual.

The narrative of Acts gives us other examples of the gift of prophecy in operation. For example in Acts 5:1–11, we read the story of Ananias and his wife Sapphira. Their secret decision to keep back for themselves some of the proceeds from the sale of land prompts Peter's surprising declaration:

> "Ananias, why has Satan filled your heart to lie to the Holy Spirit and to keep back for yourself part of the proceeds of the land? While it remained unsold, did it not remain your own? And after it was sold, was it not at your disposal? Why is that you have contrived this deed in your heart? You have not lied to man but to God." (Acts 5:3–4)

How did Peter come by this knowledge? How did he discern that Ananias had "contrived" this deed in his "heart" and subsequently "lied" to the Holy Spirit? And by what means did Peter later confront his wife, Sapphira, with the same information? I can only surmise that God revealed this information to Peter, which he then spoke to the couple, to their demise.

What we see here in Acts 5 is not unlike what we saw in John 4. In both cases information not otherwise obtainable was revealed and subsequently spoken. Is this not also what happened in the case of the conversion and healing of Saul/Paul? Here we see that the revelation came to Ananias in a "vision." He was told where he should go to find Saul and what he should say to him (Acts 9:10–12). Surely Ananias prophesied things to Saul/Paul that he could only have known by virtue of a spontaneous revelation from the Holy Spirit.

The experience of Agabus is clearly an example of the predictive use of prophecy and need not detain us (see Acts 11:27–30). But again in Acts 13, we likely see the spiritual gift of prophecy in exercise. There, while the people of God are gathered in prayer and praise, the Holy Spirit speaks: "Set apart for me Barnabas and Saul for the work to which I have called them" (v. 2). We are told in verse 1 that there were both "prophets and teachers" present. Since this is not an example of teaching, it seems probable that the revelation came to one or more of the "prophets" who in turn communicated this word to those gathered. The result was the launching of Paul's missionary journeys that would lead to the spread of Christianity throughout the ancient world.

One of the first encounters that Paul and Barnabas had as a result of this prophetic word was with "a certain magician, a Jewish false prophet named Bar-Jesus" (Acts 13:6). This man "opposed" Paul and sought to turn the proconsul away from the faith. Then we read that

> Saul, who was also called Paul, filled with the Holy Spirit, looked intently at him and said, "You son of the devil, you enemy of all righteousness, full of all deceit and villainy, will you not stop making crooked the straight paths of the Lord? And now, behold, the hand of the Lord is upon you, and you will be blind and unable to see the sun for a time." Immediately mist and darkness fell upon him, and he went about seeking people to lead him by the hand. (Acts 13:9–11)

How did Paul come by this discernment, this insight into the nature and motivation of the magician? Since the text explicitly says that before speaking he was "filled with the Holy Spirit," it only stands to reason that the Spirit revealed this to him spontaneously, in response to which Paul spoke (prophesied).

An example of where it is unclear whether the prophetic gift is employed happened while Paul was in Lystra and encountered a man "who could not use his feet. He was crippled from birth and had never walked" (Acts 14:8). As he listened to Paul speak, the apostle is described as "seeing that he had faith to be made well" (Acts 14:9). Paul then tells him to stand upright, and he was instantly healed. How did Paul see this? We don't know. Perhaps the Spirit revealed something about the man in a vision to Paul. Perhaps he impressed on Paul's heart the knowledge of the man's faith to be healed. In any case, it would appear that again Paul spoke what the Spirit spontaneously revealed. Whether or not this was a case of prophecy is hard to tell. It may be more akin to a word of knowledge, but we simply aren't told.

Here is what I take away from these examples. Unlike those scenarios I described in the earlier half of this chapter, prophecy is *always* based upon a revelation from the Spirit of God. It is not the same as enlightenment or illumination from the Spirit, which quickens and enables us to more deeply understand and appreciate the truths of God's Word. Rather in prophecy, the Holy Spirit supernaturally discloses information, facts, or insights not otherwise available by natural avenues of knowledge.

Two Remarkable, Real-Life Illustrations

Two additional illustrations of this come from individuals in my own church. I was present when the first incident occurred, as were several hundred other people, and the facts have been repeatedly confirmed by the parties involved.

We have two Sunday services at Bridgeway, one at 9:00 a.m. and the other at 11:00 a.m. During our time of singing at the first service, I was approached by one of our elders who has a strong track record of accuracy in prophetic ministry. He said, "Sam, I have a strong sense that the Lord has revealed something to me for a woman here today." I told him to return to the platform at the conclusion of the service so that he could deliver this word of prophecy/knowledge. Here is the gist of what he said:

> "The Lord impressed on my heart this morning that there is a woman present who visited her doctor about ten days ago. The prognosis given was not encouraging. The initials 'SJ' have some connection to this doctor. I'd like to pray for you today. You also have a young son who suffers from asthma. I would like to pray for him also if you'll come forward."

A woman was present that day who instantly identified with the content of that word. But it was surprising that she happened to be in the 9:00 a.m. service. In the first place, because of an extended and extremely painful illness, she had not even been at a Sunday service in several months. And when she had been able in the past to attend, she always came to the 11:00 service. In fact, she had *never* attended the earlier service. That morning she told her husband that she simply "had" to go to church, no matter the pain. But for some inexplicable reason, she felt that she should attend the 9:00 a.m. gathering.

When she heard the "word" she immediately made an effort to come forward. She struggled with her steps and barely made it to the front. She informed the man who had delivered the word that she had been to her doctor ten days earlier! More than that, although she didn't immediately make the connection with the initials "SJ", she looked in her purse at her prescription bottle and noticed that indeed those were the initials of her physician! And yes, she happened to have a young son who suffered badly with asthma.

Following prayer for her healing and that of her son, she struggled to make her way back to her seat. After the service, she made her way to the nursery to pick up her other children and noticed that her pain had diminished significantly. By the time she reached her car in the parking lot, she was entirely pain-free and remains so to this day. And yes, her young son was also instantly and completely healed of his asthma.

This is the sort of phenomenon that I would be inclined to label as a revelatory gift, be it prophecy or word of knowledge. That isn't to say that every time prophecy functions in the local church that it will be as specific and accurate as this one was. It is to suggest that what differentiates revelatory gifts from the sort of routine awakening, conviction, or enlightenment described earlier in this chapter is the specificity of the information that would not appear to be obtainable by ordinary or natural means. Keeping this distinction in mind will serve to facilitate the public and private exercise of prophecy and make the latter more readily distinguishable from the ordinary, less miraculous activity of the Holy Spirit.

The second incident I wish to share took place more recently, several thousand miles away from our church in Oklahoma City. We had sent a team of ten people to Kenya on a short-term mission trip. One of those who went was a lady who serves as the coordinator for our children's ministry at Bridgeway. I'll call her "Karen." She is remarkably mature, stable, and is not the sort who would regularly lay claim to some sensationalistic encounter with the supernatural. In fact, by her own testimony, she often struggled with doubt and was more than a little cynical when it came to claims of the miraculous.

After arriving in Kenya, the team spent time in prayer one evening in preparation for a journey into the slums the next day. They prayed that God would grant guidance, protection, as well as prophetic revelation on how and to whom they might minister. Karen suddenly heard in her head a name she had never encountered before: "Naomi Istakino."[3] When I say she heard this name, she explained that it was in her own voice but decidedly not from herself. It was, for lack of a better way of describing it, the "internal audible" voice of God. She tried to regain her composure and prayed, "Lord, what was that again?" Once more she heard these words: "Naomi Istakino."

It's important to know that this lady from Bridgeway had never once in her Christian life ever heard from God in this fashion. She had never received a word of knowledge. Hence her great surprise. She again prayed that God would confirm what she knew she had heard. Suddenly there appeared, as it were, on the inside of her closed eyelids in large white letters, "Naomi Istakino."

Karen's immediate response was to share this experience with

3 I've changed the name of the person in order to protect her identity. But I assure you that it is quite similar to the actual name of the young girl.

the others on the team. "Do any of you know anyone by this name?" No, came the unanimous answer. They then contacted one of the directors of the ministry they were there to serve and support and asked if he knew of anyone by that name. Again, the answer was no. He even checked his database to see if anyone by that name had ever had any interaction with their ministry. Again, nothing.

Two days passed and nothing happened. The lady from our church grew increasingly skeptical about her experience. She started to doubt the reality of it all and was on the verge of writing it off as a self-induced delusion. Then, on a Sunday, she heard an excited shout from another female on our team. "Karen! Come here! I want you to meet someone." As Karen approached her friend, standing with her was a young girl who had never before visited the people or the place to whom our team had gone to minister. "Karen," she said with a trembling voice, "this is Naomi Istakino!" She was sixteen years old. Karen, virtually always in control and quite calm, lost it! She leapt in the air and praised God with a loud voice. She almost fainted from joy and surprise.

Naomi didn't quite understand why. Karen then explained to her that she had come from America to help those in need and that God had revealed Naomi's name to her, a name she had never before heard. When the reality of it began to sink into Naomi's heart, she asked what we would all ask: "Why?"

Karen didn't know why. But as they continued to interact with each other, it suddenly came to Karen to say this to Naomi: "I think God just wanted you to know that he knows you. He knows your name. He knows everything about your life. Contrary to what you may have thought, you aren't alone. He knows where you live and what you need. But most of all, he just wants you to know that he cares. He loves you. And I believe he sent me halfway around the world to make it clear to you in a way that is undeniably supernatural and could never have been fabricated by purely natural or human means."

As Karen shared this, she noticed a tear in Naomi's eye that slowly began to trickle down her cheek. Such is the beauty and power and compassion of spiritual gifts in operation.

Some Practical Hints for Practicing Prophetic Gifts

Before we wrap up this introduction to prophecy, let me share a few practical guidelines for moving forward in the pursuit and exercise of these revelatory gifts.

First, acknowledge and embrace from the outset that you can do nothing to force God's hand. Whether or not he reveals something to you for the edification of another is entirely dependent on his will, not yours. If God chooses not to bless you with this gift, rest assured he has other equally important plans for you and how to use you in the life of the church.

In addition, make this a specific and consistent focus of your prayers. Cry out to God daily that he would bless you with this gifting (1 Corinthians 14:1). As I emphasized in the earlier chapters, express your desire for this gift. You might even consider fasting as an expression of your desire for the Lord and his gracious presence to manifest in this way in your life. Be sure to monitor your heart's motivation. In other words, be certain that your longing for this sort of gifting is your love for the welfare of others and not the notoriety or attention that such a gift might bring to you. The Lord gives his gifts to serve the body of Christ, as an expression of his love for his people. We minister in accord with his purposes.

Look for ways to learn from others who are already operating in revelatory gifts. Identify who they are, seek them out, ask them questions, listen to their stories, learn from their mistakes, and be encouraged by their success. In a word, hang out with people of similar passion and who have a track record of accuracy in this gifting. You can also begin learning about the many ways in which God communicates: in dreams, visions, impressions, internal audible voice, symbols, sympathetic pains, providential occurrences, etc.

Don't be surprised or put off if what you hear seems weird, but don't be weird just for the sake of being weird!

Be sure to immerse yourself in God's Word. Meditate on who God is, what he's like, and how he communicated to others in biblical history. This will help you discern whether or not it is God who is speaking. He will never reveal anything to anyone that is inconsistent with his character or his ways. And be attentive to the Spirit of God. Listen! Watch! Write down what you think may be the word of the Spirit. Be attentive to the revelatory language that God might choose to utilize for you. He doesn't always make himself known to everyone in the same way.

If you think God has revealed something to you for the edification of another, first share it in confidence with trusted and mature Christian friends who can help you process what has happened. There is wisdom in the counsel of community. And be willing to risk being wrong. Step out in faith and humility and deliver what is on your heart in words similar to these: "I may have entirely missed this, but I think God may have put something on my heart for you. If this doesn't make any sense, you won't hurt my feelings by telling me so." Resist the temptation to say: "Thus saith the Lord," or "This is the will of God for your life."

There are two things you want to avoid. Be careful about sharing negative or critical words (cf. 1 Corinthians 14:3). As this text from Paul clearly teaches, the purpose of the prophetic is positive. It is designed to build up others, not to tear them down. Also, don't assume that every random thought that passes through your brain is from God. Simply because God may have genuinely revealed something to you in the past does not mean he is always speaking. Exercise discernment and restraint.

Finally, never assume that if God is going to reveal something to you that you will experience some physiological or emotional manifestation. You may, but then again you may not. Some "see" things in their mind's eye. Others "hear" an internal audible voice.

A few will feel something in their own body that corresponds to a need for healing in the body of another. But many times the revelation will come quite naturally, in the normal flow of life. You may discover that your mind is thinking along a certain track and then, without warning, you begin to focus on something altogether different. There is no warning, physiological or otherwise, before or during the time this happens. Your train of thought feels entirely normal to you. It may be that a biblical text comes to mind, or that your attention is directed to a person, or a memory of some past incident comes into conscious thought. When you finally speak to another what is on your heart, you discover, quite to your surprise, that it is precisely what that person needed to hear. Perhaps they were thinking along the same lines. Perhaps the biblical text is one on which they were at that very moment meditating.

I'll close with a personal illustration of this final principle. About twenty-five people from our church had gathered in the home of a friend to worship, pray, and minister to one another. I had no sense or expectation that God would use me in some way to bless another, but I was, of course, open to the possibility. During our time of worship, my mind turned to a couple who had only recently begun to visit Bridgeway. I had known them for quite some time and was delighted that they had chosen to be part of our church. I began to reflect on a word of encouragement (was it a prophecy?) that I had given to the wife when I first met her more than twenty years ago. I felt increasingly stirred to share it with her and to pray for her and her husband.

After our time of singing had ended, I addressed the group as a whole and this lady in particular and told them of the word I had given her so many years earlier. I sensed that God wanted us to pray for her. I prayed that the Spirit might "fan into flame the gift of God" (2 Timothy 1:6) that had been given to her two decades earlier, a gift that by her own later admission she had somewhat neglected. After my prayer I noticed that she was visibly moved.

She then told us all that it had only been within the past two weeks that my word to her, delivered some twenty years ago, had come once again to mind. She had recovered the paper on which she had written down my word of encouragement (prophecy?) and had begun to pray that God would do precisely what I had just prayed on her behalf.

Was my impression that led to this time of prayer a prophetic revelation? Was it a word of knowledge, or perhaps a word of wisdom? I don't know. Frankly, I don't think it matters much. What matters is that she was profoundly encouraged and built up in her faith. What I want to highlight, though, is the manner in which this impression came to me. There was no vision or trance or voice or dream the night before. Physically speaking, I felt nothing. No chills. No goose bumps. No tears or trembling. I saw nothing. I only sensed that we were supposed to pray for God to reawaken this gift in her.

Though my experience is not the final word, I think it has relevance for others as well. When God uses me to prophesy, it rarely feels supernatural. It strikes me as profoundly routine. My suspicion is that this is true for many people who believe in and exercise revelatory gifts of the Spirit. We must guard ourselves from thinking that simply because the experience felt normal and ordinary and far from miraculous that it was therefore only a good guess or a hunch that turned out on target.

God may use the supernatural in an entirely natural way, as a regular and routine part of our daily interaction with him and with other believers. This isn't to dismiss that it is spectacular or amazing or to minimize its glory. It's only to say that the Spirit of God often works in and through us in the mundane affairs and relationships of life, no less so than in the more overtly miraculous circumstances we encounter.

CHAPTER 7

A PARADIGM FOR PROPHETIC PRACTICE

Up to this point in our study of the gift of prophecy and other revelatory gifts, we've looked at a number of *principles* that govern our understanding of what prophecy is and how it operates. But the time has come for us to look more closely at it in actual, real-life *practice*. And there's no better place to start than in Acts 21. Here we come face to face with the way prophecy functioned in the concrete affairs of life and ministry. This narrative is especially helpful in that we find in it an example of how the gift was used in the first century together with the proper response to prophetic words from the Lord and how to process minor mistakes. Let's closely read the narrative as Luke, the author of Acts, supplies it:

> And when we had parted from them and set sail, we came by a straight course to Cos, and the next day to Rhodes, and from there to Patara. And having found a ship crossing to Phoenicia, we went aboard and set sail. When we had come in sight of Cyprus, leaving it on the left we sailed to Syria and landed at Tyre, for there the ship was to unload its cargo. And having sought out the disciples, we stayed there for seven days. And through the Spirit they were telling Paul not to go on to Jerusalem. When our days there were ended, we departed and went on our journey, and they all, with wives and children, accompanied us until we were outside the city. And kneeling down on the beach, we prayed and said farewell to one another. Then we went on board the ship, and they returned home.

When we had finished the voyage from Tyre, we arrived at Ptolemais, and we greeted the brothers and stayed with them for one day. On the next day we departed and came to Caesarea, and we entered the house of Philip the evangelist, who was one of the seven, and stayed with him. He had four unmarried daughters, who prophesied. While we were staying for many days, a prophet named Agabus came down from Judea. And coming to us, he took Paul's belt and bound his own feet and hands and said, "Thus says the Holy Spirit, 'This is how the Jews at Jerusalem will bind the man who owns this belt and deliver him into the hands of the Gentiles.'" When we heard this, we and the people there urged him not to go up to Jerusalem. Then Paul answered, "What are you doing, weeping and breaking my heart? For I am ready not only to be imprisoned but even to die in Jerusalem for the name of the Lord Jesus." And since he would not be persuaded, we ceased and said, "Let the will of the Lord be done."

After these days we got ready and went up to Jerusalem. And some of the disciples from Caesarea went with us, bringing us to the house of Mnason of Cyprus, an early disciple, with whom we should lodge . . .

When the seven days were almost completed, the Jews from Asia, seeing him in the temple, stirred up the whole crowd and laid hands on him, crying out, "Men of Israel, help! This is the man who is teaching everyone everywhere against the people and the law and this place. Moreover, he even brought Greeks into the temple and has defiled this holy place." For they had previously seen Trophimus the Ephesian with him in the city, and they supposed that Paul had brought him into the temple. Then all the city was stirred up, and the people ran together. They seized Paul and dragged him out of the temple, and at once the gates were shut. And as they were seeking to kill him, word came to the tribune of the cohort that all Jerusalem was in

> confusion. He at once took soldiers and centurions and ran down to them. And when they saw the tribune and the soldiers, they stopped beating Paul. Then the tribune came up and arrested him and ordered him to be bound with two chains. He inquired who he was and what he had done. Some in the crowd were shouting one thing, some another. And as he could not learn the facts because of the uproar, he ordered him to be brought into the barracks. And when he came to the steps, he was actually carried by the soldiers because of the violence of the crowd, for the mob of the people followed, crying out, "Away with him!" (Acts 21:1–16, 27–36)

Beginning with Acts 21, Luke continues his narration of Paul's third missionary journey that will eventually take him to Jerusalem. The two most important stops along the way are given some additional attention: the first in Tyre and then in Caesarea. In both instances, Paul is the recipient of prophetic words that, in effect, encourage him to avoid Jerusalem.

His visit to Tyre is recorded in verses 1–6. His visit to Caesarea is described in verses 7–16. His arrival and experience in Jerusalem is found in verses 17–36. I'll begin by simply narrating the events as they unfold without making too many theological statements. We'll then return to the narrative to determine as best we can what it tells us about the gift of prophecy and its function in the life of the church.

Paul in Tyre (vv. 1–6)

The exercise of the gift of prophecy in this series of events is first noted in verse 4 where we read that "through the Spirit [the disciples of Tyre] were telling Paul not to go on to Jerusalem." Although it is not explicitly stated here, it becomes clear from the remaining narrative that they had been made aware of what awaited Paul in

Jerusalem. They were understandably concerned for his welfare and safety.

Paul in Caesarea (vv. 7–16)

The next paragraph in chapter 21 gives us a broad view of the use, operation, and identification of the gift of prophecy. There are five things to be noted here.

First, in verse 9 Luke mentions Philip the evangelist (cf. Acts 7–8), with whom Paul stayed. Philip had "four unmarried daughters, who prophesied." Yes, women can prophesy! One need only look to Acts 2:17–18 where Peter describes the fulfillment of Joel 2 on the day of Pentecost:

> *And in the last days it shall be, God declares,*
> *that I will pour out my Spirit on all flesh,*
> *and your sons and your daughters shall prophesy,*
> *and your young men shall see visions,*
> *and your old men shall dream dreams;*
> *even on my male servants and female servants*
> *in those days I will pour out my Spirit and they shall prophesy.*
>
> Acts 2:17–18, emphasis mine

There simply are no restrictions based on gender when it comes to the gift of prophecy. We also see this in 1 Corinthians 11:4ff., where women are said to "pray and prophesy." Anna is also described as a "prophetess" in Luke 2:36. What then can Paul mean in 1 Corinthians 14:29–40 where he appears to prohibit women from speaking in church and in 1 Timothy 2:12–15 where he prohibits them from teaching and exercising authority over men? I would suggest that Paul recognized a distinction between the authority of teaching (exposition and enforcement of biblical texts) and the authority of prophecy (based on the spontaneity of a revelation). This is why it is not inconsistent for Paul to restrict the formal teaching office in the church to men while permitting, indeed encouraging, women to prophesy.

Some have tried to draw a connection between Philip's daughters being "unmarried" (lit., "virgins") and their prophetic ministry. The idea seems to be that it was their sexual purity that explains their spiritual sensitivity. But this view would necessarily denigrate the beauty and joy of sexual intimacy insofar as Paul, in 1 Corinthians 11, clearly indicates that married women could also operate in this gift. There is simply no biblical basis for the idea that legitimate sexual intimacy serves to undermine or "cloud" the ability of a man or a woman to hear from God.

What did they prophesy? Did they have words for Paul? We don't know, but given the fact that the passages preceding and following contain the prophetic warning for Paul not to go to Jerusalem, we can assume that Philip's daughters spoke in similar terms.

Second, in Acts 21:10–11 we encounter Agabus and his prophetic word to Paul. This isn't the first time Agabus has appeared in Acts nor the first time he has prophesied (see Acts 11:27–30). There his prophecy was predictive and quite explicit and came to pass just as he had said. Agabus was evidently a well-respected and honored prophet and was thus listened to when he spoke. Let's again note several things in his prophetic word.

We don't know how the Spirit communicated this word to Agabus. In verse 11 we read, "Thus says the Holy Spirit." This could refer to a verbal declaration by the Spirit, whether audible or inaudible we can't know, or also to general communication via some vision or dream or impression.

Agabus doesn't simply speak the word to Paul but acts it out in rather dramatic fashion.[1] He takes Paul's belt (it may have been a

1 For similar prophetic demonstrations, see 1 Kings 11:29–31 where the prophet

money belt, typically wrapped around his waist) and binds his own feet and hands. There are two specific elements in his word: first, "the Jews at Jerusalem will bind the man who owns this belt," and second, they, the Jews, will "deliver him into the hands of the Gentiles" (v. 11). Note well that Agabus doesn't give Paul advice based on what he's heard from the Spirit. He merely describes the revelatory word. The application, if we may call it that, comes from others.

Third, the response of Luke, Paul's traveling companions, and the believers in Caesarea is uniform. They all "urged him not to go up to Jerusalem" (Acts 21:12b). They didn't receive the revelation but felt free to interpret its meaning and apply it to Paul's life.

Fourth, Paul chooses *not* to heed their advice (v. 13). However, the phrase you are "breaking my heart" may indicate that their warning was undermining Paul's resolute determination and at least momentarily caused him to pause and reconsider. Or perhaps his "heartbreak" was from his having to take a position opposed to people who he knew cared for him and loved him greatly. Perhaps we are to understand Paul's response something along the lines of: "I don't want to offend you or lead you to think that I don't love and appreciate you simply because I'm going to make a decision contrary to the one you think I should make." The simple fact is that they were making it difficult for Paul to obey what he knew to be God's will for his life. In any case, Paul says no to their urging.

Fifth, they all resigned themselves to "the will of the Lord" (v. 14). This is unusual, since the "will" of the Lord seemed already to have been discerned in verse 4 when the disciples at Tyre told Paul "through the Spirit" not to go to Jerusalem.

Ahijah the Shilonite tore his new robe into twelve pieces to show how Solomon's kingdom would be disrupted; Isaiah 8:1–4; 20:2–4, where Isaiah went naked and barefoot to show how the Egyptians would be led into captivity by the Assyrians; Jeremiah 13:1–11, where God told Jeremiah to bury his new waist band until it was soiled and ruined to symbolize how God will destroy the pride of the Jews; Ezekiel 4:1–8, where Ezekiel mimicked the Babylonian siege of Jerusalem by laying siege himself to a replica of the city. Additional examples are depicted in Jeremiah 19:1, 13; 27:1–22; and Hosea 1:2.

Paul in Jerusalem (vv. 17–36)

The distance from Caesarea to Jerusalem was about sixty-five miles, more than one day's trip. Paul's primary reason for going to Jerusalem was to deliver the money he had collected for the poverty-stricken believers there (cf. Romans 15:25–27; 1 Corinthians 16:1–4). The false rumor soon spread that Paul was telling Jewish Christians to abandon their ancestral customs and the traditions of Moses. James and the elders ask Paul to join four other men in purifying themselves in accordance with Mosaic Law. Paul agrees and does so.

If a custom was a condition for salvation or acceptance with God, then Paul always resisted (see Galatians 5:2–4). But otherwise he viewed the matter of secondary importance and adjusted his practice to those to whom he ministered as was the case in 1 Corinthians 9:20 where Paul declared:

> To the Jews I became as a Jew, in order to win Jews. To those under the law I became as one under the law (though not being myself under the law) that I might win those under the law. To those outside the law I became as one outside the law (not being outside the law of God but under the law of Christ) that I might win those outside the law. To the weak I became weak, that I might win the weak. I have become all things to all people, that by all means I might save some. (1 Corinthians 9:20–22)

As someone once said, "A truly liberated Christian is never under bondage to her own freedom." Some people are actually quite legalistic about their liberty, but not Paul. If you think you *must* at all times exercise your freedom in Christ, you aren't really free!

Whereas Paul's action proved successful with the Jews in Jerusalem, others had come from Ephesus and used the occasion to renew their opposition to the apostle. Their minds were so poisoned against Paul that nothing he did would satisfy them until he was dead. They falsely accused him of taking Trophimus, a Gentile, into the temple. There were actually four concentric rectangular inner courts in the Temple. The first was of course the Holy of Holies into which only the high priest could enter once a year. The second was the holy place for priests. The third was for Jewish men. The fourth court was for Jewish women. Gentiles were only allowed to enter the court farthest removed, beyond that of the women. A warning was posted (discovered in 1935): "No foreigner may enter within the barricade which surrounds the temple and enclosure. Anyone who is caught trespassing will bear personal responsibility for his ensuing death."

Northwest of the temple area stood the Antonia fortress which housed a cohort of Roman troops (1,000 men). The fortress was connected with the outer court by two flights of steps, making their access both quick and easy. When word reached them of the assault on Paul, the tribune took "soldiers and centurions" (approx. 200 total) to the rescue. The tribune's name was Claudius Lysias (Acts 23:26; 24:22). He arrests Paul and binds him with two chains (Acts 21:33), probably to a soldier on each side.

Note carefully: *It was the Romans, not the Jews, who bound Paul. And the Jews did not deliver him into the hands of the Gentiles but rather the Gentile Romans rescued Paul from the Jews who were trying to kill him.* Such is the narrative of events as they unfolded and as described by Luke.

The Nature of the Spiritual Gift of Prophecy

This entire narrative, together with Acts 11:28, tells us much about how prophecy functioned in the early NT church and the degree of authority it carried. Two observations will bear this out.

First, Paul clearly did not receive the warning of the disciples in Tyre as the word or will of God to him. Some have been more explicit and said that Paul simply *disobeyed* the prophetic word.

Observe closely that in 21:4 they merely "said" to Paul or "told" Paul not to go. But in verse 12 they were repeatedly *urging* or *pleading* with him not to go. There is considerable energy and concern in their efforts to convince him that God is saying that he should not make this journey.

Paul's response is found in vv. 13–14. Why did the apostle resist their warnings? The primary reason is because of Paul's own personal experience with the Holy Spirit recorded earlier in the Acts narrative. According to Acts 19:21, "Paul resolved in the Spirit to pass through Macedonia and Achaia and go to Jerusalem, saying, 'After I have been there, I must also see Rome.'" Note well that Paul's resolute determination to go to Jerusalem and from there on to Rome was "in the [Holy] Spirit." That we are understanding this correctly is confirmed by what we read in Acts 20:20–24. Paul declares that he "did not shrink from declaring" to those in Ephesus "anything that was profitable," teaching them from house to house, "testifying both to Jews and to Greeks of repentance toward God and of faith in our Lord Jesus Christ" (vv. 20–21). Then he makes this crucial declaration: "And now, behold, I am going to Jerusalem, constrained by the Spirit, not knowing what will happen to me there, except that the Holy Spirit testifies to me in every city that imprisonment and afflictions await me" (Acts 20:22).

Paul's determination to go to Jerusalem was the result of the Holy Spirit's constraint. The Spirit somehow put in his heart that it was the will of God that he go to Jerusalem. This was not something Paul concocted on his own. This was not the result of human counsel or encouragement. The Spirit "constrained" Paul to be certain that he made it to Jerusalem. This is truly remarkable in view of what we read in Acts 21:4 where, "through the Spirit," the disciples in Tyre "were telling Paul not to go on to Jerusalem." Later, after Agabus issued the warning of what would happen if Paul were to go to Jerusalem, Luke and others "urged [Paul] not to go up to Jerusalem" (Acts 21:12).

This calls for some explanation. It seems to me that there are four possible explanations for what we read.

(1) As noted, some suggest that Paul was deliberately disobedient to the will of God. They spoke "the word of the Lord" to him and he said no. This is highly unlikely. That isn't to say that an apostle was by virtue of his calling and office beyond the capacity to sin. But there is nothing in Luke's narrative that would lead us to think that Paul was being defiant or resistant to what he knew to be the will of God.

(2) I don't know anyone who would actually argue for this second option, but we have to wrestle with the possibility that the Holy Spirit made a mistake or perhaps changed his mind. Earlier in Acts 19:21 and 20:22–24, the Spirit had told Paul to go (in 20:22a Paul says he is "constrained" or "bound" by the Spirit to go) but now, for whatever reason, the Spirit speaks through these disciples and prophets and says, "No, don't go."

However in Acts 21:14, we read that when they realized they couldn't persuade Paul not to go, they entrusted him to "the will of the Lord." It seems that they initially believed it was the will of God for him not to go but later were at least willing to entertain the possibility that it *was* God's will for him to go. Had they misheard God the first time (in v. 4)? I don't think so.

(3) Some would contend that what we have here is simply not a prophecy at all but little more than advice or wise counsel from concerned friends. But in Acts 21:4 they spoke to Paul "*through the Spirit*," which is the same phrase used in Acts 11:28 where Agabus prophesied the coming famine. Even if one ends up saying this isn't a prophecy, we still have to reckon with the reality of people hearing the Spirit's voice, communicating this to Paul, and Paul in turn choosing not to believe it was the absolute and infallible word of the Lord for him, resulting in his rejection of their advice.

(4) It seems to me the best option is that through some supernatural means that is not specified, the Holy Spirit communicated

to the believers at Tyre that if Paul went to Jerusalem he would be persecuted, perhaps even killed. On the basis of this revelation, they in turn *interpreted* this to be God's warning for him not to go. They then *applied* this to Paul by issuing a stringent warning and urged him to change his plans. While the Spirit did not directly tell them to urge Paul against going, they perceived it this way and communicated it to Paul this way.

Let's consider again these three elements in every prophecy: *revelation* [the actual vision of Paul being beaten], *interpretation* [this means that if you go to Jerusalem you will suffer greatly], and *application* [it isn't God's will for you to go to Jerusalem].

On this scenario, the disciples at Tyre, and later at Caesarea, all received the same revelation. They either had a distinct impression in their hearts or heard the Spirit speak audibly or more likely had a vision of Paul being threatened and beaten and perhaps in prison as a result. This *revelation* was unmistakable. Because this revelation was from God, it was infallible and altogether true.

But they then *interpreted* the revelation as meaning that extremely perilous times awaited Paul. He was subject to severe persecution, perhaps even martyrdom. This in turn led to the *application*. They concluded that *it was not God's will* for Paul to go to Jerusalem. It simply didn't register with them that going to Jerusalem could be a good thing. Why would anyone venture into a territory where he knew persecution was certain to occur? And why would God lead him there? Combined with their love for him and their desire for his safety, they told and even urged him not to go. In other words, they got the revelation right, as well as the interpretation, but misapplied it in terms of how Paul should react.

What should they have done? Once they received the revelation, they should have prayed about it, discussed it among themselves, and then sat down with Paul and shared it with him without interpreting it and applying it. I can only conclude that whereas Paul didn't question the validity of the revelation they received, neither did he believe that they were speaking to him the very words of God such that disobedience would constitute a sin. In other words, *based on previous and oft-repeated guidance from the Spirit,* Paul knew that whereas they had heard God correctly, they had to some extent misinterpreted and assuredly misapplied what he said.

Is this not what happens in many prophetic words today? Some illustrations may help. I've witnessed instances when someone received what appeared to be a revelatory word concerning another's physical affliction (with a high degree of accuracy, in spite of the fact that they had no prior knowledge of who the person was or the nature of the condition they were suffering). When combined with the compassion of the prophet and the misguided belief that God always wills to heal, a person doesn't stop with the revelation or doesn't rest content with praying for the person but actually predicts their healing! And when that person does not receive healing, they are crushed and become disillusioned with spiritual gifts in general.

Or perhaps the revelation is interpreted as an unconditional promise when in fact it is either (1) conditional (dependent on someone's obedience or other factors falling into place) or (2) an invitation, or (3) an opportunity that may in the future present itself if other circumstances turn out favorably.

There also comes to mind the many prophetic words and dreams we received concerning our departure from Kansas City to join the faculty at Wheaton College in 2000. No one told us: "It is God's will for you to go." We interpreted them as impending offers and an opportunity that we were free to accept or reject. That decision itself would be based on other factors (desire, timing, family, wisdom, best use of my gifting, opportunity, etc.).

Second, this understanding of the nature of prophecy and how it is generally a mixture of infallible divine revelation and fallible human interpretation and application is seen in the word delivered by Agabus. As earlier noted, there are two specific elements in his word. First, "the Jews at Jerusalem will bind the man who owns this belt," and second, they, the Jews, will "deliver him into the hands of the Gentiles" (Acts 21:11). In both cases, *Agabus was wrong.*

Let's look at them in turn. First, Luke tells us twice that it wasn't the Jews who bound Paul but rather the Romans. Note again: Agabus didn't prophesy that "Paul will be bound" but rather "the *Jews* at Jerusalem will bind" him (emphasis mine). Yet we read in Acts 21:33 that "the [Roman] tribune came up and arrested him and ordered him to be bound with two chains." Again in Acts 22:29, the tribune was afraid, for he realized that Paul was a Roman citizen and that "he [the Roman tribune] had bound him."

The second element of the prophecy Agabus also seems to have misapplied. He predicted that the Jews "will deliver him into the hands of the Gentiles." Wayne Grudem has correctly pointed out that in the 119 other instances of this word "deliver" in the NT, every one of them describes an act that is conscious and intentional and willing. In his commentary on Acts, Darrell Bock writes: "The reference to Jewish involvement in the binding here is 'causative' in force: the Jews will not physically bind Paul but will be responsible for his being arrested (21:27, 30, 33). The prophecy is accurate in this sense and is not to be pressed too literally."[2] O. Palmer Robertson echoes Bock and contends that the interpretation I've placed on the story is an example of "precisionism."[3] Once more, Bock argues that "as predicted in general terms in 21:11, a Jewish reaction has led to Paul being bound."[4]

The problem with Bock's and Robertson's interpretation is that it is *not* what Agabus said. He did not speak in generalities but in very specific language! He said the Jews themselves will consciously

---

2 Darrell L. Bock, *Acts: Baker Exegetical Commentary on the New Testament* (Grand Rapids: Baker Academic, 2007), 638.

3 O. Palmer Robertson, *The Final Word: A Biblical Response to the Case for Tongues and Prophecy Today* (Carlisle, Penn.: The Banner of Truth Trust, 1993), 114.

4 Bock, *Acts*, 653.

and deliberately "deliver" over Paul to the Gentiles. The fact is that they did no such thing. They first tried to kill him (v. 31), making it necessary for the Romans, i.e., the Gentiles, to rescue him from their clutches. Luke says in verse 35 Paul was "carried" to safety by the Romans.

Would it not make much better sense if we understand Agabus to have received a revelation, perhaps a vision, of Paul surrounded by an angry Jewish mob, bound hand and foot, and then in Gentile custody, which he interpreted as meaning that the Jews would bind him and deliver him to the Gentiles? Of course, it is true that Agabus is never said to have told Paul, based on this revelation, that he should not go to Jerusalem, but Luke and his other traveling companions and most, if not all, at Caesarea did. One can only assume that Agabus would have added his voice to this chorus.

And what of Agabus prefacing his word with: "Thus says the Holy Spirit"? There is no easy answer to this. I'm inclined to believe that Agabus himself collapsed his own interpretation into the divine revelation, failed to differentiate between the two, and then spoke as if God had revealed both to him. In other words, he believed that what he saw meant that the Jews would do these two things and spoke it forth as the word of the Spirit. Luke simply records what Agabus said without necessarily endorsing the interpretation that Agabus had placed upon the details.

Those who take issue with my understanding of this story invariably point to Acts 28:17. There we read: "After three days he [Paul] called together the local leaders of the Jews, and when they had gathered, he said to them, 'Brothers, though I had done nothing against our people or the customs of our fathers, yet I was delivered as a prisoner from Jerusalem into the hands of the Romans.'"

The argument that this passage refers to the literal fulfillment of Agabus's prophecy fails to note that Paul is describing his transfer "out of" Jerusalem into the Roman judicial system at Caesarea (23:12–35) and not the events associated with the mob scene in

Acts 21:27–36. In the book *Are Miraculous Gifts for Today? Four Views*, one of the contributors, Robert Saucy, insists that "it will not do to argue . . . that Paul was actually describing the time when he was secretly escorted out of Jerusalem by the Romans to Caesarea (23:12–35), for Paul was already 'handed over to the Romans' before he left Jerusalem."[5] But as I note in my response to Saucy, "Paul's point in 28:17 is simply that he was transferred from Roman custody in Jerusalem into Roman custody in Caesarea. The fact that Paul was already, in some sense, in 'the hands of the Romans' in Jerusalem does not preclude his using the same terminology in referring to his transfer to Caesarea and the jurisdiction of Felix."[6]

One final point should be made. I find it remarkably ironic that cessationists insist on arguing that we are pressing the details of Agabus's word and that we should not expect such precision in the fulfillment of a prophecy, only then to constantly criticize and eventually reject the legitimacy of charismatic prophetic ministry today on the basis of what they see as the frequent failure to get all the details exactly right! Why do they grant Agabus leeway that they deny to us? In other words, they allow Agabus to make small errors but not contemporary continuationists! I find that oddly, and sadly, inconsistent.

What, then, may we conclude about the nature and operation of the spiritual gift of prophecy in the New Testament?

Implications for Prophetic Ministry from Acts 21

The reason why we've taken this journey into the context and interpretation of Acts 21 has been to observe the way prophecy functions in the daily experience of God's people. So often we treat subjects like this with an attitude of theoretical detachment. But neither

5 *Are Miraculous Gifts for Today? Four Views*, edited by Stanley N. Gundry and Wayne A. Grudem (Grand Rapids: Zondervan, 1996), 231.

6 Ibid., 322.

prophecy nor any other spiritual gift is a subject for mere speculation or debate. God has blessed us with these expressions of power to build us up, to encourage and console, to convict and strengthen, and to equip us to boldly proclaim the gospel of his grace. There are many practical lessons we can learn from this remarkable story.

Notice that there is no indication the people in Tyre nor Philip's daughters nor Agabus nor Luke were trying to control Paul's life. They were motivated by their love for the apostle and concern for his physical welfare. Acts 21:13–14 says that they were "weeping," which indicates that they were not trying to manipulate Paul's ministry; they wanted God's will to be done. This is a reminder that the proper exercise of revelatory gifts is aimed at the edification, not the control, of other believers.

We should also notice that Paul took their counsel very seriously, even though he believed it to be misguided. He did not casually dismiss their prophetic urging, and he was willing to process the word with others. He listened carefully to their interpretation of the vision and was grieved that he had to disagree with them and reject their advice (again, see 21:13–14). That suggests that we too should weigh carefully the counsel of brothers and sisters we trust in order to discern whether or not they are sharing a word from the Lord or their own interpretation.

In addition, we should always be open to the possibility that no matter how clearly we think we have heard from the Spirit—like Paul's companions—we may be wrong. We must cultivate *prophetic humility*. Some are simply unwilling to entertain the possibility that they made a mistake in some aspect of the revelatory experience and arrogantly seek to impose their will on others in order to preserve their reputation as uniquely gifted and anointed. This sinful and self-serving attitude will only serve to undermine the otherwise powerful and Christ-exalting exercise of prophecy in the local church.

Paul judged the validity of the word based on his own prior encounter with the Spirit. Like Paul, one of the more challenging responsibilities of all Christians is to judge, weigh, assess, or analyze the legitimacy of any claim to prophetic revelation. I've written an entire chapter in *The Beginner's Guide to Spiritual Gifts* delineating how this might be done, and I encourage you to read it carefully. It is appropriately titled, "Who Said God Said?"

We also need to be extremely careful before we move from a revelation to its interpretation and application. Don't think that you have fallen short of your responsibility to God or to others or that your prophetic gift is inadequate or incomplete if you don't get the interpretation or application. Simply because you have great clarity in the revelation does not mean God intends to enlighten you as to its application.

This is one of the most important lessons to learn in the proper exercise of prophecy in the local church. For some reason, those who are the recipient of prophetic revelation struggle to stop once the word has been shared. They feel compelled to interpret and explain and eventually apply the word either to an individual or to an entire group. I'm not suggesting that this should never happen. On occasion a person will receive both the revelation and the interpretation. But in the majority of instances, it will turn out that God has revealed something to a person but wishes that its interpretation and application be left to others.

Another implication of the passage in Acts is that simply because these prophets got the interpretation and application wrong, it does not mean they are false prophets. They are not disciplined or rebuked or set out of ministry. False prophets, technically speaking, are unregenerate people who deny that Jesus is God incarnate. Christians who on occasion (or even often) prophesy falsely should not be labeled false prophets.

But this all raises a question: Why did God give this revelation to them? If it was not to dissuade Paul from going to Jerusalem, what was the point of it all? What did God expect them to do with it? Could this have been one more example of the Spirit doing what

Paul described in Acts 20:23, only this time he did it indirectly through others rather than directly? Thus the purpose would have been to reinforce in Paul's heart what awaited him and help prepare him for the hardships ahead. In addition, this sort of revelatory experience was undoubtedly designed to stir them to intercede on Paul's behalf.

I find it highly instructive to observe that even Luke was involved in the error (Acts 21:12). This suggests that even our closest friends and coworkers can misapply a prophetic word designed for us. It is only natural for us to be more open and easily persuaded of the validity of a word when it comes from someone we know well and trust. But simply because someone loves you and desires your best interests does not give them a free pass to speak a word of direction or correction without it being subject to careful analysis.

There's no indication that those who spoke this word or those that joined them in urging Paul not to go ever changed their minds about the accuracy of their application. In other words, Paul was unable to convince them they were wrong (see 21:14). They agreed to disagree and to entrust themselves, especially Paul, to the will of God. There was no gridlock as a result of this incident. Paul's missionary journeys were not stalled or paralyzed. We should never think that perfect unanimity is required before we can respond to a word that purports to be from God.

Finally, and of supreme importance for our pursuit and practice of prophecy today, note that Luke didn't see their mistake as being fatal or a threat to the validity of prophetic ministry. At no time after Acts 21:36 does he say, "Oops," or "We repent," or "Prophecy is dangerous and to be avoided." In other words, contrary to what many suggest, errors like this do not disqualify people as prophetically gifted nor do they render prophecy unimportant for the church.

This will likely be the greatest temptation you face when learning how to implement the prophetic in your personal experience and in the life of your church. As evangelical, Bible-believing Christians who rightly prize theological precision, we are not the sort who respond well to even the slightest inaccuracies. We often conclude that in the absence of rock-solid, empirically verifiable confirmation of the absolute truthfulness of a word that purports to come from God, nothing of spiritual benefit can be gained by tolerating this gift in our midst, much less by promoting it. But revelatory gifts are inescapably subjective, and the people through whom they operate are unavoidably prone to error. We mustn't be alarmed by this. But we should remain alert. The apostle Paul, his close companion Luke, Agabus, and the many disciples who were involved in this story certainly learned and lived by this truth, and so must we.

CHAPTER 8

PRINCIPLES FOR PROPHECY TODAY

Here at Bridgeway Church in Oklahoma City, we highly value the spiritual gift of prophecy. That doesn't mean we elevate it to the exclusion or even the subordination of other spiritual gifts, but we take seriously the apostle Paul's admonition in 1 Corinthians 14:1 and the reason given for it. As you will recall, the apostle exhorts us to "earnestly desire the spiritual gifts, especially that you may prophesy" (1 Corinthians 14:1b).

It is that word "especially" that justifies the focus in this book on prophecy and in our churches as well. The point Paul goes on to make is that prophecy is "especially" beneficial to the church because, unlike uninterpreted tongues, prophecy is intelligible and thus serves to build up, encourage, and console other believers (1 Corinthians 14:3). Simply put, "the one who prophecies builds up the church" (1 Corinthians 14:4b).

But prophecy also warrants our extended attention because of the controversial nature of the gift. I've often said that whereas in the 1960s and into the 1970s speaking in tongues was the most controversial among the miraculous charismata, today it is prophecy. More questions are raised regarding prophecy than all the other gifts combined. One of the more pressing and practical issues is how prophecy ought to function in the local church. How, if at all, should it be exercised in the larger corporate gathering of the church, especially on Sunday morning when several hundred (and in some cases, several thousand) people are present? And if Sunday morning is not the ideal context for this gift, how should it be encouraged and utilized in our small group gatherings?

Because the exercise of prophecy in small group settings is a bit simpler than its practice in corporate worship, I'll begin with a few words regarding the best way, in general, to facilitate and watch over the prophetic when few people are present and follow up with several guidelines that will make its use in the corporate gathering of the church more effective and less subject to abuse and criticism.

Facilitating the Prophetic in our Small Groups

When people ask me how we facilitate the exercise of prophecy in our church, I begin by encouraging them to focus on its presence in small groups rather than in the larger corporate gatherings. We should remember the first-century context in which Paul wrote his instructions to the church at Corinth. Though we can't be 100% certain, most scholars agree that no more than 150 people could have been accommodated in the homes of the first century. Most homes would max out at far less than that. So when we read Paul's writings about prophecy, we need to keep in mind that he likely did not have in mind the modern day megachurch or even one that exceeded 200 believers. His instruction most closely relates to smaller gatherings where virtually everyone knew everyone else.

Let me share an example of what I'm talking about. Many people have been puzzled by Paul's counsel regarding the use of tongues in a gathered assembly. In 1 Corinthians 14:27–28 we read: "If any speak in a tongue, let there be only two or at most three, and each in turn, and let someone interpret. But if there is no one to interpret, let each of them keep silent in church and speak to himself and to God."

The question I'm often asked is this: "How could one even know if there was another present who had the gift of interpretation? Without this advance knowledge, it would appear to make Paul's instruction in this text difficult to obey."

That's true. But that's where the context in which he wrote matters. We need to keep in mind the likelihood that, given the comparatively small size of house churches in Corinth, virtually everyone who attended a church would be personally acquainted with everyone else there. Each person would likely know what spiritual gift was regularly exercised by every other individual. If one believed that she had a tongue that should be exercised publicly, she could easily determine if those who regularly exercised the gift of interpretation were present. In any case, in a substantially smaller crowd the opportunity for the exercise of all spiritual gifts would be significantly greater.

So what does this suggest for how we should proceed with the exercise of prophecy in our small group meetings? The first thing I recommend is that the leader of the gathering explicitly and frequently inform those gathered that this is a "safe" environment in which everyone should feel free to take risks. As odd as that may sound, it will go a long way toward putting at ease the hearts of people who live in fear that if they make even the smallest of mistakes they will be rebuked or mocked or in some manner marginalized from the group.

Remember that there will always be varying degrees of confidence in people regarding the question of whether or not they have truly heard from God. Paul wrote this in Romans 12:6 concerning the exercise of prophecy: "Having gifts that differ according to the grace given to us, let us use them: if prophecy, *in proportion to our faith*" (emphasis mine). In my contribution to the book *Are Miraculous Gifts for Today? Four Views*, I write this about the relationship between our faith and the exercise of prophecy:

> Paul seems to be saying that "some who had the gift of prophecy had a greater measure of faith (that is, trust or confidence that the Holy Spirit would work or was working in them to bring a revelation which would be the basis of a prophecy)." In other

> words, there will always be greater and lesser degrees of prophetic ability and consequently greater and lesser degrees of prophetic accuracy (which, it seems reasonable to assume, may increase or decrease, depending on the circumstances of that person's life). Thus, the prophet is to speak in proportion to the confidence and assurance he or she has that what is spoken is truly from God. Prophets are not to speak beyond what God has revealed; they must be careful never to speak on their own authority or from their own resources.[1]

If this is what Paul has in mind, we should take it as an incentive to deal tenderly and patiently with those who are somewhat uncertain if they have a genuine prophetic word from God intended for another person or for the group as a whole. We should tell our people on a regular basis, "Don't be afraid to step out in faith and give expression to what you believe God has revealed to you. If you don't get things perfectly, you need not fear that anyone will judge you or disregard you. You won't be put in a special class of subspiritual Christians who are not permitted ever again to exercise their gifts lest we be damaged by the errors you espouse."

People need to know that they are loved and valued and that their contributions are appreciated. In the absence of this relational atmosphere, many will simply keep their mouths shut and decline ever to participate in a meaningful way. They need to know that their courage in stepping out in faith will be honored and that they need not fear being exposed to public humiliation.

In addition to encouraging people to take risks and contribute, you may want to think about the structure of your small group setting. If the entire gathering is dominated by a single person, or if the time is entirely devoted to the teaching of the Scriptures, there will be fewer opportunities for the Spirit to speak through

---

1 *Are Miraculous Gifts for Today?*, 210.

revelatory gifts and to build up those present. We should not try to excuse this by saying: "But if the Holy Spirit wants to minister through a prophetic gift, he will do it in some manner with or without our assistance. He can interrupt our proceedings any time he pleases."

While in one sense, that's true, I don't believe that is the Spirit's preferred manner of ministering in, to, and through us. The Spirit does not overwhelm or intrude or treat us as puppets. There may well have been people in first-century Corinth who appealed to an argument like this. Paul was attempting to put in place certain restrictions on the number of those who might prophesy in any one gathering, lest they dominate the meeting and make difficult, if not impossible, the exercise of a wide range of gifts by multiple individuals. To those who might respond to him by saying, "But I just couldn't help myself. The Spirit overwhelmed me and I couldn't refrain from speaking, notwithstanding your instruction that only two or three prophesy before the others pass judgment," Paul replied, "No, you aren't out of control; you can exercise restraint; after all, 'the spirits of prophets are subject to prophets. For God is not a God of confusion but of peace'" (1 Corinthians 14:32–33).

In our church we regularly encourage our small group leaders to "make space" or provide ample time and opportunity for the prophetic gift to be exercised. For those who do not have a leadership position and want to speak a word to someone, it's a great idea to ask permission. This will help the hearers, if it really is a word from God, receive what you're saying. It also respects the leader whom you may be able to influence in a good way, whereas you otherwise might not if you do not work within the leadership structure established by your church.

If your group regularly spends time in singing or prayer at any one gathering, it may be helpful to pause in the middle or even wait until the end, and then say: "Let's stop for a moment and remain silent. Each person should pray quietly and ask the Spirit if he wishes to make known something that would be of benefit and for the building up of others present tonight."

After a few minutes you can then ask: "Does anyone have a sense from the Lord about the direction of our meeting tonight?" "Is anyone hearing from the Lord for ministry?" "Did anyone have a dream recently or feel burdened or impressed in some way?" Don't be afraid of or offended by the awkwardness of silence. Maybe God isn't speaking at this time. And if he isn't, don't feel as if you have failed if no prophetic ministry is forthcoming. But if someone shares a revelation from God, give time for the others to ponder its content, to pray, perhaps even to search the Scriptures to see if what was said is true.

If someone did hear from God and the word bore special importance for a particular individual, take time to pray this truth into their life. Either gather around that person or, better still, have them sit in a chair in the middle of the room while others lay hands on them and ask the Spirit to bring insight into the full meaning of the prophetic word and how the person in view might properly respond to what was said. When this is done, we have seen instances where the Spirit continues to reveal something of value and practical application for that person's life.

How to Introduce and Deliver a Prophetic Word

A great deal of damage has been done to believers in many different churches by the careless, controlling, and overly authoritative delivery of prophetic words. Most Christians have a deep and sincere desire to respond with humility and complete obedience to whatever God may be saying to them. Recall that Paul told the Thessalonian believers to "hold fast [to] what is good" (1 Thessalonians 5:21). This means that once a prophetic utterance has been tested and weighed and it has been determined that it is good, we are to embrace it and obey it. Most Christians readily agree with this and want to be seen as responsive to what God may have revealed.

That's why it is very important that when we are communicating what we believe is a word from God we do it in a gentle and caring manner, without manipulation and authoritarianism.

Dramatic pronouncements aren't helpful. Avoid saying things like "Thus saith the Lord," or "This is the word of the Lord for your life," or "God specifically told me to tell you that you should . . ." Just don't say them. They aren't helpful. This doesn't mean that the person who heard from God should waver or question the accuracy of what they believe God has revealed. It is simply a question of pastoral etiquette and a way of avoiding manipulation or coercion in sharing what you've heard or seen.

We have found that it is better to introduce prophetic utterances with statements such as:

> "I have a strong inner impression that I believe is from the Lord."
> "I have a picture in my mind that I think may be for someone here."
> "I had a sense from the Holy Spirit about what he wants to accomplish tonight."
> "I had a dream which involved several of you, and I would like to share it."

Speaking in this way puts people at ease and reassures them that they are not disobedient if they choose to wait or to consult others regarding the truth of what was spoken. Prophetic words may be highly symbolic and require extensive prayer and investigation. People should not be made to feel guilty if they respond with less than immediate and wholehearted affirmation.

How to Respond to Questionable "Words"

On occasion you will experience an immediate check or hesitation in your heart regarding the authenticity of an utterance that purports to be from God. This doesn't mean you are by nature a cynic or that you doubt the validity of the gift of prophecy. It more likely indicates that your knowledge of Scripture, together with common sense, has detected something amiss in what was said. If this should occur, I suggest you take the following steps.

Some alleged prophetic words will need immediate correction, especially if they are biblically misguided. Suppose your small group is praying for a woman whose marriage is in deep trouble, although it is clear that neither she nor her husband have committed adultery. If someone says, "I have a strong sense from the Lord that you should divorce your husband," you can rest assured that this sense was *not* from the Lord. You can respond to occasions such as this by saying: "I appreciate your zeal and your desire to help our sister, but we know from God's Word that she does not have biblical grounds for divorce, and thus your 'sense', though undoubtedly intended to be of help, is *not* of the Holy Spirit."

Even in these situations be gentle, kindhearted, and encouraging. Don't crush the spirit of the person or respond in a way that would make them fearful and hesitant to ever prophesy again. Of course, if their word is unequivocally unbiblical and contrary to what is clearly taught in Scripture, you will need to bring correction clearly, and it will inevitably cause some measure of relational discomfort or internal pain. Such occurrences are unavoidable. But you can still bring truth to bear in a way that everyone involved feels loved and supported.

If the "word" is general or vague or merely a repetition of some biblical text or principle already well known, don't dismiss it, but encourage the group to commit to pray about it and re-visit it at a later time. I've seen people mock prophetic ministry because the word spoken did not feel sufficiently supernatural. But nowhere in Scripture are we told that the exercise of a spiritual gift will always appear or feel supernatural in the sense that it could not have been exercised by virtue of a person's own natural talents. Sometimes the most helpful and encouraging revelatory words are those that pertain to some issue or need that could conceivably have been spoken by a person without the gift of prophecy.

If the prophetic word shared is weird or unintelligible or embarrassing, you can simply say: "Thanks for sharing. Let's discuss this in private at a later time. I'm not sure this is the direction the Spirit is leading us at this time." But don't be surprised if you later discover that the weird or slightly embarrassing word was genuinely of God and proves to be beneficial to those for whom it was intended.

Guidelines for Prophecy in the Corporate Assembly

Although the small group setting is the context best suited to the exercise of prophecy (and most other spiritual gifts as well), there will be times when the gift may also be exercised in a corporate gathering of all God's people. Obviously, there will be some limitations on how it is practiced due to time constraints and the size of the crowd. All of these will make it more difficult to steward this gift on a Sunday morning, but not impossible.

Many churches place an open microphone somewhere near the platform to which people in the congregation have access. At any time during the service (with the exception of the sermon), people can approach the mic and deliver what they believe is a prophetic word. I was blessed to preach at one such church that practiced the prophetic in this way. On two or three occasions during the time of singing, the worship leader's attention was drawn to the presence of a man or woman at the mic. He would quickly conclude whatever song was being sung to accommodate the prophetic utterance.

While there is nothing inherently unbiblical about this practice, I do not recommend it for at least three reasons. First, it is too tempting to impetuous and immature visitors or church members who would abuse an opportunity to speak authoritatively into the life of the church. Some people with an inflated sense of their own importance are convinced that they have a calling from God to speak into the life of other churches. Of course, most churches that provide an open mic monitor its use closely. They will do everything in their power to restrict access to those in the church with whom they are already quite familiar who might misuse it. But the potential still exists for an arrogant, pushy, or unbalanced individual to seize the opportunity and disrupt the service.

One last comment on this practice. We've found that more times than not, the individual who bypasses our guidelines for the delivery of a prophetic word is either a first-time visitor or someone who has only rarely attended our corporate gatherings. They often envision themselves as uniquely gifted and called by God to set other Christians straight. They feel compelled to share and regard it as disobedience if they do not seize the opportunity to speak what is on their heart.

We recently had a young man visit our church for the first time, and he immediately made his way to the front of the platform where he knelt during our time of worship. I felt no need to stop him, as he never disrupted the proceedings or spoke out loudly. However, both I and our security team were prepared to step in and restrain him if he chose to address the congregation without our approval. Our sound engineers have standing orders that if anyone not approved by me or the elders takes hold of a microphone, they are to cut the power immediately. On this occasion I'm happy to report that the young man kept himself in check and as of this writing has not returned to our church (although he is certainly welcome to do so).

In addition to allowing anyone access, an open mic does not give the leadership of the church any opportunity to assess the prophetic word before it is delivered. I'll say more about this later and give suggestions for how this assessment can be done in a healthy and productive way.

Finally, on a personal note, I must admit that I do not find it helpful to the spiritual atmosphere of the service to repeatedly interrupt the flow of worship with prophetic words. At Bridgeway Church here in Oklahoma City, our singing is not haphazard or random. Those who lead our worship are strategic in the songs they select. Songs are intentionally chosen and are thematically designed to construct a gospel narrative that leads our people to see and savor Jesus Christ. The sequence of the songs is designed to tell a story. There is narrative development as the time of singing progresses in which certain biblical truths are unpacked, illustrated, and reach their climax. Interrupting this liturgical flow undermines the communication of the message. Indeed, our worship pastor always selects songs and adapts his contribution to the topic and biblical text of my sermon. To allow prophetic voices to insert themselves into this pattern, without first being vetted to determine if their word is relevant to the moment and the ministry goals to which we are moving, most often proves counterproductive.

An Appropriate Practice of Prophecy in the Public Assembly

So, if an open mic is not the best way to facilitate the prophetic gift in a corporate gathering, how can we do this in a way that is fruitful and respectful? Here are several suggestions that guide how we practice and facilitate prophetic words in our church.

We start by having *a designated point person* at each worship celebration, someone who has the responsibility and authority to make the final decision on how prophetic ministry is to be facilitated. This will usually be either myself, one of our senior leaders, one of the elders, or a member of the prophetic team. Whoever is selected for this role needs to be biblically informed, spiritually mature, and of such a temperament that they can deal kindly but firmly with those who may insist that if they are not permitted to speak they are disobeying God.

We also prepare our people by instructing them that if they believe the Lord has revealed something to them, they should share this word with the appointed individual. We prefer that they put what they want to share in writing, but if that is not possible, we encourage them simply to go to the leader and communicate what they believe the Lord is saying. I have grown accustomed to feel a tap on the shoulder or a tug on my arm as someone whispers in my ear, "Sam, I think the Lord has laid something on my heart that ought to be shared with the congregation as a whole." When this happens, I or the designated point person will make an immediate judgment as to whether the individual has indeed heard from God. I encourage everyone to remember that neither I nor any other pastor or elder is infallible in making such judgments and that errors can and have been made in this regard. We simply ask that people not be offended or take it as a personal rejection if we determine that they have not heard from the Lord.

If we determine that the Lord has truly spoken to a person, our first task will be to decide whether or not the revelation is for that individual *personally* or if it is designed for the church *corporately*. Often times what a person hears from God is intended for personal edification or should become a focus in their own personal prayer life. If it is determined that a word is suitable for the whole body, several other decisions have to be made.

First, a judgment will be made as to *when* the word should be shared with the entire body. That is to say, should it be shared now or perhaps next week (or sometime thereafter), once additional time is given to prayer and discussion among the staff, elders, and prophetic team? Then, assuming that the word is appropriate for the entire church at the time the person received it, a judgment will be made as to the most fitting time *during the service* when it should be communicated. Should it be shared immediately, or should we wait until after our time of singing, or perhaps after the sermon, or at some other time during the course of the morning service? Once it is decided when the word is to be shared, the final decision concerns *who* should speak it forth. On occasion we will permit the individual who received the word to share it publicly. This will often depend on how well we know the person and if they have a demonstrated history of accuracy and maturity in the exercise of their spiritual gift. At other times, the point person will assume responsibility for communicating the word to the body as a whole.

If a word is shared publicly, we believe that every believer in the congregation has a personal responsibility to pay close attention to the prophetic word and to judge or evaluate the biblical validity of its content (cf. 1 Corinthians 14:29; 1 Thessalonians 5:19–22). However, only men are permitted to articulate publicly this evaluation or judgment in the corporate gathering (1 Timothy 2:11–15; 1 Corinthians 14:33–35). In our church, if there is a word spoken that I or the other elders find inaccurate or unacceptable, we would typically respond in this way:

> "Folks, please know that we highly value prophetic ministry. We want to do everything we can to encourage it and to learn from one another. But we also have a responsibility as your spiritual leaders to guard you from error. Our brother (or sister) obviously acted and spoke in a way they thought was what God desired, and I want to honor them for their sincerity. However, I don't believe that what was said is altogether accurate. Let me take just a moment and explain what I believe is more consistent with God's Word."

Of course, if we were doing what we should do, it would never come to this, as we would have evaluated the prophetic word before it was ever spoken to determine if it was truly of God.

Finally, I'll often mention that the Scriptures are clear that, at most, "two or three prophets" should speak during the course of any one corporate gathering (1 Corinthians 14:29). I ask that everyone abide by this rule and that they not be offended or take it personally if we choose to limit the number of those who prophesy.

Don't Criticize, Coerce, or Publicly Confront

While the guidelines I just shared are useful for corporate gatherings, there are also several additional suggestions that apply more generally to the exercise of the prophetic. These could be considered matters of etiquette that help the person sharing a word to do so in a way that achieves its biblically stated purpose of "upbuilding and encouragement and consolation" (1 Corinthians 14:3).

When I teach on how to share a prophecy or a word, I tell people to avoid publicly criticizing or correcting church leadership by name. It is better to take such issues privately to the elders. Paul is quite clear how we should rebuke and correct those in authority: "Do not admit a charge against an elder except on the evidence of two or three witnesses" (1 Timothy 5:19). Remember that the New Testament doesn't say, "be subject to the prophets" but rather "be subject to the elders" (1 Peter 5:5).

I would also suggest that you avoid publicly exposing someone's sin by name. Speak of the sin in general or anonymous terms and ask the Spirit to bring conviction to the person(s) in mind (1 Corinthians 14:24–25). If you are persuaded that someone is in serious moral or theological error, go to them privately, share the word, and seek to resolve the matter in a way that does not unnecessarily expose the individual to unwarranted public shame. If they do not repent, and there is objective evidence to support your sense that they are in sin, take it to the elders of the church for them to process and respond (Matthew 18:15–20).

Similar to the point just made about sharing sin publicly, avoid prophesying about marriages, babies, moves, or job changes. The only people who should speak authoritatively into whether a particular man and a particular woman should get married are that man and that woman! This isn't to say that God would never provide *confirmation* of the propriety of an engagement to someone other than the couple getting engaged, but the principle that must be observed when it comes to marriage is that if you are not the man or woman in question, it's none of your business!

Several years ago there was a young man in our church who was well educated, mature, zealous for the Lord, and, from what the women have told me, extremely handsome. I can't begin to tell you the number of single young ladies who told others (one even told the man himself!) that they had experienced a dream in which they saw themselves married to him. I don't doubt that such dreams took place. They likely were very real and quite vivid. But there is no reason to believe they were revelatory or were designed to be prophetic in nature. As things turned out, the young man married a precious lady whom no one would have guessed would turn out to be his bride.

Notice that I also included a prohibition against prophesying about pregnancies as well. I want to be clear that I include this warning because such prophecies can be dangerous and detrimental. There is a natural tendency born of Christian compassion and love to speak a word of encouragement to the barren and infertile in our midst. We have grieved with them and prayed with them and suffered heartbreak when they became pregnant and subsequently miscarried. But be extraordinarily careful that you do not mistakenly identify your understandable desire that someone conceive with a revelation from God that such will in fact come to pass. Our love for others and our confidence in God's power are not a legitimate basis on which to speak prophetically into their lives. By all means let these realities energize your prayers on their behalf, but refrain from turning your own well-meaning confidence or hope into a prophetic promise. I have often seen how a failure to observe this rule has resulted in emotional devastation for many couples that long to have children.

This is true when it comes to changing occupations or career trajectories as well. I am convinced that God loves his children sufficiently well that if he is leading them to resign one position in the hope that he/she will be offered another, better, higher paying occupation, God will make it clear to them. Certainly we should all seek the counsel and wisdom of other believers and solicit their prayers on our behalf. But aside from what admittedly may be an exceptional case, I am confident that you can trust God to lead you in such a decision without the input of others who would remain largely unaffected if the choice you make turns out to be a disaster.

Interpretation and Application Are Not Always Needed

There may be times when God reveals that a friend or someone you know has a sickness or physical illness. Several times I've witnessed situations where God has revealed a person's affliction or disease to someone who had no prior knowledge of it. When this occurs, the recipient of the revelation will sometimes jump to the immediate conclusion that it is God's will to heal this person. Why else would he make known the existence of a physical or emotional affliction if he didn't intend to deliver that person, for their good and God's glory? While this might seem to be a reasonable conclusion, it isn't always the case. God may be sharing this knowledge with you so that you can better encourage your friend or volunteer to provide meals or do yard work or other tasks that they otherwise are unable to accomplish. It may be God's intent for you to pray regularly for that individual, not only that he be healed of the affliction but also, in the absence of healing, that he be enabled to persevere through the pain and serve as a platform for the display of God's grace and the sufficiency of his love (see 2 Corinthians 12:8–10).

I point this out because it is an example of a common mistake that prophetically gifted people make when they respond to a revelation from God. Earlier, I mentioned the three elements of a prophecy. First is the revelation itself: what God said or showed you or the content of what was impressed on your heart or that you saw in a dream. Second is the interpretation of that revelation: What is its meaning? Third is the application of the interpretation: How does this truth impact one's life? What should one do in response to it? How should the individual proceed in life in light of the content of the revelation?

Remember the principle we established: It is extremely difficult for a prophetically gifted person to communicate the revelation and stop. Typically, a person will feel a responsibility to share the word, interpret its meaning, and then tell the individual how they should live or act in the light of it. They will often feel as if they have fallen short in their commitment to the church or that they have disobeyed God himself if they do not follow up the revelation with practical, life-changing instruction. But while there may be some situations where interpretation and application are needed, in most cases a person should simply share what God has shown to them and leave it there. Leave the task of interpretation and application to others.

This means that unless you have explicit biblical warrant, do not tell a person what God's will is for their life. For example, I do not need a prophetic revelation to know that it is God's will for Christians to abstain from fornication. All of us have already been told this in biblical texts such as 1 Thessalonians 4:3. Prophetic revelation isn't needed for us to know that God's will is that we never pay back evil for evil. Paul has declared God's will on this matter in Romans 12:17.

This is not meant to rule out the giving of advice or making recommendations to other believers based on one's own past experience or common sense. It is always a good rule of thumb to seek out the wisdom and insights of more mature and seasoned believers when we are making momentous decisions in our lives. But do not go to them expecting God to reveal his will for your life through a prophetic word they deliver to you. By all means they should pray for you. By all means they should carefully assess your situation and speak truth and caution and encouragement into your decision-making process. By all means they should draw on their knowledge of God's Word and its principles and seek, together with you and others, to find the most Christ-honoring application to your situation.

Let me give you an example. Let's say you are a high-school senior and you are weighing multiple options about where to attend college. You should start out by talking with trusted friends and counselors who have your best interests at heart. Seek as much information as you can. Pray relentlessly. I don't believe that God's *typical manner* of providing guidance is to give someone other than you a revelatory dream about which school is the right school. If God should choose to lead you in such a manner, he will likely give that dream to you, an experience for which you can then seek confirmation or refutation from people of wisdom and knowledge.

Avoid Making Public Predictions

Be careful about prophesying public, political, or natural disasters. Notice that I said, "Be careful." I would not go so far as to say that this form of prophetic utterance is altogether illegitimate or out of bounds. Predictive prophecy does exist, and sometimes God will use it for the benefit of his people (see Acts 11:27–30 and the predictive prophecy by Agabus of an impending famine). Could God conceivably use you or someone in your church to make known in advance some event of great impact and social significance? Yes. But in my experience this type of prophecy is rare and is not the typical expression of the prophetic gift that we find in the New Testament church.

Why do I suggest caution about these types of predictive prophecies? Because you need to be prepared to be proven wrong. All it takes is for your prediction to fail to come to pass to demonstrate that you did not hear from God. So how should we respond when someone prophesies some public, political, or natural disaster? Simply wait and see if it happens! That being said, I should point out that it doesn't take a spiritual gift to predict that California (and now my own home state of Oklahoma) will soon experience a substantially severe earthquake. Anyone who pays attention to current events can prophesy that a terrorist attack in the Middle East (or even in America) is soon to happen.

Don't Use Prophecy to Establish Doctrines or Rules

Avoid using prophecy to establish doctrines, practices, or ethical principles that lack explicit biblical support. I'm extremely reluctant to pay much, if any attention, to someone who tells me that God told them that playing pool is a sin. I'm not inclined to put much credence in an alleged "prophetic" utterance to the effect that attending all movies is inherently wicked. For someone to claim they heard God tell them that buying insurance is indicative of a failure to trust in divine sovereignty is beyond what we should expect of the prophetic as it is portrayed in the NT.

Again, this does not mean that playing pool or attending movies or buying insurance is God's will for all Christians. The Bible simply doesn't address such matters. What the Bible does indicate is that each believer must make the best use they can of what is explicitly commanded in God's Word as well as whatever prompting or practical guidance they receive while in prayer. But even if one is confident of God's direction for their life, that doesn't mean it is God's direction for another's life.

Related to this is the danger of setting behavioral standards on secondary issues such as whether one should drink alcohol in moderation or listen to secular music. I'm simplistic enough to believe that if God thought it essential to our sanctification that we either indulge in such activities or refrain from them, he would have made it clear in Scripture or would have provided us with principles on the basis of which we could make definitive application. God will never reveal new ethical rules for what is right and wrong and binding on the conscience of all Christians in every age. What is good and what is evil has been finally and forever settled in the written Word of God.

The Regular Practice of the Prophetic

Let me close with some final, commonsense suggestions when you begin exercising the gift of prophecy on a regular basis. First, be cautious about excessive dependence on prophetic words for making routine, daily decisions in life. There are, of course, certain exceptions to this rule. This is what I said in *The Beginner's Guide to Spiritual Gifts*:

> Typically . . . Paul emphasizes the importance of "reckoning" with the circumstances of whatever situation one is facing. Consider the needs of people, the principles of Scripture, and seek the counsel of those who have a track record of wisdom (see Phil. 2:25; 1 Cor. 6:5). Concerning his travel plans, Paul writes, "And if it is fitting for me to go also, they will go with me" (1 Cor. 16:4). Here Paul will make his decision based on a sober evaluation of what is fitting or advisable in view of the circumstances and what he feels would please God. Of course, nothing he says rules out the possibility that prophetic insight could play a role. In other texts Paul appeals to "knowledge," "discernment," and "spiritual wisdom and understanding" (Phil. 1:9–10a; Col. 1:9) as essential in the decision-making process. Certainly, revelatory insight from the Lord can be crucial in such deliberation, but God does not want us to be paralyzed in its absence.[2]

2 *Beginner's Guide to Spiritual Gifts*, 130.

Be careful that you don't let your identity be dependent on your gifting. Most of us can readily embrace this principle without a struggle. But it is often (not always) different when it comes to people who are gifted prophetically. I want to be careful not to stereotype prophetic people, but I've observed over the years that they can often be far more sensitive than others when it comes to how the exercise of their gifting is received and how they are personally assessed.

Of course, I'm not at all surprised by this once we think deeply about the nature of the prophetic. To be the recipient of prophetic revelation from God, whether in dreams, impressions, trances, visions, or words of knowledge and words of wisdom, can be nothing short of euphoric. The experience brings feelings of nearness to God and a heightened sense of spiritual intimacy that isn't often the case with other of the charismata. Most everyone who has received revelatory insights in these ways will testify to this. The result is that men and women with this gifting, especially if it occurs on a regular basis, can be more self-defensive than others. I am not suggesting that all who are prophetically gifted are of the same temperament or personality, but I do observe a general pattern in their demeanor and behavior. To question whether or not they truly heard from God feels like personal rejection. If someone exercises mercy toward me or perhaps blesses me with a generous financial gift, I don't pause to test or assess whether or not they did this in the power of the Holy Spirit. But when a claim is made that God has spoken, it is our collective responsibility to closely examine and biblically assess the truthfulness of what is communicated.

On a couple of occasions when I've been the recipient of prophetic revelation and in turn observed how blessed were those to whom I ministered, I confess that it was exhilarating and felt profoundly supernatural (of course, as noted earlier, one can truly prophesy and feel nothing out of the ordinary). When something so deeply and inwardly personal happens to you, it is easy to become overly sensitive to any criticism or doubts that may come your way. The result is often that prophetically gifted folk struggle to separate themselves from the work of the Holy Spirit through them. Apart from the latter, they feel a sense of loss and lack of direction. Their personal value as individuals and their place in the body of Christ are too closely wrapped up in the spiritual gift with which they've been blessed. So we must lovingly, gently, and consistently remind them that *they are not their gift*. Their identity is fundamentally wrapped up in Jesus Christ and their relationship to him and not in any ministry or service that he might choose to accomplish through their efforts.

Don't despise prophetic utterances when things go badly, when people are offended, or when someone gets it wrong (1 Thessalonians 5:19–22). Needless to say, this is easier said than done! We who embrace and build our lives and ministries on the inerrant Word of God and thus highly prize theological accuracy are disinclined to be tolerant of those who go astray. I'm not suggesting that we compromise our convictions or ignore serious theological error. Rather, I have in mind those minor mistakes people make with regard to what we might call secondary issues. If someone prophesies that Jesus is not returning a second time, or that he is returning and they know the "day and the hour" of the event, immediate correction and discipline are called for. But when mistaken words are spoken on matters of admittedly less importance, it is crucial that we not let our reaction lead us to despise the prophetic gift altogether or to enact rules or changes to our bylaws that would inhibit the proper exercise of the gift in the future.

Along with this, we need to be patient and remember that much of this will seem strange and unusual to people who have never experienced it before. Make sure that you are devoting sufficient time to helping visitors, unbelievers, or cessationists understand prophetic ministry. They will often feel confused or find it weird. Make sure there is time to dialogue and debrief about what has (or has not) happened. I've often found it helpful when such folk are present to preface the meeting with a statement such as this:

We are so happy that all of you are with us tonight. We hope and pray that this will be a time of practical benefit and spiritual encouragement to you. But we are also aware that you may not understand or agree with what may happen. We believe that the Holy Spirit can speak to us through revelatory spiritual gifts such as prophecy, word of knowledge, and word of wisdom. It may be that someone will share a dream they recently had that has relevant application to our lives. We want you to understand that we will not allow anything to go unaddressed that conflicts with Scripture. The Bible is our highest and final authority for determining truth. So put your hearts at rest, and know that nothing contrary to God's written and inspired Word will be tolerated.

That being said, some things might occur that simply make you feel uncomfortable. That often happens when we experience or witness something that we've never encountered before. We hope you will be patient with us. We are by no means perfect in what we do or believe. But if you will allow us to minister as we believe God is leading, we'll be certain to provide ample time for you to ask whatever questions you might have or to voice whatever concerns are on your heart.

Finally, don't let prophetic ministry dominate any meeting of the local church. There *are* other spiritual gifts! This is undoubtedly the rationale for Paul's comments in 1 Corinthians 14:29, "Let two or three prophets speak, and let the others weigh what is said." Limiting prophetic ministry to "two or three" will ensure that there is plenty of time and opportunity for other believers to exercise their spiritual gifts as well.

Conclusion

The passion and love the apostle Paul had for the churches he established and in which he ministered is unquestioned. He worked with his own hands so that the people would not find it necessary to support him financially. He cared little for his personal reputation and was even willing to sacrifice his life to bring them the gospel of God's grace (see Acts 20:24). One passage in particular comes to mind. In spite of their mistreatment of him and their suspicions regarding his apostolic credentials, he wrote this to the church in Corinth: "I will most gladly spend and be spent for your souls" (2 Corinthians 12:15a).

I mention this in order that we might more fully appreciate the force of Paul's exhortation in 1 Corinthians 14:1. We are all familiar with his exhortation to "earnestly desire the spiritual gifts," but we dare not ignore the phrase that follows: "*especially* that you may prophesy" (1 Corinthians 14:1, emphasis mine). Why "especially"? Why such an emphasis on this one spiritual gift? I could even ask the question, "Why did I write this chapter? Why the focus in this book on practical guidelines for exercising this gift in the local church? Why devote such meticulous concern to how prophecy is communicated and sustained in the lives of God's people?" The simple answer is because Paul himself believed that it was uniquely beneficial to the spiritual growth and maturity of God's people (see 1 Corinthians 14:3). As much as Paul loved his brothers and sisters in local churches everywhere, we can rest assured that he would not have made this a focal point of his exhortation were it not for the fact that he believed in its powerful capacity to bring encouragement, instruction, and consolation to Christian lives.

So I urge you to resist any temptation to minimize or, worse still, to dismiss entirely the spiritual gift of prophecy as if you and your church can get along well enough without it. Paul thought otherwise. So perhaps the appropriate response would be to read this chapter again, to make it a point of conversation in your small group, to make room for it in your corporate gatherings as a church, and then to step out in faith and take those risks, apart from which people may well go without the blessings that prophecy can bring.

CHAPTER 9

USER-FRIENDLY DELIVERANCE

When we begin to cultivate an openness to the supernatural power of God's Holy Spirit in our lives and in our churches, we should expect that God's work will be opposed. There will be some pushback. And it won't just be the people who don't like the changes or those who feel uncomfortable and leave. We must never forget that we live in a world at war and a spiritual battle rages on all around us each day.

As J. I. Packer once said, whenever God moves, Satan keeps pace. The enemy of our faith will do whatever is in his power to discourage you, to frighten you, and to enslave as many as he can in fleshly bondage and spiritual darkness. And one of the most significant ministries of the church is to liberate people from this bondage, from their enslavement to the demonic. My aim in this chapter isn't to persuade you that born-again Christians can be demonized. I believe that believers can be demonized, and I've addressed that issue in detail in a chapter in another book I've written called *Tough Topics*.[1] In what follows, I take for granted that we are engaged in a serious spiritual battle and that demonic assault of God's people is a daily reality that we ignore to our great harm.

There is no explicit reference in the New Testament to a spiritual gift of deliverance. I must say, however, that I have known several individuals who have demonstrated a powerful, extraordinarily authoritative,

1 *Tough Topics: Biblical Answers to 25 Challenging Questions* (Wheaton, Ill.: Crossway, 2013), 166–183.

and undeniably effective ministry in helping others find freedom from demonic oppression. Whether or not they were operating in the power of a spiritual gift or simply taking advantage of that authority given to all Christians in the name of Christ is of little concern to me. What matters is that we, as individual believers and as a church, come to understand the importance of this ministry and how to effectively facilitate the deliverance of those who suffer from demonic attack.

Six Reasons Why Christians Avoid Deliverance Ministry

I know that some of you reading this book will be tempted to skip this chapter. (Others may have turned immediately here.) For some people, it's just not something of interest. But my suspicion is that most who quickly turn the page do so because they are frightened by the subject of spiritual warfare and feel ill-equipped to handle the ugly and often disruptive outbursts that occur when the Holy Spirit confronts the realm of principalities and powers. But it is essential that we enter and engage in these spiritual battles. We cannot stick our head in the sand and ignore this reality. Evil beings have the power to affect our relationship with God—if we are ill equipped to engage with them.

If we ever hope to encourage people in our local churches to deal courageously and effectively with demonic activity, we need to educate them on why they feel so reticent to get involved in the first place. Many Christians avoid deliverance ministry because they have been offended by those who have taken it to unbiblical and damaging extremes. Make no mistake, the professing church has been damaged by the so-called ministries of men and women who argue that every sin is demonically induced. We hear them speak of the "spirit of nicotine" or the "spirit of greed" or the "spirit of anxiety." Virtually every moral weakness, addiction, or spiritual failure, together with every other grievous transgression, is attributed by such folk not to the fleshly impulses of our selfish, fallen selves but to some demon who is responsible for its presence and enslaving power in our lives. Can Satan or one of his demons aggravate and intensify our chosen acts of rebellion and unbelief? Yes. Can he cripple us with feelings of shame and guilt and blind us to the liberating grace of the cross of Christ? Yes. But no one can justifiably exonerate their bad behavior by insisting that "the devil made me do it!"

Lingering in the memories of some people are horrible scenes of a helpless man or woman being angrily berated by a deliverance expert or having a crucifix pressed painfully on their forehead. One thing I do know about the devil: he's not hard of hearing. Increased decibel levels spewed from the mouths of spiritual showmen accomplish nothing. Sadly, this type of manipulative excess has turned off many believers from ever giving serious consideration to what can be done to serve and set free those who are genuinely and grievously afflicted by the demonic.

Others avoid deliverance ministry because they wrongly believe that deliverance is a special ministry for special people with special spiritual gifts. Whenever there is a manifestation of demonic activity, they instinctively turn to see if that especially "spiritual" person is available to deal with the problem. They feel inadequate and often excuse their withdrawal by insisting that they simply don't have that particular spiritual gift. At the bottom of this hesitation is a failure to understand the full extent and efficacy of the authority given to all believers by Jesus himself.

I've also come across some Christians who avoid deliverance ministry because of a wrong interpretation of 2 Peter 2:10–11 and Jude 8–9. Peter speaks of holy angels who, "though greater in might and power, do not pronounce a blasphemous judgment against them [fallen angels / demons] before the Lord." Even more daunting is what we read in Jude:

> Yet in like manner these people also, relying on their dreams, defile the flesh, reject authority, and blaspheme the glorious

> ones. But when the archangel Michael, contending with the devil, was disputing about the body of Moses, he did not presume to pronounce a blasphemous judgment, but said, "The Lord rebuke you." (Jude 8–9)

At first glance, it might sound like Peter and Jude are warning us against confronting or speaking against angelic beings, even fallen, demonic ones. But a careful reading shows that these texts do *not* mean that we, as Christians, are forbidden to rebuke or verbally resist or pronounce judgment against demonic beings. Neither unbelievers (the "false teachers") nor even the holy angels have the authority that we have received by virtue of our being in Christ. In Christ, with his authority, we both can and must resist and rebuke the enemy (see Luke 10:1–20; Acts 5:16; 8:7; 16:16–18; 19:12). Jude does not extend to Christians the restriction he places on Michael.

Still others avoid deliverance ministry because they wrongly assume that Christians cannot be demonized. While I've addressed this elsewhere, I will make a few brief points here. First, we should observe that every case of demonization described in the New Testament involves someone under the influence or control, in varying degrees, of an indwelling evil spirit. The word "demonization" is never used in the NT to describe someone who is merely oppressed or harassed or attacked or tempted by a demon. In every case, reference is made to a demon either entering, dwelling in, or being cast out of the person. Matthew 4:24 and 15:22 at first appear to be exceptions to this rule, but the parallel passages in Mark 1:32–34 and 7:24–30 indicate otherwise. *To be "demonized," in the strict sense of that term, is to be inhabited by a demon with varying degrees of influence or control.*

Even if it should be proven that a Christian cannot be indwelt by a demonic spirit, almost everyone would concede that the born-again can be oppressed, tormented, and in a variety of ways spiritually and mentally assaulted by the powers of darkness. I raise this to point out that *regardless of where the demon might be, believers are often in need of deliverance and the freedom that Christ died to obtain for them.*

We must also honestly acknowledge that some avoid deliverance ministry because they are afraid of encountering the demonic. Hollywood portrayals of ritual exorcism have not helped in this regard. And of course Satan himself loves nothing more than to intimidate Christians with offensive images, sounds, and a variety of physical manifestations for which they feel altogether ill equipped. But none of the preceding excuses would ever have Satan's desired effect on Christians if the latter were fully aware of their identity in the risen Christ and the unchallenged authority that is theirs in Jesus' name. So that's where we must begin. The foundation of biblical deliverance ministry is a clear understanding of Christian identity and the authority believers have in Christ.

The Believer's Identity and Authority in Christ

Of the many biblical texts that address the availability of Christ's power over evil beings to believers, none does so with the clarity and conviction of Luke 10. In the first verse of that chapter, we read: "After this the Lord appointed seventy-two others and sent them on ahead of him, two by two, into every town and place where he himself was about to go" (Luke 10:1). By "others" Luke means other than the twelve apostles. These were non-apostolic disciples, followers of Jesus. Luke 10:1 stands in contrast to Luke 9:1 where Jesus "called the twelve together and gave them power and authority over all demons." I mention this distinction because some Christians try to excuse their lack of engagement in deliverance ministry or their feelings of spiritual impotence by pointing to the fact that "the twelve" were given "power and authority over all demons" but not themselves.

"I'm not an apostle," I've heard on countless occasions. "What reason do I have for believing that I might have that kind of authority?" Well, the reason is Luke 10, where average, non-apostolic followers of Jesus are given the same authority as the apostles over Satan and his forces.

Jesus sent these disciples out "two by two" to provide mutual protection, encouragement, and support, and also to establish legal attestation and binding testimony to what might subsequently occur (see Deuteronomy 17:6; 19:15). It would appear that the commissioning, authorizing, and empowering of the seventy-two (some texts read "seventy") is a prelude to the ministry of the larger universal body of Christ. As Susan Garrett explains, "Luke may have conceived of the mission by 'seventy (-two) others' as foreshadowing the period of the church, when not only the twelve but *many* sons and daughters would receive the Spirit of the Lord and prophesy, and would thereby be enabled to carry out Jesus' work."[2]

The narrative of their experience picks up in verses 17–20 of Luke 10.

> The seventy-two returned with joy, saying, "Lord, even the demons are subject to us in your name!" And he said to them, "I saw Satan fall like lightning from heaven. Behold, I have given you authority to tread on serpents and scorpions, and over all the power of the enemy, and nothing shall hurt you. Nevertheless, do not rejoice in this, that the spirits are subject to you, but rejoice that your names are written in heaven."

In my opinion, this is the most important passage in all of Scripture when it comes to equipping and encouraging average Christian men and women to engage the enemy. Here's why! For starters, you can't escape the obvious excitement shown by the

2 Susan Garrett, *The Demise of the Devil: Magic and the Demonic in Luke's Writings* (Minneapolis: Fortress Press, 1989), 48.

seventy-two when they return. "*Even* the demons are subject to us in your name!" (emphasis mine). In other words, "Wow!" Perhaps they had low expectations for the outcome of this ministry journey and were genuinely surprised by the effectiveness of the power they were given. But notice the clear excitement they have afterward. They understand that what they've experienced is something new.

We should also notice that they do not simply say the demons are "subject to us." No, they are "subject to us" only "in your [Christ's] name" The authority and the power that produced results belonged to Christ. His name empowered everything they did. Jesus had imparted it to or invested it in them.

It is unlikely that the "fall" (v. 18) of Satan referred to in Luke 10 is a reference to his original, pre-temporal, fall into sin, since Jesus' comment was directly in response to their report concerning the success they had experienced in casting out demons. As Sydney Page points out, "the context demands a reference to a fall that is the result of being defeated, not a fall that is the result of sinning."[3] So when Jesus tells them that he "saw" Satan fall what does he mean by this? The verb used here (*theoreo*) is not used elsewhere for visions Jesus had (although it is used to describe the visions that others experienced: see Acts 7:56; 9:7; 10:11). Whether or not Jesus experienced a vision or simply is using figurative language is unimportant. Of more significance is the nature and time of this fall of the enemy.

This fall that Jesus speaks about could refer to a visionary experience in which Jesus "saw" the impending fall or demise of the devil, an event yet to be fulfilled (cf. Daniel 7:2, 4, 6, 7, 9, 11, 13). Perhaps Jesus was looking forward to the judgment Satan would incur by virtue of the atoning sacrifice of the cross and the subsequent resurrection of Jesus from the dead. Other biblical interpreters see here a reference to Satan's fall that occurred because of

3 Sydney H. T. Page, *Powers of Evil: A Biblical Study of Satan and Demons* (Grand Rapids: Baker Books, 1995), 109.

his defeat in the wilderness when he failed in the tempting of Jesus. Still another possibility is that this fall is a reference to his defeat each time his house is plundered (Matthew 12:22–32) as a result of successful deliverance ministry. Whichever view is correct, Jesus is not saying that because of this fall from heaven Satan is no longer active or a threat. In fact, in verse 19 Jesus issues a promise that makes sense only if there are real dangers from which his disciples need to be protected. He says to his disciples: "I have given you authority" (Luke 10:19a).

Authority simply means delegated power. This not only refers to responsibility (the prerogative) but also entails *the spiritual power to enforce compliance.* Authority is the right and power to act and speak as if Jesus himself were present (v. 16). I once heard author and pastor Neil Anderson say something about authority that bears repeating here: "Spiritual warfare is not a horizontal tug of war but a vertical chain of command." In other words, we must never envision ourselves as operating on a level playing field with Satan and his demons. Alone and in the power of our own identity, we don't stand a chance against him. But in Christ and on the basis of who we are in him and in light of the authority of the risen Lord that has been bequeathed to us, Satan and his demons are a defeated lot. They must obey us. Don't ever think of yourself as at one end of a rope and Satan at the other, both of you struggling to overpower the other. No! You are in Christ who is over all. Satan is beneath you, in Christ's name.

Over what or whom have we been given this authority? What are the "serpents" and "scorpions" mentioned in Luke 10:19? These references are not to be taken literally but are a vivid and symbolic way of describing demonic beings. Serpents and scorpions were familiar sources of evil and pain in Palestinian life and frequently symbolized all kinds of adversity and affliction (see Numbers 21:6–9; Deuteronomy 8:15; Psalms 58:4; 140:3). The scorpion was also a means of divine chastisement in 1 Kings 12:11, 14 (see also Luke

11:11–12). And we are all familiar with Satan's identification with the serpent (Genesis 3; 2 Corinthians 11; Revelation 12 and 20). Satan's domain is that of snakes and scorpions (see especially Psalm 91:12–13).

If you still have doubts, notice that Jesus explains the meaning for us. He connects the "serpents and scorpions" of Luke 10:19 with the "demons" of verse 17. "Serpents and scorpions" are parallel to "all the power of the enemy," an undeniable reference to Satan and his hosts. And in verse 20, Jesus again indicates clearly that "serpents and scorpions" are a reference to demonic "spirits" (Revelation 9:3, 5, 10 lends support to this interpretation).

Jesus' warning in verse 20 isn't suggesting that it is wrong or sinful to rejoice in the authority we have over the demonic. If it were, Jesus would never have given such authority to his disciples in the first place. The point of this verse is that *in comparison with* being saved, such power is far less significant. Authority over the demonic spirits is great. But being saved, forgiven, and having one's name recorded in the book of life is greater!

So what is the significance of all this? Do we, the church, have this same authority today? Or was this a temporary endowment? My answer is not that we have the *same* authority, it's that we have even *greater* authority! I say this for several reasons. First of all, remember that this commission and the authority and power it entailed was given to the seventy-two, not simply to the twelve. It isn't possible to restrict this authority to a select few. Jesus' selection of seventy-two is done in anticipation of the worldwide mission of the entire body of Christ. The seventy-two were not uniquely gifted or specially called people with high office or position in the body of Christ. They were ordinary followers of Jesus, just like you and me.

In addition, we now live and operate on *this* side of the cross, subsequent to the defeat of Satan. In other words, their authority and power, prior to the cross, can hardly be regarded as equivalent to ours, subsequent to the cross. We also live and operate on *this* side of Pentecost. We operate with the fullness of the indwelling power and presence of the Holy Spirit. They did not have that indwelling presence. We have the fullness of divine authorization as stated unequivocally in the Great Commission (Matthew 28:18–19).

Christians often forget this. We fail to fully appreciate the fact that we have been raised up and seated with the exalted Lord, under whose feet all principalities and powers have been subjected (Ephesians 1:19–2:7; Colossians 2:9–10). The proof of the pudding is in the eating. In other words, the *evidence* of authority is the *exercise* of authority. One need only read numerous texts of the authority and power operative in the early church, following the ascension of Jesus, to see confirmation of this point. (I suggest you read closely Acts 5:16; 8:7; 16:18; 19:12–16; 2 Corinthians 10:3–4; Ephesians 6:10–13; James 4:7; 1 Peter 5:8; 1 John 2:13–14.)

The Exercise of Authority: Binding, Resisting, Rebuking

To this point I've labored to establish that every believer possesses authority over the demonic by virtue of our relationship to Jesus Christ. But how is this authority manifest? Some people use a variety of different words—a diverse vocabulary—when they engage in deliverance ministry. They speak of "rebuking" the enemy or "binding" the demonic. So is the use of these terms a legitimate biblical expression of our authority over the enemy? Some say no. They argue that we should simply pray and ask God to do the work of deliverance. "Why not just pray, 'O God, please resist, rebuke, and bind this evil spirit for me'?" They insist that we should always defer to God and never personally confront or resist the enemy ourselves.

But consider Ephesians 6:10–20. Here, Paul calls upon the church to take an active role in standing firm and struggling against the enemy. We should pray and ask for God to work, of course, but we must not stop there. We also need to avail ourselves of the power and weaponry secured for us by Christ's victory. Let us not forget that, as we've just seen in Luke 10, God has *delegated* his authority to us. It is not God's plan to settle all our spiritual disputes apart from our involvement. He wants us to *utilize* the authority he has invested in us. One reason may be that God wants us to share in and to enjoy the thrill of victory (Jesus is obviously pleased with the response of the seventy-two in Luke 10).

Another way of saying this is that God is pleased to utilize *means*, namely us, in the pursuit of his ends. In other words, God wants to involve us in the work of the kingdom. We are his representatives, spokesmen, ambassadors in evangelism, ministry, and so too in spiritual warfare. No one would ever think of saying: "O God, preach the gospel to the lost," or "O God, teach the truth to your people," or "Lord, would you please visit the sick today as I'm simply too busy." We would rightly consider a person who prays and does nothing to be disobedient. Rather, God desires to use us in proclaiming the gospel and in teaching the principles of Scripture and in ministering in mercy to those who are hurting. We have been entrusted with his authority, his power, and his gifts to minister to his people in his name and to participate in expanding his kingdom.

"O.K.," you say, but "is it biblical to *bind* the enemy?" Should we use that term? Well, let's take a look at where that term comes from. The only texts in Scripture where the term "bind" is used are in Matthew 12:29; 16:19; and 18:18. In the first of these it is Jesus who bound the devil, most likely a reference to his victory over him in the wilderness. Whereas Jesus is nowhere recorded as saying, "I bind you," he did, in point of fact, "bind" or restrict or inhibit the ability of the enemy to keep people in bondage.

In Matthew 16:19 we read of the "keys" (see Luke 11:52) granted to the leadership of the church. These are likely a reference to the power to know, understand, and proclaim the terms on the basis of which entrance into or exclusion from the kingdom of God is granted. Whatever we "bind" (prohibit) or "loose" (allow) through the proclamation of the gospel will prove to be an earthly application or confirmation of what heaven has already decreed. We have been given authority to pronounce forgiveness or judgment depending on a person's response to the truth (cf. John 20:23). The context of Matthew 18:18 is church discipline. Jesus is speaking about the decision of the church in adjudicating a dispute between two people. In this context, to "bind" is to declare someone guilty. Conversely, to "loose" is to declare them innocent. The decision of the church on earth reflects the decision already made in heaven. That is to say, when we conform to biblical guidelines and accurately declare the terms on which membership and fellowship in the church are possible, our decisions will be an earthly expression of heaven's prior decree.

In studying these passages, I find nothing in these three texts that gives explicit endorsement to the practice of saying, "Satan, I bind you in Jesus' name." However, before we dismiss this as an unbiblical practice, we need to observe a few other explicit commands of Scripture. In Ephesians 6 we are told to "stand" (v. 11) against the schemes of the devil. We have also been equipped with this spiritual armor that we might "withstand" in the evil day (v. 13). More explicit still is the statement by James that we should "resist the devil," together with the assurance that if we do "he will flee from" us (James 4:7). Likewise, Peter says, "Resist him," that is, our "adversary the devil" (1 Peter 5:8–9). To "resist" means to stand against or to oppose, to set oneself against someone or something. To resist Satan or his demons thus means to employ the authority and power given us by God to restrict his/their activities, to restrain his/their efforts, to thwart his/their plans.

So, while there is nothing in Scripture that requires us to use the term "bind" or speak of "binding" the demonic, there are plenty of passages that speak of resisting, opposing, and employing the authority Jesus has given us over the demonic. And because "bind" means to inhibit or to restrain someone from an action or activity, I think we have sufficient warrant to use the term if we wish to. So it is true that neither Jesus nor anyone else in the New Testament ever says: "Satan (demon), I bind you." On the other hand, both Jesus and Christians do, in terms of practical and experiential impact, "bind" him/them, primarily by the truth of God's word spoken (Matthew 4:1–11) and moral resistance (Ephesians 6:10–20). To put it simply, while we should not be too dogmatic about terms and should avoid appealing to the three texts cited above in Matthew's gospel to support our practice, I believe it is theologically permissible to use the terminology of "binding" when we resist the enemy.

What about "rebuking" the enemy? Is this biblical? The term "rebuke" (*epitimao*) is used frequently by Jesus in his encounters with demonic spirits (Matthew 17:18; Mark 1:25; 3:12; 9:25; Luke 4:35, 41; 9:42). The term functions as a word of command by which evil forces are brought into submission. Thus "it combines the idea of moral censure expressed by the word *rebuke* with the notion of the subjugation of demonic powers. It shows that Jesus has authority over the evil spirits and that they are powerless to resist his control."[4]

As an example of "rebuking" a spirit, consider Paul's deliverance of the slave girl in Acts 16:18—"And this she kept doing for many days. Paul, having become greatly annoyed, turned and said to the spirit, 'I command you in the name of Jesus Christ to come out of her.' And it came out that very hour." Clearly, the apostle didn't say, "Evil spirit, I bind you," or "I rebuke you." But notice what he *did*. He effectively bound and rebuked the spirit when he said, "I command you in the name of Jesus Christ to come out of her." Paul's words were a rebuke to the demon, which bound (restricted or restrained) the evil spirit's activity as it pertained to

4 Page, *Powers of Evil*, 143.

the slave girl. That's my point here. Whatever term we choose to use to describe it, this same power and authority exercised by Paul has been given to all Christians by the risen Lord.

Jesus' Approach to Deliverance

Jesus provides the best model for us in learning to interact with the demonic. There are numerous instances in the gospels where Jesus encountered the demonized, but one of the more helpful is Mark 5. There are several things that we learn from this passage (as well as a few others in Mark's gospel) that characterize Jesus' approach to deliverance. Not all of these are employed in every instance where Jesus encounters a demon, but each of them is important to remember for our own ministry.

The first thing we should notice in Mark 5 is that Jesus secures the name of the demon, or seeks to identify the spirit. In this case, it is a man who is indwelt by a "Legion" of demons. Jesus asks him, "What is your name?" (Mark 5:9). Why did Jesus do this? Some scholars point out that in the ancient world people believed that to know and speak someone's name was to gain spiritual authority over them. But Jesus already had this authority. Perhaps he did this to let those watching know the full extent of demonic power he was confronting. By asking for a name, Jesus makes it known that this man was under the influence of a virtual army of demons. The word "Legion" referred to a contingent of Roman soldiers, numbering upwards of 6,000. Or Jesus may have simply asked to reveal to the man himself how serious his condition was.

After asking the demon for a name, Jesus binds the spirit, which is to say, he prohibits it from some activity and thus curbs or breaks its power (see also Matthew 12:29). Then, he rebukes the spirit. Another way of saying this is that he censures or warns or denounces the demon. We see this explicitly again in Mark 1:25: "But Jesus rebuked him [the demon], saying, 'Be silent and come out of him!'" We also observe this approach in Matthew 17:18; Mark 9:25; and Luke 9:42. This sort of *rebuke* is not just a verbal reproof but also a technical term for subjugation of the evil power.

After binding and rebuking the demon, he silences it. In Mark 1:34 we read that "he healed many who were sick with various diseases, and cast out many demons. And *he would not permit the demons to speak*, because they knew him" (emphasis mine). We don't know with certainty why he refused to let them speak, but Peter Davids cites three possible reasons.[5]

> First, "the teachers of the law" associated him with Beelzebub, "the prince of demons" (3:22). Any tendency to show that he accepted the demonic would have given extra evidence to these opponents.
>
> Second, to accept the testimony of demons about himself would give a precedent to his followers to accept (or even seek) testimony of demons about other things. This would threaten to make Jesus' movement an occult movement.
>
> Third, and most important, Jesus' whole mission was a call to faith based on evidence, not on authoritative testimony. . . . Therefore the demons were short-circuiting Jesus' whole methodology. His command to them was a sharp "Shut up!" His invitation to the crowd at their expulsion was, "See and believe that the Kingdom of God has come."

After silencing the demonic spirits, Jesus would typically cast them out (see Matthew 8:16; Mark 1:25; 7:29), and after casting them out, he would refuse to let the spirit return. We read this in Mark 9:25—"And when Jesus saw that a crowd came running together, he rebuked the unclean spirit, saying to it, 'You mute

---

5 Peter H. Davids, *More Hard Sayings of the New Testament* (Downers Grove, Ill.: InterVarsity Press, 1991), 27.

and deaf spirit, I command you, come out of him and *never enter him again*'" (emphasis mine). There are even some occasions in Scripture when Jesus would directly send a demon into the abyss. We read in Luke 8:31 that the demonic spirits themselves "begged him not to command them to depart into the abyss." Why do the demons fear the abyss? Perhaps it is a place of imprisonment where they would be temporarily consigned, awaiting the final judgment. Or it may refer to the place of final punishment. We can't be certain. Aside from its appearance here and in Romans 10:7, the word *abyssos* is found only in Revelation 9:1–2, 11; 11:7; 17:8; 20:1, 3.

Regardless of the exact meaning of the word, we should note that Jesus did not always consign exorcised demons to the abyss or in some place of permanent detention. As seen above in the account of the demonized young boy in Mark 9, Jesus simply said, "I command you, come out of him and *never enter him again*" (v. 25, emphasis mine). This implies that the recurrence of demonization after deliverance was a possibility, and steps had to be taken to prevent such from happening. Evidently, often after being cast out from a person, a demon was free to return to the person or to enter someone else.

Notice in Mark 9 that Jesus criticizes the disciples for their lack of faith in dealing with this demonized boy (vv. 19, 28–29). Evidently, due to their previous success in deliverance ministry, they had come to believe that divine power was at their disposal to use as they saw fit, apart from constant reliance on God. But this kind of demon, says Jesus, can come out only by prayer (v. 29). This is intriguing, insofar as *there is not a single instance of deliverance by prayer in the New Testament*. Deliverance elsewhere always occurs by the word of *command*. It is also interesting to note that deliverance from an indwelling spirit is never granted in response to the faith of the one who is demonized, although it is sometimes related to the faith of others. One can only conclude that in particular cases where an especially powerful demon is involved, prayer may be needed.

Sydney Page notes that "Mark focuses on the need for prayer

because it clearly demonstrates that divine power is not under human control; it must always be asked for. Manifestations of the power of God, such as are needed when dealing with the forces of evil, come only in response to the attitude of trust and reliance upon God that is expressed in humble prayer."[6] Jesus doesn't specify precisely what should be asked for in prayer, but we can assume that it is for the power and presence of the Holy Spirit to enable us to do what we in our own power could never accomplish (see Luke 11:13).

It surprises many to discover that even for Jesus, deliverance was not always instantaneous or without considerable resistance (see Mark 1:26; 5:8 [Lk. 8:29]; 9:26). If this is difficult to grasp, consider the analogy of a parent and his/her child. When my daughters were young and still in the home, and I would exercise parental authority and tell them to do something, or to cease from some activity; it was not unusual for them to delay their obedience. They would resist complying with my command, using any number of tactics. Soon, though, they began to obey, but then hesitate. They stalled, made excuses, and insisted on arguing about whether or not it was right or necessary for them to obey me. They might try to distract me from the issue at hand by diverting my attention to something of equal or greater urgency. They moved slowly, hoping I'd forget. They might even play me off against their mother, telling me that she had given her approval. If I persisted in the exercise of my authority as their parent, they would eventually do as I said or suffer the consequences!

I think something similar may be at work in the exercise of spiritual authority. Our approach should not be, "Speak the word of command in Jesus' name, *and* it is done," which usually leads to frustration and disillusionment. Our approach should be, "Speak the word of command in Jesus' name *UNTIL* it is done."

We should also remember that Jesus' approach was never ritualistic or mechanical or magical. He employed no elaborate religious

6 Page, *Powers of Evil*, 164.

formula. No incantations. No candles. No mood music playing in the background. No charms. No religious formulas. No chanting. No dancing. No cutting off of a chicken's head. He didn't have to shout or jump up and down. He didn't physically restrain the demonized man or press a cross against his forehead. He didn't use "holy" water or incense. He simply said: "Shut up! Get out!"

It is little wonder, then, that the people of his day were amazed by how Jesus dealt with deliverance (see Mark 1:27; Matthew 9:32–33). According to Matthew 8:16, Jesus "cast out the spirits *with a word*" (emphasis mine). Jesus never appealed to a higher authority when expelling demons, unlike Paul, for example, who cast out a demon from the slave girl in Acts 16 by appealing to "the name of Jesus Christ" (v. 18).

Encounters with the Demonic and Deliverance in the Book of Acts

In addition to the encounters of Jesus in the gospels, there are several examples of demonic deliverance in the Book of Acts (see Acts 5:16; 8:5–8; 13:6–12; 16:16–18; 19:12). The story in Acts 19:13–17 is worthy of special attention:

> Then some of the itinerant Jewish exorcists undertook to invoke the name of the Lord Jesus over those who had evil spirits, saying, "I adjure you by the Jesus whom Paul proclaims." Seven sons of a Jewish high priest named Sceva were doing this. But the evil spirit answered them, "Jesus I know, and Paul I recognize, but who are you?" And the man in whom was the evil spirit leaped on them, mastered all of them and overpowered them, so that they fled out of that house naked and wounded. And this became known to all the residents of Ephesus, both Jews and Greeks. And fear fell upon them all, and the name of the Lord Jesus was extolled.

Acts 19:13 contains the earliest known occurrence in Greek literature of the word "exorcist" (*exorkistes*) and the only occurrence of it in the New Testament. Whereas here it is used of the Jewish "exorcists," it is never used to refer to Christians engaged in deliverance ministry (perhaps because of its magical connotations).

Acts 19:12 tells us that Paul was engaged in a successful deliverance ministry in Ephesus. Although the connection is not explicit, Luke appears to link the presence of disease with that of demons as well as the healing from disease with the expulsion of demons. He also mentions that there were some itinerant exorcists present in the vicinity of Ephesus, but these were not Jewish Christians, otherwise they would have simply appealed to the name of Jesus as the one whom *they* preached. Any reference to Paul would have been unnecessary (v. 13). Also, we can see from the way the demon speaks of them that they were not true believers.

The demon that is referenced in this passage is portrayed as an intelligent being who is able to converse openly and clearly with humans. The demon is able to distinguish between Christian and non-Christian, between true faith and false profession. Strangely, this demon also appears to have something of a sense of humor. Note the sarcasm in his reply: "Jesus I know, and Paul I recognize, *but who [the heck] are you*?" (v. 15, emphasis mine). The question the demon asks is not for the purpose of learning their identity (names) or obtaining personal information about them. He is challenging their right to use the name of Jesus: "I know Jesus. I must bow to his authority and obey. And I know Paul acts in Jesus' name. But who are you that I should obey what you say or pay any attention to your demands?" As John Stott points out, "To be sure, there is power—saving and healing power—in the name of Jesus, as Luke has been at pains to illustrate (e.g., [Acts] 3:6, 16; 4:10–12). But its efficacy is not mechanical, nor can people use it second-hand."[7]

---

7 John Stott, *The Spirit, the Church, and the World: The Message of Acts*

Christians, such as Paul, most certainly do have a right to the name of Jesus, and demons must obey.

This narrative demonstrates that demons are by nature violent and can infuse their victims with superhuman strength (v. 16). Although this does not mean we should never make physical contact with the demonized (Jesus certainly did; see Luke 4:40–41), it is certainly a cautionary note that we should never act presumptuously or carelessly when dealing with the supernatural power of the enemy.

Neil Anderson's Approach to Deliverance

Among the many approaches to deliverance ministry, I have found much that is helpful in the approach proposed by author Neil Anderson.[8] Anderson advocates what he calls the *truth encounter* method of deliverance as opposed to the *power encounter*. A truth encounter requires that the demonized or oppressed individual personally renounce the enemy, repent of all known sin, affirm the truth, and submit to the Lordship of Jesus. No one else need be engaged in the process. It is a form of self-deliverance.

A truth encounter can be contrasted with a power encounter, which is when you confront the demon directly and verbally command that it identify itself (name, function, point of entry, etc. [although this is not essential to the power encounter]) and cast it out (to the abyss, or to wherever Jesus sends it). Jesus often employed the power encounter approach, as did Paul in Acts 16. To engage in a power encounter you would typically follow this approach: (1) *Expose* (discern and document that demonic activity is present), then (2) *engage* (identify, name, function, point or ground of entry), and then (3) *expel* (in the name and authority of Jesus).

(Downers Grove, Ill.: InterVarsity Press, 1990), 307.

8 See especially, *The Bondage Breaker* (Eugene: Harvest House, 2000); *Victory over the Darkness: Realizing the Power of Your Identity in Christ* (Ventura: Regal Books, 1990); and *Ministering the Steps to Freedom in Christ* (Ventura: Gospel Light, 1998).

Anderson advises against power encounters in deliverance for two primary reasons. First, he argues that conversing with demons is never advisable because demons are liars (John 8:44). While I agree that demons will certainly try to lie, I believe they can be compelled to speak the truth when subjected to the authority of Christ. For an example of this, see Mark 1:24 where demons spoke the truth.

Anderson also argues that the epistles are our guide to deliverance, not the gospels or Acts. The epistles stress what we do for ourselves, not what others do for us. Anderson insists that he has not attempted to "cast out" a demon in years, instead helping people find freedom in Christ by enabling them to resolve their personal and spiritual conflicts. He believes that success in attaining freedom is dependent on the cooperation of the person who is oppressed. Anderson gives no textual or biblical arguments for rejecting the gospels and Acts as a pattern for deliverance. His position is probably the fruit of his dispensational approach to biblical interpretation, but I'm not convinced that we should limit deliverance ministry in this way.

While it is obviously ideal for an individual to participate in deliverance, what should we do for a younger child or someone who can't perceive the truth sufficiently to work through Anderson's "Steps to Freedom"? What if the bondage is so intense as to have crippled the person's ability and strength to work through the steps, or if a person is so thoroughly deceived that he/she doesn't believe the truth or effectiveness of the steps? What if the person has been blinded by the enemy (2 Corinthians 4:4)? Anderson's truth encounter is certainly good and helpful and ought to be employed whenever possible. But in cases of severe demonic stronghold or intractable resistance, a direct power encounter may also be required.

Anderson asks the question, "If *you* expel or cast out a demon from someone, what is to prevent the demon from returning?" In other words, he says that without the involvement of the person, without the responsible activity and mental participation of the victim, the problem may disappear for a while only later to re-emerge.

My response is that what prevents a demon from coming back is the same authority and power by which it was compelled to leave in the first place. In Mark 9 Jesus commanded the spirit saying, "never return." So, too, should we. Of course, a person can always willingly re-open that door, but that possibility should not prevent us from helping them get free.

A final caution with Anderson's approach is that it is cognitive, a form of self-deliverance. *We are not exorcists*, says Anderson, *but facilitators*:

> In a truth encounter, I deal only with the person, and I do not bypass the person's mind. In that way people are free to make their own choices. There is never a loss of control as I facilitate the process of helping them assume their own responsibility before God. After all, it isn't what I say, do or believe that sets people free—it's what they renounce, confess, forsake, whom they forgive and the truth they affirm that sets them free. This "truth procedure" requires me to work with the whole person, dealing with body, soul and spirit.[9]

But of course, in the final analysis, it isn't what "I" say, do, or renounce even in the power encounter, but what "I, *in the name and authority of Jesus*," say and do that brings deliverance. We need to remember that there is no power inherent in truth. All power is in God, and it is the God of truth who has power to set the captives free.

A Practical Model for Deliverance

Now that you've gained some familiarity with biblical examples of deliverance and we've looked at one of the most popular models for

---

9 Neil Anderson, *Released from Bondage* (San Bernardino: Here's Life Publishers, 1991), 17.

deliverance, we are ready to articulate the model for deliverance ministry employed at Bridgeway. I acknowledge that this certainly isn't the only way to approach those who are severely oppressed, but it's the approach that I've found most helpful.

Pray for Discernment

As you are getting started in the ministry of deliverance, I highly recommend the value of having someone skilled in deliverance and gifted in discernment present with you. It's one thing to read about this in a book or even in the Bible, it's another thing to practice it. Those who are new in deliverance ministry often presumptuously and incorrectly connect demonic spirits with certain emotional and/or psychological symptoms and bizarre behaviors. Experience is helpful. Whereas we don't want to ignore demons if they are present, even greater damage can be done by assuming that they are the cause of a problem when they aren't.

I mentioned having someone with the gift of spiritual discernment, so let me take a moment and briefly explain the spiritual gift of discerning of spirits. Unfortunately, nowhere in the New Testament is this gift defined, and the only place it is even mentioned is in 1 Corinthians 12:10. Because we know so little about this gift, we should avoid dogmatism in our efforts to identify and account for how it should operate in our lives. That being said, I suggest that this charisma is most likely the Spirit-empowered ability to distinguish between what the Holy Spirit does, on the one hand, and the works of another spirit (demonic) or perhaps even the human spirit, on the other. We must come to grips with the fact that not every supernatural display of power is produced by the Holy Spirit. My sense is that this is the type of discernment that the gift of discerning of spirits is designed to accomplish: to provide us with insight into the ultimate origin or cause of any particular spiritual phenomenon.

There is a sense in which all Christians are responsible to "test the spirits to see whether they be of God" (1 John 4:1), and the ability to draw these conclusions does not require a special gift. We need only ascertain whether or not a person "confesses that Jesus Christ has come in the flesh" (1 John 4:2). Those who do not, says John, are "not from God" but are operating in the "spirit of the antichrist" (1 John 4:3). The apostle Paul, on the other hand, has in mind a unique ability that is fundamentally intuitive or subjective in nature, a Spirit-energized ability that is only given to some in the body of Christ, not all. The spiritual gift of distinguishing of spirits is probably a supernaturally enabled sense or feeling concerning the nature and source of any particular spirit under consideration.

Again, we can't be certain about this, but it is likely that we see examples of this gift in operation in the following texts. In Acts 16:16–18 Paul was able to discern that the power of a young slave girl was not divine but derived from a demonic presence. We also read in Acts 13:8–11 where Paul through the Holy Spirit saw that Elymas the magician was demonically empowered in his efforts to oppose the presentation of the gospel. In Acts 14:8–10 Paul "saw" (discerned?) that a man had faith to be healed. And in Acts 8:23 Peter is portrayed as in some sense "seeing" that Simon Magus was "in the gall of bitterness and in the bond of iniquity." How did he come by this knowledge? Perhaps it was through his exercise of the gift of discerning of spirits. Then there is Jesus himself. In John 1:47 he looked at Nathanael and described him as a man "in whom is no deceit." Again in John 2:25 it is said that Jesus "knew what was in man."

Here are some important steps we should take in the process of discernment:

- Pray for the Holy Spirit to open your spiritual eyes and speak to you regarding the individual. He may be pleased to reveal to you the cause of the oppression or what sins(s) might have occurred that gave the devil an "opportunity" or "foothold" (NIV; literally, a "place") in this person's life (Ephesians 4:27).

- Pray with your eyes *open*. The presence of a demonic spirit will often lead to physical, visible manifestations. If it does, don't react in disgust or surprise. Satan would love nothing more than to intimidate you into thinking that you are incompetent for the task of securing freedom for this individual. Don't ever conclude that any case of demonic oppression or demonization is above your spiritual pay grade! Simply take authority over the spirit(s) in Jesus' name. You may recall from the story in Mark 9 that when a father brought his demonized boy to Jesus for deliverance, the demon suddenly "convulsed the boy, and he fell on the ground and rolled about, foaming at the mouth" (Mark 9:20). Even after Jesus commanded the demon to "come out of him and never enter him again" (9:25b), the physical manifestations didn't immediately cease: "And after crying out and convulsing him terribly, it came out" (9:26a).
- Learn (by experience) the signs and symptoms of oppression and demonization. This will only come with time, as no two cases are always precisely the same. I can say, however, that in most instances of serious demonization, I've discovered that the enemy will do everything possible to resist the truth of the gospel. As noted below, under point (3), when asked to read aloud of how "all rule and authority and power and dominion" have been "put under" the feet of the risen and exalted Christ (Ephesians 1:21–22), the afflicted person will often stutter, stumble, get distracted, complain of dizziness, or angrily refuse.

Instruct the Person

After you have prayed for discernment, take time to explain to the individual what you are doing and why. This will help alleviate their fears and any anxiety they might be feeling. Explain to them that *if* they have a demon, this does not mean they are dirty, more sinful than other Christians, subspiritual, or unloved of God. Instruct the person to cooperate with what is happening by constantly giving you feedback: what they are feeling, thinking, physical sensations, intrusive thoughts, violent or sinful impulses, etc.

Articulate Your Authority in Christ

Begin by verbally declaring the authority of Christ and his supremacy over all demonic spirits. I encourage either you or the person who is suffering to read aloud Luke 10:17–20, Ephesians 1:15–23 (esp. v. 21), and Colossians 2:9–15. Direct, authoritative prayer and Bible-reading should stir and agitate demonic spirits if they are present. Ask the person if they are hearing or feeling anything unusual when you read the Bible or speak of Jesus and his blood.

Explore Other Possible Causes

Don't immediately assume that the problem is demonically caused. Conduct an interview of sufficient depth that you explore the possibility of other potential sources for the problem such as: physiological (have they had a physical examination recently?), prescription medication (are they on any?), other organic causes, stress, fatigue, circumstantial issues, relational dynamics, etc. Be aware of the fact that even if the presenting problem is caused by something other than a demonic spirit, the enemy can still aggravate, intensify, and exploit such factors.

Ask the Right Questions

Ask the person to give you a personal testimony of faith in Christ. Do they struggle in doing so? Are they able to affirm without agitation or hesitation their submission to the lordship of Jesus? Ask the person if they experience any special hindrances when they engage in spiritual activities such as praying, reading the Bible, worship, etc. Ask them if at any time he/she is feeling anger or hate toward you. Do they feel prompted to assault you either verbally or physically?

Determine as best you can if any behavior or beliefs of the person may have opened the door to demonic activity. Focus particularly on *family history* (any involvement of ancestors in the occult or unbiblical practices) and *personal sins* (idolatry, witchcraft, unforgiveness, sexual immorality, etc.). If something in particular is discovered, lead the person in a prayer of confession, repentance, and repudiation of whatever it is that may have led to demonic intrusion. In short, lead them in a prayer by which *they* close any doors that may have been opened.

Confront the Enemy

I have found the most effective strategy is to engage the person in eye-to-eye contact. Explain to them that whereas you will be looking *at* them, you will not be speaking *to* them. You will be addressing any demonic spirit that might be present. (This is what Paul did in Acts 16:18.)

Look directly into their eyes and say: "In the name of the Lord Jesus Christ and through the power of his shed blood and resurrection life, I take authority over any demonic spirit either present in or around __________ (name of person). In the name of the Lord Jesus Christ, I command any and every demonic spirit to leave __________ (name of person) and never return."

You may find it necessary to repeat this prayer of command more than once. Demons are quite good at misdirection and will try to deceive you into thinking they have left when they are actually still present.

These commands and prayers for deliverance may take any number of forms. You may want to be specific in naming any sins that may have led to the problem. You may want to pray for the Holy Spirit to shine the light of revelation and truth into the person's heart and mind, dispelling all darkness and confusion, etc. You may wish to pray prayers of protection over the person. Remember: the key is not in particular words or formulas but in the simple, irresistible authority of the risen Christ in whose name you act.

If there is a demon present, you can usually expect some form of resistance or physical manifestation. Encourage the person to report to you any impressions, thoughts, emotional impulses, physical sensations, voices, etc., that occur in the course of your prayer.

Assessment

One of three things is true. It may be that the demon(s) really did leave. Its departure may be loud, violent, and visible, or silent, simple, and unseen. Don't be too quick to draw conclusions about whether it left based on how the person felt or reacted. If you suspect it might still be present, repeat the above procedures.

There is also the possibility that the demon(s) is still there. If it is still present, there are at least three possible reasons: (1) the person doesn't want it to go; (2) the demon(s) has moral grounds for staying; or (3) this is an especially powerful demon that requires more prayer, faith, fasting, and concentrated effort on the part of all involved (see Mark 9:28–29).

Finally, you may have to reckon with the fact that the demon(s) was never there in the first place and that the nature and cause of the affliction (whether it be emotional or physical) is of a different order, calling for a different approach.

Concluding Prayer

It might be helpful to close with a prayer such as this:

> *Father, I thank you that ____________ (name of person) is your child, redeemed by the blood of Christ Jesus, forgiven and justified by faith in his name, and indwelled by the precious and powerful Holy Spirit. Guard him/her. Protect*

him/her. Surround your child with your angelic hosts. Fill him/her with a renewed sense of your love and the peace that surpasses all understanding.

Conclusion

We should passionately cherish and regularly give thanks for every promise spoken to us in Scripture. In view of Satan's determination to "devour" us (1 Peter 5:8), there is perhaps one promise that we should especially lay hold of and praise God for its fulfillment. Learning how to obey the command to "resist the devil" (James 4:7a) was the principal aim of this chapter. But the promise that follows the exhortation should be precious to every child of God: "and he will flee from you" (4:8b). I've tried to make it clear in this chapter that "the devil," or Satan, is a very real, very cunning, and very powerful enemy. But he is no match for the Christian who stands firmly in the authority of Christ and resists him. That's not arrogance or spiritual bravado. It's simply a matter of believing and acting on the promise of God: "he *will* flee from you." Whatever power Satan may have, ours in Christ is greater.

James does not suggest that Satan *might* flee from us if we resist him. He does not *hope* that such will be the case. He does not say that *perhaps* we will be successful in our opposition to his nefarious plans. He declares without hesitation or doubt that if we resist our enemy he *will* flee from us. If little else of practical benefit comes to you who read this chapter, I pray that you will move forward in your Christian life and in whatever ministry God has given you with a newly found and biblically grounded confidence in the authority and power given to every believer in the name of Jesus. Don't live in fear of the devil and his minions. Stand firm. Resist them. Rejoice and be glad in the exercise of the authority given to you in Christ, but even more so in the incomparable truth "that your names are written in heaven" (Luke 10:20).

CHAPTER 10

DO NOT QUENCH THE SPIRIT!

There are numerous metaphors and analogies employed by the biblical authors to describe both the nature and ministry of the Holy Spirit, the three most common being wind, water, and fire. When it comes to *wind*, one thinks immediately of our Lord's words to Nicodemus and the mysterious way in which he brings new birth to spiritually dead sinners:

> "Do not marvel that I said to you, 'You must be born again.' The wind blows where it wishes, and you hear its sound, but you do not know where it comes from or where it goes. So it is with everyone who is born of the Spirit." (John 3:7–8)

When the apostle Paul wanted to describe the Spirit's work in imparting the new birth or the experience of being born again, he turned to the cleansing properties of *water*:

> But when the goodness and loving kindness of God our Savior appeared, he saved us, not because of works done by us in righteousness, but according to his own mercy, by the washing of regeneration and renewal of the Holy Spirit, whom he poured out on us richly through Jesus Christ our Savior. (Titus 3:4–6; see also 1 Corinthians 12:13)

These are precious truths to our hearts, cherished by all believers. No less so is the association of the Spirit with *fire* (in addition to the text in 1 Thessalonians 5:19–20 from which the chapter title comes, see also Matthew 3:11–12; Acts 2:1–4; 2 Timothy 1:6–7).

Whether it is the fire that burns up and consumes the dross of sin in our lives or the fire of power and energy that fuels our efforts to labor for the glory of Christ and the good of his people, the Holy Spirit is a glorious gift, the consummate treasure whom we hold dear.

My aim in this chapter is twofold. First, to issue a warning about the many ways, whether consciously or not, that we quench the flame of his presence. And second, to provide a measure of practical guidance about what we might do to stoke the fire of his power in our personal lives and in the experience of the local church.

Though we've spent most of this book talking about ways to welcome and encourage the supernatural ministry of the Holy Spirit, we also need to be aware that there are many subtle and often unconscious ways in which we *quench* the presence of the Holy Spirit. I don't say this as a judgment but as a simple fact of reality. There may be fears in the hearts of our people, or warnings we've heard against charismatic excess. It might be the unspoken rules that govern your Sunday morning worship or the principles articulated in our church bylaws. It may be patterns of indwelling sin that are present in your church community. All of these can quench the fire of the Holy Spirit's work, sometimes snuffing it out altogether.

How serious a problem is this in our churches today? I'll answer that by pointing you to a statement by Octavius Winslow written in the mid-nineteenth century. Winslow's words give expression to a truth that all Bible-believing, gospel-centered evangelicals need to hear and heed. He writes:

> All that we spiritually know of ourselves, all that we know of God, and of Jesus, and His Word, we owe to the teaching of the Holy Spirit; and all the real light, sanctification, strength and comfort we are made to possess on our way to glory, we must ascribe to Him. . . . Where He is honored, and adoring thoughts of His

> person, and tender, loving views of His work are cherished, then are experienced, in an enlarged degree, His quickening, enlightening, sanctifying and comforting influence.[1]

Think about what Winslow is saying here. Everything we know of God the Father and of Jesus does not come naturally. We owe *everything* to the ministry of the Spirit. Everything we understand in God's Word, whatever degree of insight we gain into the measureless truths it embodies, we must attribute to the ministry of the Spirit. Whatever positive moral change we've experienced in life, whatever conformity to Christ we've seen develop in our spiritual walk, the Holy Spirit has done that. Whatever strength we receive when our weakness threatens to overwhelm, whatever encouragement we feel at times of despair and doubt, whatever sanctifying influence we sense in our souls, we owe to the third person of the Godhead. "Where he is honored," says Winslow, "and adoring thoughts of His person, and tender, loving views of His work are cherished," Christian men and women will experience in "an enlarged degree" the glorious benefits of his work.

The antithesis of honoring the Spirit is quenching him (1 Thessalonians 5:19–20). The antithesis of entertaining adoring thoughts of his person and cherishing his work is quenching him. One can hardly conceive of a more serious sin than that of quenching the Spirit of God!

The language of quenching the Holy Spirit comes straight out of your Bible, not just mine! Paul gave this energetic word of exhortation to the Christians in Thessalonica: "Do not quench the Spirit. Do not despise prophecies, but test everything; hold fast what is good. Abstain from every form of evil" (1 Thessalonians 5:19–22).

To use Paul's metaphor here, the Spirit is like a fire whose flame we must be careful not to quench or extinguish. The Holy Spirit

---

1 Octavius Winslow, *The Inquirer Directed to an Experimental and Practical View of the Work of the Holy Spirit* (New York, 1840), iv–v.

wants to intensify the heat of his presence among us, to inflame our hearts and fill us with the warmth of his indwelling power. We don't want to be a part of the bucket brigade that stands ready to douse his activity with the water of legalism and fear and extra-biblical rules. Obviously, one of the ways we do this is with a flawed theology that claims that his gifts have ceased and been withdrawn.

Sadly, I've known people who, as soon as they feel the slightest tinge of warmth from the Spirit's supernatural work, quickly grab their theological and denominational fire hose and douse his flame! I understand their concerns. They have grown weary of fanatical extremes and unbiblical sensationalism and feel compelled to pull in the reins on the Holy Spirit. They struggle with doubt and are increasingly cynical about the supernatural. The result is that they have become practical cessationists who rarely pray for the sick with expectant faith and rarely make room for the operation of spiritual gifts such as prophecy.

When we look at the Scriptures, there are at least six ways in which people can sin against the Holy Spirit, six *specific* sins that people can commit. The first one that the New Testament talks about is *insulting* the Spirit (see Hebrews 10:29). Jesus himself warned us of the second, that there are dire consequences for *blaspheming* the Spirit (Matthew 12:31). Stephen charged his accusers with *resisting* the Spirit (Acts 7:51–53). And the apostle Paul warned the church in Ephesus about *grieving* the Spirit (Ephesians 4:29–32). Peter accused Ananias and Sapphira of *lying* to the Spirit (Acts 5:3). Finally, there is the text we just read where Paul cautions the Thessalonians about the tendency to *quench* the Spirit (1 Thessalonians 5:19–22). My reading of these texts leads me to conclude that only non-Christians can commit the first three of these sins, but the latter three are within the power of Christians to commit. And it is with the sixth that we are most concerned in this chapter.

Before we look in detail at *how* we quench the Spirit, we need to look briefly at the fact that the Spirit *can* be quenched. Why is this a problem? Well, let me remind you that this is the *sovereign* Spirit of God, who as God works all things according to his will. Yet here we are told that he has granted to the Christian the power and authority *either to restrict or release* what he does in the life of the local church! Here we are told that the Spirit comes to us as a fire, either to be fanned into full flame and given the freedom to accomplish his will or to be doused and extinguished by the water of human fear, control, and flawed theology. How are we to reconcile this ability to quench the Spirit with the truth that God is sovereign, that none can resist his will?

We begin by acknowledging that the Spirit can certainly accomplish all that he wills to accomplish. But it is no less true that in certain instances, especially when it comes to spiritual gifts and the manifestation of the miraculous and supernatural, he will rarely, if ever, force himself upon us against our will or judgment. As we saw earlier when we looked at the spiritual gift of prophecy, Paul says in 1 Corinthians 14:32 that "the spirits of prophets are subject to prophets." His point is that the Holy Spirit does not act upon or through us as if we were puppets. The sovereign Spirit happily subjects himself to our decisions. This is a frightening thought and an awesome responsibility! We can make choices that will determine whether and to what extent the Spirit will operate freely and powerfully in our midst. Notice that Paul doesn't say, "Hey, don't worry about your theology of the Spirit. Don't give a second thought to how you structure and orchestrate your corporate worship services or your small group ministries. The Spirit's going to do whatever he wants regardless of what you do or say."

What, then, is our responsibility? Paul tells us: we are to fan the flame of the Spirit's fire! Intensify the heat! Rekindle what has grown cold from neglect and indifference (2 Timothy 1:6). Facilitate! Teach! Encourage! Make it safe for people to step out in faith and expectation. Don't create an atmosphere of fear in which people are terrified of making a mistake and being publicly denounced for their failures. Don't forbid speaking in tongues;

don't despise prophetic utterances. Instead, when you discern the Spirit's presence, when his fire is detected, pour gasoline on it!

Five Ways We Might Quench the Holy Spirit

So what does it mean to quench the Holy Spirit? How do we do this, and even more important, how do we avoid doing it? While there may be more than this, I want to look at five ways in which we quench the Spirit's work.

First, we quench the Spirit whenever we diminish his personality and speak of him as if he were only an abstract power or a source of divine energy. Gordon Fee refers to the struggle one of his students had with understanding the personhood of the Spirit: "God the Father makes perfectly good sense to me," said the student, "and God the Son I can quite understand; but the Holy Spirit is a gray, oblong blur."[2] There are times when the precious Spirit of God is treated as if he were no more than an ethereal energy, the divine equivalent to an electric current: stick your finger of faith into the socket of his "anointing presence" and you'll experience a spiritual shock of biblical proportions! The mechanical manipulation and virtual depersonalization of the Spirit has frightened many evangelicals and made them understandably skeptical of any claims to miraculous activity. In view of such patterns of ministry, any talk of *experiencing the Spirit* is summarily dismissed as dishonoring to his exalted status as God and a failure to embrace his sovereignty over us rather than ours over him.

This can be easily overcome by a brief consideration of how the New Testament consistently describes the Holy Spirit. The Holy Spirit is portrayed as having all the qualities of a personal being. If you were asked to define *personhood,* what words would you employ? How would you differentiate a person from a mere

2 Gordon D. Fee, *God's Empowering Presence: The Holy Spirit in the Letters of Paul* (Peabody, Mass.: Hendrickson Publishers, 1994), 5–6.

power or a machine? I suspect you would argue that a person has the capacity for independent thought and self-reflection; a person experiences genuine affections and can exercise his/her will in the making of decisions. All of these are predicated of the Spirit in Scripture: he has a *mind* (he thinks, reasons, and knows)[3]; he has *feelings* or *affections* or *emotions*[4]; and he makes choices, decisions, and exercises his *will* in accordance with his desires[5]. The Spirit also performs all the *functions* of a personal being. He talks[6], testifies[7], can be sinned against (Matthew 12:31), lied to (Acts 5:3), tested/tempted (Acts 5:9), and insulted (Hebrews 10:29). The Spirit enters into relationship with other persons (2 Corinthians 13:14), and can encourage (Acts 9:31), strengthen (Ephesians 3:16), and teach them (Luke 12:12; John 14:26; 1 Corinthians 2:13).

Second, we quench the Spirit whenever we neglect or overlook, or worse still deny, some feature of his multifaceted ministry. A good many folk actually think it unbiblical to think much of the Spirit. They aren't being blasphemous in this regard but are simply trying to honor what they believe is the point of what Jesus said in John 16:13–15. In the upper room discourse, not long before his arrest and crucifixion, Jesus said this of the Spirit:

> "When the Spirit of truth comes, he will guide you into all the truth, for he will not speak on his own authority, but whatever he hears he will speak, and he will declare to you the things that are to come. He will glorify me, for he will take what is mine and declare it to you. All that the Father has is mine; therefore I said that he will take what is mine and declare it to you." (John 16:13–15)

---

3 See Isaiah 11:2; John 14:26; Romans 8:27; 1 Corinthians 2:10–11.
4 See Acts 15:28; Romans 8:26; 15:30; Ephesians 4:30; and possibly James 4:5.
5 See Acts 16:7; 1 Corinthians 12:11.
6 See Mark 13:11; Acts 1:16; 8:29; 10:19; 11:12; 13:2; 21:11; 1 Timothy 4:1; Hebrews 3:7; Revelation 2:7.
7 See John 15:26.

The point they derive from this statement is that the Spirit will never draw attention to himself. His divinely appointed task in the economy of redemption is to shine a light on Jesus. "He will glorify me," said Jesus. Therefore, anything that tends to glorify the Spirit himself is not of God. The Spirit is supremely *Christocentric*. Any ministry today, any teaching, vision, mission, or otherwise that elevates the Spirit above the Son, is decidedly unbiblical.

This is a healthy reminder for many in the charismatic movement who have severed the person and work of the Spirit from the person and work of the Son. Those who make experiencing the Spirit an end in itself have failed to grasp the goal for which the Spirit has come.

However, we must be careful to avoid the error of *reductionism*, as if the whole of the Spirit's ministry can be reduced to Christology, as if the Spirit does *nothing but* glorify Christ. It's the mistake of arguing that the *primary* purpose of the Spirit's coming is the *sole* purpose of his coming. The principal aim of the Spirit in what he does is to awaken us to the glory, splendor, and centrality of the work of Christ Jesus. But this does not mean that it is less than the Spirit at work when he awakens us also to his own glory and power and abiding presence.

We should remember that the Holy Spirit inspired hundreds of biblical passages that speak about himself and his work! The Holy Spirit makes himself known through a variety of spiritual and physical manifestations. People often could see the presence of the Spirit (cf. Acts 8:14–18 and 10:44–46). Consider his descent on Jesus in the form of a dove at his baptism, or his appearance with rushing wind and tongues of fire at Pentecost.

In Acts 13:1–2, it is the Holy Spirit who gives direction in response to fasting and worship. Acts 15:28 suggests that the apostles and elders of the Jerusalem church sought the Spirit in their decisions to find out what "seemed good to the Holy Spirit."

The Spirit also bears witness with our spirit that we are children of God (Romans 8:16), and cries, "Abba, Father" (Galatians

4:6). He provides a guarantee or a down payment of our future fellowship with him in heaven (2 Corinthians 1:22; 5:5), and reveals his desires to us so that we can be led by those desires and follow them (Romans 8:4–16; Galatians 5:16–25). He gives gifts that manifest his presence (1 Corinthians 12:7–11). And from time to time he works miraculous signs and wonders and miracles that strongly attest to the presence of God in the preaching of the gospel (Hebrews 2:4; compare Romans 15:19; 1 Corinthians 2:4).

Third, we quench the Spirit whenever we suppress or legislate against his work of imparting spiritual gifts and ministering to the church through them. "Sam, are you saying that the doctrine of cessationism is a quenching of the Spirit?" I don't believe cessationists consciously intend to quench the Spirit, but yes, cessationism as a theology quenches the Spirit. Most cessationists will say that they desire for the Spirit to work in whatever ways they believe are biblically justified. But the unintended, practical effect of cessationism is to quench the Spirit. As a theology it restricts, inhibits, and often prohibits what the Spirit can and cannot do in our lives individually and in our churches corporately. Despite good intentions, the practical effect is that the Spirit is quenched.

As I look at the American church today, I see that it is in a desperate state. We need all the help we can get! We need the full range of the Spirit's marvelous and miraculous activity. We desperately need the energizing and empowering manifestation of the Spirit as outlined by Paul in Romans 12:3–8; 1 Corinthians 12:7–10; 12:27–31; and Ephesians 4:11. That is one of the reasons why I've written this book and why I believe every church needs to operate in the fullness of the spiritual gifts.

Fourth, we quench the Spirit whenever we create an inviolable and sanctimonious structure in our corporate gatherings and worship services and in our small groups that does not permit spontaneity or the special leading of the Spirit in how we pray, preach, and praise.

This may not seem obvious at first, so let me illustrate this in three practical ways.

First, let's consider how we often pray for the Spirit to come and bring revival to our churches. Our tendency is to pray for revival, because we think that is the religious thing to do, only later to say, after revival has come: "Oh my! This isn't at all what I had in mind!" We *say* we want revival . . . but on *our* terms. We don't pray this way, but this is what our hearts are saying to God:

- "Come Holy Spirit . . . but only if you promise in advance to do things the way we have always done them in our church."
- "Come Holy Spirit . . . but only if I have some sort of prior guarantee that when you show up you won't embarrass me."
- "Come Holy Spirit . . . but only if your work of revival is one that I can still control, one that preserves intact the traditions with which I am comfortable."
- "Come Holy Spirit . . . but only if your work of revival is neat and tidy and dignified and understandable and above all else socially acceptable."
- "Come Holy Spirit . . . but only if you plan to change others; only if you make them to be like me; only if you convict their hearts so they will live and dress and talk like I do."
- "Come Holy Spirit . . . but only if you let us preserve our distinctives and retain our differences from others whom we find offensive."

Or consider how we quench the Spirit in our small group gatherings. It happens when we create an atmosphere of fear and control. People are hesitant and disinclined to speak up or contribute because they are terrified of being judged and put to shame. They are afraid to be honest, to talk about the things they are struggling with, the doubts they have, the sins they need to confess. There is a lack of transparency and grace.

For those who are responsible for preaching, I want to challenge you as well. The truth is that pastors often quench the Holy Spirit in the way we preach. Years ago, I heard John Piper refer to the habit of some who will endorse and encourage the exercise of spiritual gifts in their preaching and then unconsciously quench the Spirit with what he called "the public verbalized institutionalization of caution." He had in mind those long, impassioned warnings and caveats and qualifications concerning the work of the Spirit. He had in mind the ten-minute exhortation regarding spiritual gifts followed by the thirty-minute, heavy-handed and somber warning about their potential errors and excess. If you are responsible for preaching, what do you tend to emphasize?

Finally, consider some of the parameters you place on what is permitted and what is not in corporate gatherings. I'll say more about this in the last chapter on "Worship in the Spirit," but for now I want to draw your attention to Paul's reference in Ephesians and Colossians to "spiritual songs" (Ephesians 5:19; Colossians 3:16). Why does Paul call these songs spiritual? I believe he does this to differentiate between songs that are previously composed as over against those that are spontaneously evoked by the Spirit himself. Spiritual songs are most likely unrehearsed and improvised, perhaps short melodies or choruses extolling the beauty of Christ. They aren't prepared in advance but are prompted by the Spirit, and thus are uniquely and especially appropriate to the occasion or the emphasis of the moment.

So is there any room in your church—or even in your personal, private devotional practices—given to this sort of prophetic singing? I call it prophetic because these are songs that often are the fruit of a revelatory impression or sense of guidance from the Spirit. They were not planned in advance. No one had any advanced sense that room should be given to their place in the corporate assembly. Could it be that we quench the Spirit's work either by denying the possibility that he might move upon us in this way or by so rigidly structuring our services that there is virtually no time allowed for God's sovereign interruption of our liturgy?

Fifth, and finally, we quench the Spirit whenever we despise prophetic utterances.[8] We now come to the primary point of Paul's comments in 1 Thessalonians 5. Take another look at that passage and observe the parallel between verses 19 and 20. Paul's exhortation in verse 19 is that we not quench the Spirit, and then what comes next? It immediately connects with our response to prophecy in verse 20. While his exhortation to avoid quenching the spirit undoubtedly has application to the exercise of other spiritual gifts in the church, its first and primary reference is to the gift of prophecy.

I find that the most important word in that section is the word "but" that opens verse 21. Clearly Paul is setting up a contrast here. *Rather than* quenching the Holy Spirit by despising prophetic utterances, examine everything. That word "everything" or "all things" in verse 21 is a reference to the prophetic utterances in verse 20. This leads us to the conclusion that the "good" in verse 21 to which we are to hold fast and the "evil" in verse 22 from which we are to abstain are also references to the prophetic utterances mentioned in verse 20. Most have appealed to verses 21–22 as a general exhortation to help us in our response to good and evil in the world. But when looked at in the light of the overall context, we see that the "good" are those prophetic utterances that truly come from God and encourage, edify, and console, whereas the "evil" refers to what alleges to be revelation from God but in fact is not, having been shown to be inconsistent with Scripture.

Stop and think about that for a moment. The fact that Paul felt compelled to write this is itself remarkably instructive. It tells us that not everyone in the early church was completely happy about

8 Some of what follows has been adapted from my book *The Beginner's Guide to Spiritual Gifts*, 138–144.

the gift of prophecy. Some were clearly disenchanted with its use in the church and were actually taking steps to suppress its exercise. This is remarkable for no other reason than that it was happening in the church at Thessalonica, one of the most godly and mature early congregations (see Paul's praise of them in 1 Thessalonians 1:1–10). Why were some in Thessalonica "despising" (ESV and NASB) or treating "with contempt" (NIV) prophetic words? Probably for the same reasons that people do so today!

Undoubtedly the prophetic gift had been abused in Thessalonica, prompting some to call for its elimination altogether. Some were likely using it to control other people's lives, claiming to know God's will for other Christians. My guess is that some appealed to the gift to increase their sphere of influence and power in the church. Perhaps it was being overused and over-emphasized. People had thus grown tired of it. Or it may be that, contrary to the instruction of Paul in 1 Corinthians, certain prophetically gifted people tended to dominate the corporate assembly of God's people. Perhaps "words" of prophecy weren't being judged at all but were being naively embraced no matter the content. Some probably thought it weird and were embarrassed by the gift, or at least by the hyper-spiritual-holier-than-thou posturing of some in the church. If it is anything like today, I assume that some who had the gift of prophecy probably claimed they were spiritually special, highly favored, uniquely anointed, and thus had a right to the hearing of all others. Then, of course, others were disillusioned when special words spoken over them didn't come to pass.

But let's not miss the force of what Paul is saying here. Simply put, it doesn't matter how badly people may have abused this gift. *It is a sin to despise prophecy.* This is a divine command. Don't treat prophecy with contempt; don't treat it as if it were unimportant; don't trivialize it. In other words, there is a real, live baby in that murky, distasteful bath water. So be careful that when you throw out the latter you don't dispense with the former!

What's the Alternative Then?

So what is the alternative to not quenching the Holy Spirit when he speaks prophetically through someone? Well, it isn't an "anything goes" attitude. No, we must still exercise wisdom and discernment, and we need to test, judge, and examine every word. *Paul doesn't correct abuse by commanding disuse*, as is the practice of many today. We are neither to gullibly believe every word that is spoken nor cynically reject them altogether, as if they have no spiritual benefit. Paul's remedy for sinful despising isn't unqualified openness. His remedy is *biblically informed discernment.*

The NASB renders the phrase here as "prophetic utterances" and the ESV has "prophecies." Literally, this is the plural form of the word "prophecy," which refers not to the gift of prophecy but to the individual utterances or words that come forth in the life of a church. I believe our responsibility not to quench the Spirit, stated positively, is threefold.

First, we are to test, to examine, to evaluate, to assess, to weigh, or to judge these utterances. The body of Christ today urgently needs prophetic ministry, but perhaps even more importantly, churches who embrace this gift must practice discernment. A church must be theologically literate and sufficiently familiar with the Bible so that they can effectively judge and evaluate both the source and meaning of dreams, visions, and subjective impressions. Why have some today failed to adequately judge prophetic words? Some people fear to judge a prophetic word because they don't want to quench the Spirit. Confrontation is also difficult and painful, and they might not want to hurt someone's feelings or shut them down. Or they don't want to lose the blessing that otherwise might come from humble submission to what God is saying. Then there is what I call prophetic awe (virtual reverence for gifted people; "who am I to judge him/her?").

But consider the Bereans' response to Paul in Acts 17:10–11.

They didn't hesitate to take what he said and measure it against the Scriptures. So how do we judge or weigh or assess or evaluate prophetic words? The same way! The first standard of judgment is to assess all claims to prophetic revelation in light of apostolic teaching as found in Scripture (cf. 2 Thessalonians 2:15). The greatest deterrent to prophetic excess is a biblically literate, theologically informed local church. We should also judge prophetic words in light of their tendency to edify (1 Corinthians 14:3). That is to say, does the word build up or tear down, encourage or discourage, foster unity or division? This is the test of love. There is also the test of community in which we solicit input from the community of believers in the body of Christ instead of relying solely upon a single individual's judgment. Finally, there is a place for personal experience, especially with predictive prophecy. Does what the person has said actually come to pass? Sometimes you can't judge a word until after the fact.

Second, Paul tells us that we are to "hold fast to that which is good" (1 Thessalonians 5:21 NASB). Once you have determined that the word is *good*, that it is biblical and meets all other criteria and is therefore most probably from God, believe it, obey it, and preserve it. The flip side of this is that we are to "abstain from every form of evil" (v. 22). The word "abstain" (ESV) or "avoid" (NIV) is also found in 1 Thessalonians 4:3 ("abstain from sexual immorality") and 1 Timothy 4:3 ("abstaining from foods"). Hence this directive could be translated, "shun every kind of prophetic utterance that is evil," that doesn't conform to Scripture, that doesn't build up and encourage and exhort and console.

This suggests that prophets can speak both "good" and "evil" words. Remember, *evil* can come in various shades of black! There is a type of "evil" that simply means it isn't good or effective in doing what Scripture says prophecy should do. In this case, as we look at the context of what Paul is saying, we see that "evil" means "ineffective" or "unfruitful." Or it may simply mean that it is contrary to

Scripture. But it doesn't necessarily mean hateful, mean, sinister, wicked, or motivated by a desire to inflict harm on you. It simply means a word that fails to accomplish what true prophetic words are designed by God to accomplish.

This also means that there is a vast difference between prophesying falsely and being a false prophet. Most of those I know with a prophetic gifting (including myself) have, at one time or another, prophesied falsely. We have spoken words we thought were from God which, in fact, were not. But that doesn't make us false prophets. It just makes us human! False prophets in the New Testament were non-Christian enemies of the gospel (cf. Matthew 7:15–23; 24:10–11, 24; 2 Peter 2:1–3; 1 John 4:1–6).

In conclusion, it is crucial to the life of the individual believer and especially to the spiritual health of the corporate body that we make it our aim not to quench the Holy Spirit by treating prophetic utterances with disdain and contempt. May God help us to test them, judge them, weigh them, and embrace what is good, godly, and edifying, while at the same time we reject what is bad, misguided, and destructive.

CHAPTER 11

MANIPULATION OR MINISTRY?

It's unfortunate, but sadly all too common, that sinful or misguided people will take advantage of people and use them for selfish purposes. As you are growing in your understanding of the Holy Spirit and how to exercise the gifts of the Spirit, it is necessary to learn how to discern between true ministry and manipulation. In this chapter I hope to provide guidance as to how to recognize biblically warranted ministry that facilitates the experience of the Holy Spirit and his many gifts. I also will try to help you differentiate contrived, fleshly efforts to elicit a response or induce a physical reaction that has more to do with bringing honor to the "pastor" or "teacher" than it does with glorifying God.

The task isn't an easy one. There is always the danger of passing unwarranted judgment on the motives of certain people, together with the consequent heavy-handed and legalistic imposition of extrabiblical rules that quench the work of the Spirit. Conversely, some are equally inclined to naively embrace all claims to the legitimacy of spiritual activity, thereby perpetuating the harmful so-called ministries of those who seek their own praise rather than that of Christ himself.

Because Christians are afraid of fanaticism and excess, they are often tempted to manipulate the situation to maintain some sense of control. Of course, none of us enjoys the feeling that we aren't in control. But that feeling is compounded by the sad reality that many believers are afraid of the Holy Spirit. They lack familiarity with how the Spirit works, and when the Spirit moves in power, they are scared. This is true of many Evangelicals, although few would openly admit that they're frightened at what God might do in their life or in the experience of their local church. We like to think of ourselves as open to whatever God might choose to do, but secretly we keep our foot on the brake pedal, lest things careen out of control and bring reproach on the name of Jesus and embarrassment to ourselves and our ministry.

One of the primary aims of this book has been to identify the many reasons why fear paralyzes the hearts of people when it comes to the experience and exercise of spiritual gifts. Fear creates hesitation and limits what we are comfortable allowing in our lives and in the life of our church. One of the most common concerns I run into is the concern that we avoid manipulation. We want to avoid anything that is fake or artificial. We want to avoid fabricated emotional highs and forms of so-called ministry that are the contrived product of human scheming or fleshly efforts to demonstrate that one is truly anointed of God.

Where does this concern come from? I suspect that it is rooted in negative experiences we've had seeing some religious celebrities or TV personalities (I refuse to honor them with the name "evangelists") whose on-air antics and claims of supernatural power reek of artificiality and smack of self-promotion. Vulnerable, and often gullible, people rush to these charlatans with heightened expectations of being delivered from ill health, poverty, or whatever other challenging circumstances they believe are outside the will of God and often end up disillusioned and devastated beyond recovery. What they mistakenly looked for in terms of biblical and loving ministry turned out to be a manipulative effort to separate them from their hard-earned money.

I share these concerns. I'm frustrated and angered by those who manipulate emotions and trick people into believing lies or giving money in exchange for a touch of God's power. We need to look carefully at how we can avoid manipulative techniques that pass themselves off as ministry to God's people. But knowing the difference between heartfelt and sincere ministry on the one hand and fleshly manipulation for self-serving ends on the other isn't always easy. In this chapter I want to provide a few helpful tips that will heighten your discernment and enable you to maintain your zeal for the legitimate work of the Spirit *without* sacrificing your theological integrity.

I earlier noted that no matter how diligent and passionate we are about the Holy Spirit, we cannot make the wind blow. We cannot coerce, control, or manipulate his presence or power in our lives. Notwithstanding this obvious truth, some persist in their efforts to make it happen. I've witnessed this during times of revival. Perhaps the word "renewal" is better, but in either case I'm talking about seasons in the life of God's people when the Spirit appears to be uniquely operative and more than ordinarily overt in his ministry and the display of spiritual power. It should come as no surprise that during these times there are frequent criticisms that manipulation is occurring. This is why identifying manipulation and avoiding it is of crucial importance.

Webster's defines the verb *manipulate* as follows: "to manage or control artfully or by shrewd use of influence, especially in an unfair or fraudulent way." But what does it mean to say a pastor or preacher or teacher is manipulative? We must be careful how we answer that question, because to accuse someone of being manipulative is to raise doubts about their *intent* in ministry. To say someone is being manipulative brings into question both their character and sincerity. This is an issue that goes beyond merely an analysis of differing styles of how to conduct a Sunday morning service. It is an issue that deals directly with the heart. As we will see in a moment, manipulation is more concerned with one's *motives* than with one's *methods*. It isn't so much *how* you conduct a service but *why*.

We are repeatedly warned in Scripture about the dangers of unrighteous judgment and a critical spirit.[1] So I approach this subject with great caution. I do not want to be guilty of impugning the integrity of someone simply because I am uncomfortable with their methods or am offended by idiosyncrasies in their personality or am of a different opinion on some secondary theological concept. Nevertheless, having said this, we can't escape the fact that, in seasons of spiritual renewal and heightened zeal, charlatans appear suddenly on the scene. We often hear that someone was *pushed* over, rather than falling under the sovereign power of the Holy Spirit. Others speak of the loud and often flamboyant tactics of certain ministers whose style of preaching or praying draws more attention to themselves than to God and his glory. Who will ever forget the exposure of one TV evangelist who received words of knowledge about his audience by means of a radio transmitter that he passed off as a hearing aid!

The apostle Paul talks about integrity of ministry in his second letter to the Corinthians. "Since we have this ministry," Paul writes, "we do not lose heart, but we have renounced the things hidden because of shame, not walking in craftiness or adulterating the word of God, but by the manifestation of truth commending ourselves to every man's conscience in the sight of God" (2 Corinthians 4:1–2 NASB). We must be diligent to be good stewards of the grace and gospel of God. We must strive to serve and minister and preach and pray in a way that is characterized by integrity, sincerity, and above all a desire that Jesus Christ be center stage. In a word, we must strive by God's grace to avoid even the semblance of manipulation. We must avoid that sort of so-called ministry that will bring reproach on the name of Christ Jesus.

Characteristics of Manipulation

I want to begin by identifying several types of manipulation and highlighting some of their most common characteristics. Often there is a very fine line between human manipulation and the work of the Holy Spirit, sometimes so fine that it may be difficult to know precisely when one crosses the boundary into the other. My desire is not to create fear in your heart about being manipulative, far less to say or do anything that might quench the Spirit's work. My goal is simply to articulate some principles that I trust will increase and sharpen our spiritual discernment.

That being said, if you are still wondering why I'm spending an entire chapter on manipulation in this book, the simple answer is that it's extremely common for people to be confused on this issue and resist the Spirit as a result. They grow skeptical or fearful of the spiritual gifts because they suspect that what has occurred is artificial or the result of human technique or "religious sleight of hand" rather than the precious Holy Spirit himself. So it's important that we understand how manipulation occurs and what it looks like.

To begin, one of the most common forms of manipulation is *the attempt to covertly lure a person to forego the reasons or suspend the arguments they have for not doing something which they believe is wrong or suspect.* There is nothing wrong or manipulative in seeking to convince a person that such reasons or arguments are incorrect. But when one deliberately circumvents such arguments in order to undermine their influence in the decision-making process of the person who embraces them, the action is manipulative. Indeed, it may even be termed malicious.

For example, someone leading a service or a time of corporate prayer may sarcastically denounce people who disagree with him/her as having a religious spirit or being in bondage to tradition. Of course, there is always the possibility they may be right! But a minister can make that point without the use of ridicule or that condescending tone of voice, which intimidates people into suspending the use of the Bible or sanctified wisdom in assessing what is being said.

I have in mind a particular TV personality who adopts an easy-going, down-home style, together with what appears to be a feigned misuse of grammar and pronunciation, all with a view to convince his audience that he speaks from "simple faith in Jesus," while his opponents are overly educated Pharisees whose only desire is to undermine the faith of "plain folk like you and me." This is manipulation, and it should be avoided at all costs.

A second way in which we manipulate others is when *we attempt to persuade someone to attribute to God an experience that is in fact the work of the flesh.* In doing so the person hopes to eliminate what would otherwise be legitimate resistance to his or her ministry. It should be noted that there need not be malicious or deceitful intent on the part of the leader. He/she may truly believe that a work of the flesh is, in point of fact, the work of God. In their sincere and passionate desire to see people blessed, they may go overboard, as it were, in labeling something the work of God that under careful and more deliberate scrutiny would prove to be human hysteria or fleshly indulgence. Thus their own lack of discernment can open them to the charge of being manipulative.

Another form of manipulation is *the attempt to produce in someone an experience or behavior, the result or effect of which will bring more benefit to the person ministering than to the person receiving the ministry.* In other words, manipulation is when a minister exploits for personal gain the sincere need and desire for God in another Christian. We are all too painfully familiar with the scandals that rocked the church in America in recent years. The result is an increased sensitivity among most people to anyone who even remotely appears to draw attention to himself/herself. This has put all of us in a difficult situation. On the one hand, we don't want to be duped by a self-serving charlatan. On the other hand, we want to avoid that sort of hypercritical, self-righteous judgment that has the potential to tear down the body of Christ.

It is also important to remember that a leader or minister may receive considerable praise and public notoriety, not because he is a self-seeking shyster or a wolf in sheep's clothing, but because of the anointing of the Spirit in their ministry. Billy Graham is an articulate and world-famous evangelist. But I dare say no one would accuse him of pursuing his ministry for personal gain above the glory of God.

Another related point is the tendency some have to draw attention to the manifestations of the Spirit in order to prove they are anointed. The effect on a congregation is to make them feel as if the absence of such manifestations in their own lives is an indication of a spiritual defect or a lack of faith.

A fourth type of manipulation is *the use of illegitimate means to achieve a legitimate end*. The minister tends to think: "If I can get them to God, how I do it is of secondary importance." Often this reduces to pure pragmatism, the philosophy that measures truth by results. "If it works," reasons the pragmatist, "it must be true." Religious pragmatism says, "If it works, it must be *God*!" Some measure success of ministry by the quantity and intensity of physical manifestations. Those who depend on such signs are especially tempted to do whatever is most effective in producing them.

If the leader assumes that "God didn't show up" because the manifestations were minimal, he creates an atmosphere in which he will unconsciously employ tactics that in any other setting he would never use. We must be careful in our evaluation of the alleged success or failure of meetings. Success is *never* to be measured by the presence or absence of physical phenomena such as weeping, laughing, shaking, or falling down. Success is achieved when the Lord Jesus Christ is magnified and his people are ignited with a burning passion for him and holiness. Frequently such transformation is attended with powerful and bizarre physical manifestations. But the absence of the latter does not prove the absence of the former. Nor does the presence of the former demand the presence of the latter.

Manipulation also occurs *when one takes advantage of human weakness, insecurity, or timidity to achieve an effect*. In seasons of renewal or revival, many come to church with heightened and often unbiblical expectations and thus are more easily swayed by emotionally charged religious tactics than they would be under normal circumstances.

This is not to say that we should never seek to increase godly expectations or desires in other believers. If the Word of God makes a promise (e.g., Luke 11:13), it is certainly proper to take steps in ministry that will enlarge a person's expectation of its fulfillment.

But we can all too easily become manipulative if we believe in a mechanical, cause-and-effect relationship between a certain ministry style and the release of the Holy Spirit. Believing that certain formulas guarantee the manifestation of spiritual power opens one to the charge of being manipulative. This is especially the case if the teacher is successful in persuading the congregation of the biblical legitimacy of his chosen method.

While I believe that God often suspends his activity and the release of his power on the prayers of his people (see, e.g., Isaiah 30:18–19; Jeremiah 29:12–13; James 4:2), we must always affirm the sovereignty of the Spirit. He will not be tamed or domesticated by our methods. Any attempt to eliminate the mystery from God's ways by reducing his activity to certain so-called divine laws that nowhere appear in Scripture will ultimately lead to false guilt and shame in those who supposedly missed out. If doing *x* always results in blessing *y*, the absence of *y* can only be due to my failure or sin or lack of faith in regard to *x*. People who think in those terms are primed and ready for the manipulative tactics of unscrupulous and ill-taught ministers.

A leader is also being manipulative when he/she uses techniques that supersede the volitional input of the congregation. Manipulation makes people feel as if they have no choice, as if they have been led to do or believe something under subtle coercion. Unfortunately, music has often been exploited to achieve this effect. I believe in the power of music. I believe such power is

God-given. Music has the potential to shape our thinking as well as stir our passions. God loves music and has ordained that we praise, worship, and encounter him by means of it. But music, much like doctrinal truths found in Scripture, can be used (perhaps we should say abused) to create an atmosphere that is so emotionally charged and intense that people are induced to say and do things that in any other context they would find objectionable.

I'm not suggesting that we are purely rational beings. I believe God created and redeemed our emotions no less than our minds. But nowhere do I read in Scripture that music was created to persuade us to ignore or violate what our minds have learned from the Bible concerning truth and falsehood, good and evil. I've actually heard people say, "I was so caught up in the mood of the moment and the flow of the music that I found myself agreeing with what was happening in the meeting before I could even think about whether or not it was biblical." When music is used in this way it has become dangerously manipulative.

I mention this next point because it is all too common. It is manipulative *when a person is put on public display and made to feel as if the lack of a physical response will embarrass or in some way reflect adversely on the leader.* The use of this form of social and emotional pressure to elicit a response is undeniably manipulative. Although the leader may have good and holy intentions, the person who is the object of such focused and concentrated attention is subjected to an unnatural constraint to conform to the expectations of those present.

However, being witness to a legitimate touch of God on a person's life can be a tremendous encouragement. In his book *Prepare for Revival*, Rob Warner refers to the practice of the Airport Vineyard in Toronto during a season of extended renewal in the 1990s in which two or three people are invited to the front to give testimonies of what God has done in their lives. This may be viewed as "lighting new fires from warm coals, building faith in the congregation by a verbal witness and visible demonstration of the powerful presence of God." So here we are faced again with a very difficult question: "What is the dividing line between legitimate, God-glorifying, encouraging *ministry*, on the one hand, and illegitimate, man-centered *manipulation*, on the other?"

Related to this is the false belief that some have that every bodily sensation or physical impulse is a touch of God. This belief system is unbiblical and it creates a false interpretation of what *is* happening and a false expectation of what *should* happen. Don't teach or pass along the mistaken assumption that God wants everyone to experience physical or bodily manifestations. Certainly God wants everyone to receive his presence and his power through the infilling of the Holy Spirit. But it is unbiblical to assume that *receiving the Spirit* necessarily entails physical phenomena. A *powerful* encounter with the Holy Spirit may yield the *quiet fruit* of holiness and humility instead of the overt display of signs and wonders.

An excellent example of this is what the apostle Paul says in Romans 15. When we read about the "power of the Holy Spirit" in Scripture we mistakenly assume that the result will always be an overt, miraculous, somewhat sensational manifestation of divine energy. Often times, that is precisely what occurs. In Romans 15:18–19 Paul talks about his ministry to the Gentiles, which took place "in the power of signs and wonders, in the power of the Spirit" (NASB). But the "power of the Holy Spirit" is no less in operation when Christians are enabled to love one another and to treat one another with kindness and humility. If in Romans 15:18–19 Paul attributes signs and wonders to the power of the Holy Spirit, in Romans 15:13 he attributes joy, peace, and hope to the same divine power. There we read, "Now may the God of hope fill you with all joy and peace in believing, so that you may abound in hope by the power of the Holy Spirit" (NASB).

We are manipulating people when we say or do something that leads people to think that they are subspiritual if a phenomenon does not occur or that they are spiritual or the recipient of God's favor if a certain phenomenon does occur. In some charismatic circles, there is a tendency to refer to people who do not experience powerful and visible physical manifestation as HTRs, that is to say, people who find it "Hard to Receive." I want to suggest a slight change in terminology and refer to them as HTMs, people who find it "Hard to Manifest."

Most likely, these people are very open to receive from God. Their hearts are repentant, humble, and hungry for the presence and sanctifying influence of the Holy Spirit. If such is true, they will most certainly receive a touch from God. But that doesn't mean they must manifest physical phenomena. They *may*, but if they don't, it isn't necessarily because they are closed to what God is doing. I would classify myself as an HTM. But I am certainly open to receiving everything God has made available. God wants all his people to receive. But he doesn't necessarily want all his people to manifest. They *may*, and if they do, praise God. But they may *not*, and if they don't, praise God!

A person may also be manipulative when he/she compensates for the lack of anointing by using natural skills or tactics to arouse or inspire or excite an audience. For example, several years ago there was a phenomenon in many charismatic circles known as the "laughing revival." I'm not here to pass judgment on its legitimacy but only to draw attention to one particular tactic that I found to be decidedly unbiblical. I have in mind those occasions when the Lord did not appear to be inducing laughter in his people, so the minister resorted to telling jokes or laughing infectiously in hope of inducing the same in everyone else. That, my friend, is sinful manipulation and serves only to bring reproach on the name of Christ and his gospel.

Some people are being manipulative when *they do things that make others feel indebted*. People have been manipulated when they find themselves saying: "He did this for us; so we feel obligated to do likewise for him." Or they create an environment where a person lacks the freedom to make decisions without feeling they are missing God's best. For example, when people are told not to biblically analyze or evaluate a phenomenon but simply receive it, on the supposition that the mind is the enemy or obstacle to intimacy with God, they are being manipulated.

A leader can also manipulate by *suggesting to people how they are supposed to feel*. Not wanting to "miss" God, they are tempted to fabricate or artificially produce such feelings, or perhaps imitate those who they are convinced are receiving a genuine touch from God. If none of this works, they frequently leave feeling isolated, unloved, and sub-Christian. Somewhat related to this is the temptation to identify by discernment what God is doing before anyone else can hear, see, or feel any spiritual activity. For example, in a meeting that otherwise seems to be uneventful, a leader may say: "I sense that God is imparting a spirit of travail," or "I sense that the joy of the Lord is being poured out." Such pronouncements may predispose people to acquiesce to the slightest tinge of either sadness or laughter on the assumption that: "It must be God. Didn't the minister say so?" All of this is often an attempt to "jump-start" an otherwise dead meeting. It may also be highly manipulative.

I use the word *may* because, God occasionally does speak prophetically to a leader about what he is doing for the purpose of giving direction and meaning to what the naked eye and the natural mind alone cannot see. So once again, we are faced with the struggle to differentiate between divine guidance and human control.

If you are a leader or minister, avoid putting people in a position where the only way they can disagree with you is by challenging your integrity. You may well be an honest and sincere person who has no desire to be deliberately deceitful. And those you lead may have no desire to question your character or to pass judgments on your motives, especially in a public setting. But the words or actions you use to communicate are phrased or presented in such a way that to disagree with you is tantamount to calling you a liar or a charlatan. The result is that people feel unnecessary pressure either not to say anything at all or to concede to your viewpoint.

Avoid speaking in such a way that our listeners are compelled, often on the spot, to take a side: (a) It *must* be God, or (b) It *can't* be God. Christians who are somewhat timid and not well grounded biblically will tend to capitulate to that form of spiritual pressure and take the path of least resistance.

I've presented a variety of ways in which it is possible to manipulate people, many of which I've observed personally in my own life or in the lives of others. Looking at the variety of ways in which manipulation manifests, I believe we can summarize this by grouping these habits into five categories that we must work to avoid: selfish manipulation, coercive manipulation, deceptive manipulation, blaspheming manipulation, and shaming manipulation.

1. SELFISH MANIPULATION

- Attempting to produce in someone an experience or behavior, the result or effect of which will bring more benefit to the leader than to the person himself
- Trying to make others feel indebted

2. COERCIVE MANIPULATION

- Using natural skills or tactics to arouse or inspire or excite an audience
- Using illegitimate means to achieve a legitimate end
- Taking advantage of human weakness, insecurity, or timidity to achieve an effect

- Employing techniques that supersede the volitional input of the congregation
- Putting people in a position where the only way they can disagree is by challenging the leader's integrity

3. DECEPTIVE MANIPULATION

- Attempting to covertly lure a person to forego the reasons or suspend the arguments they have for not doing something that they believe is wrong or suspect
- Telling or suggesting to people how they are supposed to feel

4. BLASPHEMING OR EXALTING MANIPULATION

- Believing in a mechanical, cause-and-effect relationship between a certain ministry style and the release of the Holy Spirit
- Attempting to persuade someone to attribute to God an experience that is in fact the work of the flesh
- Suggesting that every bodily sensation or physical impulse is a touch of God

5. SHAMING OR GUILT-PRODUCING MANIPULATION

- Making someone feel as if the lack of a physical response will embarrass or in some way reflect adversely on the leader
- Implying others are subspiritual if a phenomenon does not occur or that they are spiritual or the recipient of God's favor if a certain phenomenon does occur
- Making others fear they are missing God's best in making a decision

Manipulation and Facilitation

Given the numerous ways in which we can be guilty of manipulating others in ministry, I have found it helpful to clarify the difference between *manipulation* and *facilitation*. Facilitation is the attempt to make the reception of a biblical truth or experience easier and more effective. Legitimate means are used to achieve legitimate ends with no attempt to coerce or trick the congregation. It is not necessarily manipulative when a leader, in order to facilitate a legitimate biblical experience, speaks loudly or becomes emphatic in his actions, tone, or gestures.

For example, when I preach, my aim (with the help of the Holy Spirit) is to influence and shape the life of my listeners. Therefore, I use those words, phrases, and illustrations that I believe will be most effective in persuading them of the truth of the message and the importance of obeying it. This is not manipulation.

People who charge someone with being manipulative are often those who are disdainful of the *means*. That is to say, they believe that "if God really wants me to experience this phenomenon, he is more than capable of making it happen without your help." Or again, they say, "If it were God, *you* [the minister] wouldn't be necessary."

In other contexts with other spiritual activities, they would probably never raise such an objection. They believe, for example, that God utilizes evangelism as a means for achieving the end of saving souls. They believe that God ordains prayer as a means for the goal of bestowing certain blessings. They believe God sanctions Bible study as a means for achieving spiritual growth. I suspect the reason why they become disdainful of means when it comes to this time of renewal is less theological than personal. It isn't because God is opposed to the use of means. It is because *they* are personally opposed to the strange and seemingly undignified things they observe happening in renewal meetings, and this objection provides them with what seems to be a legitimate excuse to keep it all at arms' length.

In other words, if someone is skeptical of renewal or offended by some of the more unusual phenomena that occur, they will often use the charge of manipulation to justify their opposition. Accusing the leader of being manipulative is an easy and effective way of excusing oneself from having to wrestle with the truth or falsity of the renewal. It provides warrant in the mind of the skeptic for not opening himself/herself to the influence of the Spirit. If a skeptic simply does not want what is happening for himself, the charge of manipulation provides him with an apparent good reason for maintaining his distance.

Lessons for Today from the First Great Awakening

One would be hard-pressed to identify in history a season of renewal or revival in which physical manifestations did not occur. Once we recognize the presence of such phenomena both in biblical times and in the history of the church, we will be less inclined to rush to judgment concerning the validity of what we see occurring.

During the First Great Awakening in the early 1740s, pastor and theologian Jonathan Edwards (1703–58) addressed the tendency people have to reject events as not of God simply because the Bible doesn't provide explicit analysis or precedents for everything they see and hear. Listen to his counsel (which I have slightly modernized to make for easier reading).

> Many are guilty of not taking the Holy Scriptures as a sufficient rule whereby to judge whether or not this is the work of God, in that they judge by those things which the Scriptures don't give as signs or marks to judge one way or the other, . . . namely, the effects that religious exercises and affections of mind have upon the body. Scripture rules respect the state of the mind,

> and persons' moral conduct, and voluntary behavior, and not the physical state of the body. . . . Christ knew what instructions and rules his church would stand in need of better than we do; and if he had seen it needful for the church's safety, he doubtless would have given ministers rules to judge of bodily effects, and would have told them how the pulse should beat under such and such religious exercises of mind; when men should look pale, and when they should shed tears; when they should tremble, and whether or not they should ever be faint or cry out; or whether the body should ever be put into convulsions. He probably would have put some book into their hands that should have tended to make them excellent anatomists and physicians: but he has not done it, because he did not see it to be needful.[1]

Edwards insists that as long as we are careful to monitor the state of one's mind and moral conduct, insisting that such be in conformity with Scripture, our fears and suspicions prompted by extraordinary bodily effects seem entirely groundless.

But is it reasonable or biblical to think that people under the influence of the Spirit will experience intense bodily effects? Edwards answers:

> Let us rationally consider what we profess to believe about the infinite greatness of the things of God, divine wrath, divine glory, and the infinite love and grace in Jesus Christ, and the vastness and infinite importance of the things of eternity; and how reasonable is it to suppose that if it pleases God a little to withdraw the veil, and let light into the soul, and give something of a view of the great things of another world in their transcendent

1 Jonathan Edwards, *The Great Awakening: Some Thoughts Concerning the Present Revival of Religion*, edited by C. C. Goen (New Haven: Yale University Press, 1972), 300.

> and infinite greatness, that human nature, that is as the grass, a shaking leaf, a weak withering flower, should totter under such a discovery? Such a bubble is too weak to bear the weight of a view of things that are so vast. Alas! What is such dust and ashes, that it should support itself under the view of the awful wrath of the infinite glory and love of Jehovah![2]

He cites as biblical examples the physiological and emotional reactions recording in such texts as Exodus 33:20; Psalm 119:131; Daniel 10:6–8; Habakkuk 3:16; and Revelation 1:17, and then writes:

> God is pleased sometimes in dealing forth spiritual blessings to his people, in some respect to exceed the capacity of the vessel, in its present scantiness, so that he not only fills it full, but he makes their cup to run over, agreeable to Ps. 23:5; and pours out a blessing, sometimes, in such a manner and measure that there is not room enough to receive it, Mal. 3:10.[3]

One particular objection often raised during the time of the Great Awakening concerned the "distress that they have been in for the souls of others."[4] Edwards was stunned that "Christian" people would actually object to other Christian people being so overwhelmed with grief for lost souls that their bodies fainted under the sorrow. He cites several texts that point to an intensity of concern for the lost sufficient to overwhelm the body: Esther 4:1; Psalm 119:53, 136; Isaiah 22:4; Jeremiah 4:19; 9:1; 13:17; 14:17; Romans 9:3. "And why then," asks Edwards, "should persons be thought to be distracted, when they can't forbear crying out at the consideration of the misery of those that are going to eternal destruction?"[5]

---

2 Ibid., 302.
3 Ibid., 303.
4 Ibid., 305.
5 Ibid., 306.

I want to direct our thoughts once again to the issue of what constitutes a successful meeting or time of ministry. Edwards faced the objection in his day that there were many who boasted of success simply because they could point to physical manifestations as alleged "tokens of the presence of God." His response to this objection is worthy of citation in full (again, with slight revisions):

> Concerning this I would observe, in the first place, that ministers are accused of many things concerning physical manifestations that they are not guilty of. Some would have it that they speak of these things as certain evidences of a work of the Spirit of God on the hearts of their hearers, or that they regard these bodily effects themselves to be the work of God, as though the Spirit of God took hold of, and agitated the bodies of men; and some are charged with making these things essential, and supposing that people can't be converted without them; whereas I never yet met a man who held either of these views.
>
> But when it comes to speaking of such effects as probable tokens of God's presence, and arguments of the success of preaching, it seems to me they are not to be blamed; because I think they are so indeed. Therefore, when I see them excited by preaching the important truths of God's Word, urged and enforced by proper arguments and motives, or are consequent on other means that are good, I don't hesitate to speak of them, and to rejoice in them, and bless God for them as such. For at times . . . I have found that these are evidences that the people in whom these effects appear, are under the influence of God's Spirit. In such cases . . . I confess that when I see a great crying out in a congregation, in the manner that I have seen it, when those things are held forth to them that are worthy of their being greatly affected by, I rejoice in it, much more than merely in an appearance of solemn attention, and a show of affection by weeping. . . . To rejoice that the work of God is carried on calmly,

> without much ado, is in effect to rejoice that 'tis carried on with less power, or that there is not so much of the influence of God's Spirit: for though the degree of the influence of the Spirit of God on particular persons, is by no means to be judged of by the degree of external appearances, because of the different constitution, tempers, and circumstances of men; yet if there be a very powerful influence of the Spirit of God on a mixed multitude, it will cause, some way or other, a great visible commotion.[6]

If we were to apply the lessons from the First Great Awakening to our culture today, let's consider several possible scenarios that one might encounter in a prayer meeting or perhaps during an ordinary Sunday corporate gathering of God's people:

> "I prayed, 'Come, Holy Spirit,' and people fell down, laughed, and trembled." Did the Spirit come?
>
> "I prayed, 'Come, Holy Spirit,' and no one fell down, laughed, or trembled." Did the Spirit not come?
>
> "I didn't pray, 'Come, Holy Spirit,' yet people fell down, laughed, and trembled." Did the Spirit come anyway?

We must be careful not to draw any dogmatic conclusions about the presence or absence of the Holy Spirit based on the presence or absence of such phenomena.

It is not necessarily manipulative if people are led to experience extraordinary bodily manifestations simply by observing the example of others who are receiving God's touch. Whereas they may be copying the behavior of others, perhaps out of desire to be accepted, noticed, or affirmed, such is not always the case.

Once again, Edwards faced this issue during the First Great Awakening. He pointed to numerous examples in Scripture where

6 Ibid., 399–400.

we are exhorted either to set examples for others to follow or are exhorted to follow the example that others have set (Matthew 5:16; 1 Corinthians 4:16; 11:1; 2 Corinthians 8:1–7; Philippians 3:17; 1 Thessalonians 1:7; 2 Thessalonians 3:9; 1 Timothy 4:12; Titus 2:7; Hebrews 6:12; 1 Peter 3:1). He writes:

> 'Tis therefore no argument against the goodness of the effect, that one affects and stirs up another; or that persons are greatly affected by seeing others so; yea, though the impression that is made upon them should be only by seeing the tokens of great and extraordinary affection in others in their behavior, taking for granted what they are affected with, without hearing them say one word.[7]

In conclusion, perhaps the best and most biblical course of action in our church services and prayer meetings is neither to *produce*, *prevent*, nor *perpetuate* the manifestations. We are to pray, "Come, Holy Spirit," and be confident that he will, whether or not manifestations follow. If they do, we should not prevent them from occurring. But neither should we take steps to artificially induce them.

7 Johnathan Edwards, *The Great Awakening: Distinguishing Marks of a Work of the Spirit of God*, 238–39.

CHAPTER 12

THE IMPORTANCE OF WORSHIP IN THE SPIRIT

We've come to the final chapter. My hope is that, to this point, you've found yourself growing in your understanding and desire for the supernatural gifts of the Holy Spirit. I've tried to provide a mix of biblical teaching with practical advice and suggestions on using the gifts and things to avoid.

In this last chapter, I want to turn to the topic of worship. Now some may wonder, why include a chapter on worship in a book designed to help facilitate the exercise of spiritual gifts? Surely, Sam, you aren't suggesting that worshiping is a spiritual gift? No, I'm not. But worship, no less so than the variety of charismata, is awakened, sustained, and energized by the same Spirit of God. The power we are exploring in this book, that we all want to experience more of, is the power of the Holy Spirit who not only informs our minds and inflames our affections for the majesty of Christ but also energizes and accounts for all spiritual gifts. And in this last chapter I want to show you that the relationship between the two is more important than many have until now conceded. Let's begin by looking at several important biblical texts.

Notice how many biblical texts directly connect the Spirit of God with worship (emphasis added):

> Jesus said to her, "Woman, believe me, the hour is coming when neither on this mountain nor in Jerusalem will you worship the Father. You worship what you do not know; we worship what we know, for salvation is from the Jews. But the hour is coming, and

is now here, when the true worshipers will worship the Father *in spirit and truth*, for the Father is seeking such people to worship him. God is spirit, and those who worship him must worship in spirit and truth." (John 4:21–24)

Therefore, one who speaks in a tongue should pray that he may interpret. For if I pray in a tongue, my spirit prays but my mind is unfruitful. What am I to do? I will pray with my spirit, but I will pray with my mind also; *I will sing praise with my spirit* [more literally, "in the spirit"], but I will sing with my mind also. (1 Corinthians 14:13–15)

And do not get drunk with wine, for that is debauchery, but *be filled with the Spirit*, addressing one another in psalms and hymns and *spiritual songs*, singing and making melody to the Lord with your heart, giving thanks always and for everything to God the Father in the name of our Lord Jesus Christ. (Ephesians 5:18–20)

For we are the circumcision, who *worship by the Spirit of God* and glory in Christ Jesus and put no confidence in the flesh. (Philippians 3:3)

And when they had prayed, the place in which they were gathered together was shaken, and they were all *filled with the Holy Spirit and continued to speak the word of God with boldness.* (Acts 4:31)

While Peter was still saying these things, the Holy Spirit fell on all who heard the word. And the believers from among the circumcised who had come with Peter were amazed, because *the gift of the Holy Spirit* was poured out even on the Gentiles. For they were hearing them speaking in tongues and *extolling God*. (Acts 10:44–46a)

While they were *worshiping the Lord* and fasting, *the Holy Spirit said*, "Set apart for me Barnabas and Saul for the work to which I have called them." (Acts 13:2)

I've only quoted a few passages here, but I do it to make a point. The biblical witness simply cannot conceive of genuine, Christ-exalting worship apart from the energizing presence of the Holy Spirit. Absent the Spirit, worship degenerates into a religious performance, an empty ritual that exalts man and his talents rather than God and his beauty. But worship that is fueled, sustained, and carried along, as it were, by the Spirit not only honors Christ but also awakens and prepares the human heart to be ever more receptive and vulnerable to the work and voice of the Spirit.

Perhaps a word of personal testimony would be helpful here.[1]

One of the more powerful catalysts in my personal spiritual growth was the discovery of God and his beauty, power, and love during times of worship. This was not simply a cognitive discovery in the sense that I learned new things about God. It was that, to be sure, but far more. It was also a deeply experiential encounter that affected not merely how I *envisioned* God but how I *enjoyed* him. I had always worshiped God. Or so I thought. I had always loved music, especially the great hymns of the church. But all too frequently worship for me was little more than singing songs *about* God. Of course, we ought to sing about him. But I rarely had any expectation of meeting God or experiencing his presence or engaging my heart with his. I could recite from memory 1 Peter 1:8. I could exegete and expound its truth. But never before had I *felt* in the depths of my soul this "love" for Christ or this "joy" that Peter describes as "inexpressible and filled with glory"!

It never dawned on me that enjoying God was permissible, much less possible. I could understand fearing God and obeying God, even loving God. But enjoying God struck me as inconsistent with the biblical mandate both to glorify God, on the one hand, and deny myself, on the other. How could I be committed above all else to seeking God's glory if I were concerned about my own

1 What follows has been adapted in part from my book *Convergence: Spiritual Journeys of a Charismatic Calvinist* (Kansas City, Mo: Enjoying God Ministries, 2005).

joy? My gladness and God's glory seemed to cancel each other out. I felt compelled to choose between the two. Embracing them both struck me as out of the question. Worse still, enjoying God sounded a bit too lighthearted, almost casual, perhaps even flippant, and I knew that Christianity was serious business.

It was first Jonathan Edwards, and then C. S. Lewis[2] and John Piper,[3] who helped me to see that *God's glory and my gladness are not antithetical*. In fact, they are very much connected. They helped me see that at the core of Scripture is the truth that *my heart's passion for pleasure* (which is God-given and *not* the result of sin) and *God's passion for praise* converge in a way that alone makes sense of human existence. Two statements from Edwards should suffice to account for what I'm saying:

> Now what is glorifying God, but a rejoicing at that glory he has displayed? An understanding of the perfections of God, merely, cannot be the end of the creation; for he had as good not understand it, as see it and not be at all moved with joy at the sight. Neither can the highest end of creation be the declaring God's glory to others; for the declaring God's glory is good for nothing otherwise than to raise joy in ourselves and others at what is declared.[4]

Here it is again, in slightly different words:

> God is glorified not only by his glory's being seen, but by its being rejoiced in. When those that see it delight in it, God is more glorified than if they only see it. God made the world that

---

2 See especially Lewis's essay, "A Word About Praising," in *Reflections on the Psalms* (New York: Harcourt, Brace and World, 1958).

3 John Piper, *Desiring God: Meditations of a Christian Hedonist* (Colorado Springs: Multnomah, 2011).

4 Jonathan Edwards, The "Miscellanies," Entry Nos. a-500, *The Works of Jonathan Edwards*, vol. 13., no. 3, edited by Thomas A. Schafer (New Haven: Yale University Press, 1994), 200.

> he might communicate, and the creature receive, his glory . . . both [with] the mind and the heart. He that testifies his having an idea of God's glory [doesn't] glorify God so much as he that testifies also his approbation [i.e., his heartfelt commendation or praise] of it and his delight in it.[5]

Edwards' point is that *passionate and joyful admiration of God, and not merely intellectual apprehension, is the aim of our existence.* If God is to be supremely glorified in us, we must be supremely glad in him and in what he has done for us in Jesus. Enjoying God is not a secondary, tangential endeavor. It is central to everything we do, especially worship. In one way, *it is worship.* We do not do other things hoping that joy in God will emerge as a by-product. Our reason for the pursuit of God and obedience to him is precisely the joy that is found in him alone. To worship him for any other reason than the joy that is found in who he is, is sinful.

This theological digression was important, because it articulates the transformation in my understanding and experience of worship. There's no other way to say it: I suddenly felt the freedom to *enjoy God*. I actually *felt* his presence. I actually *felt* his enjoyment of me in my enjoyment of him (cf. Zephaniah 3:17). I began to sense a *power* and *spiritual intensity* that at first was a bit frightening. Although I have always been a romantic and somewhat emotional, when it came to worship—especially in a public setting—I was always diligent to rein in my emotions. I felt compelled to preserve a measure of so-called dignity and religious sophistication.

But then God *visited* me in worship! As I drew near to him, he drew near to me (James 4:8). I began to experience an intimacy and warmth of relationship with God that reminded me of Paul's prayer for the Ephesians:

---

5 Ibid., no. 448, 495.

> (I pray) that according to the riches of his glory he may grant you to be strengthened with power through his Spirit in your inner being, so that Christ may dwell in your hearts through faith—that you, being rooted and grounded in love, may have strength to comprehend with all the saints what is the breadth and length and height and depth, and to know the love of Christ that surpasses knowledge, that you may be filled with all the fullness of God. (Ephesians 3:16–19)

David tells us that in God's presence there is "fullness of joy" and at his right hand are "pleasures forevermore" (Psalm 16:11). I began to move beyond the affirmation of this truth to the tangible, experiential enjoyment of it. It suddenly dawned on me that, whereas I had trusted God with my mind, confident that he was sufficiently sovereign to protect my theology, I had not trusted him with my affections. A few years later I came across a statement in one of Jack Hayford's books that perfectly expresses what I was sensing at that time:

> It began to dawn on me that, given an environment where the Word of God was *foundational* and the Person of Christ the *focus*, the Holy Spirit could be trusted to do *both*—enlighten the intelligence and ignite the emotions. I soon discovered that to allow Him that much space necessitates more a surrender of my senseless fears than a surrender of sensible control. God is not asking any of us to abandon reason or succumb to some euphoric feeling. He is, however, calling us to trust Him—enough to give *Him* control.[6]

I still sing *about* God. I always will. But there's something different in singing *to* God. Yes, I still join with others and sing "*We*

---

6 Jack Hayford, *A Passion for Fullness* (Dallas: Word Books, 1990), 31.

love him." After all, we must never lose sight of the fact that we are a *community* of worshipers. But I much prefer engaging God one-on-one, my heart touching his, and singing "*I* love *you*!"

I made a discovery about worship that I believe is found repeatedly in Scripture. Unfortunately, whereas I had read it, I never experienced the reality of it. I'm referring to the outpouring of divine *power* during times of praise. When God's people exalt and enjoy him, he releases the power of his Spirit to heal them, to encourage them, and to enlighten them, among other things, in a way that is somewhat unique. When God's people worship, he goes to war on their behalf (2 Chronicles 20). When God's people worship, he enthrones himself in their midst (Psalm 22:3). When God's people worship, he speaks to them and guides them (Acts 13:1–3). When God's people worship, he delivers them from their troubles or comforts and sustains them in the midst of hardship (Acts 16:19–40).

And it is this conjunction between our praise of him and the experience of his power in us that makes the subject of worship so important for our discussion of how spiritual gifts operate in the local church.

Worship Wars?

People either start or stop attending certain churches for a variety of reasons. For some, it is the preaching of the Word or the absence of it that determines their decision. For others, it is the availability of parking or the children's ministry or friendliness of the people that governs where they ultimately land. Believe it or not, in some cases it's the brand of coffee they serve in their café!

But in the past thirty or so years, the one factor that has probably been the decisive factor more than any other is the style of worship that a church displays. The sad fact is that the church in the West has been ripped apart in many instances over such debates as:

Should our worship be long or short?
Should our worship be formal or free?
Should our worship use acoustic guitars or a Baldwin piano?
Should we use hymns or contemporary songs?
Should we have praise teams or robed choirs?
Should our worship be characterized more by the fear of God or the enjoyment of God?

And the list of choices could go on seemingly without end. Oftentimes, though, the divide is along the lines of Word and Spirit. Word-oriented churches that are often cessationist in their theology take one particular approach, while Spirit-oriented churches that practice spiritual gifts take yet another approach.

What both groups share in common is their conviction that worship must be *theocentric*: it is concerned with glorifying God. Where they differ is on the ways and means. Cessationists believe God is most glorified when biblical truths about him are accurately and passionately proclaimed in song, liturgy, and recitation of Scripture. The focus of worship is to *understand* God and to represent him faithfully in corporate declaration. Worship is thus primarily didactic and theological, and *their greatest fear is emotionalism.*

Charismatics, on the other hand, believe God is most glorified not only when he is accurately portrayed in song but when he is experienced in personal encounter. Charismatic worship does not downplay understanding God but insists that he is truly honored when he is *enjoyed*. Worship is thus emotional and relational in nature, and *their greatest fear is intellectualism.*

Admittedly this is perhaps a bit too tidy. Cessationists would no doubt agree that God is to be enjoyed, but they see this as primarily a cognitive experience. Charismatics contend for a more holistic enjoyment. God is not merely to be grasped with the mind but felt in the depths of one's soul. The mind is expanded but the affections are also stirred (and the body may well move!).

Perhaps the best way to illustrate this difference is the way both groups think of God's *presence* in times of corporate praise. Think of it this way. When you gather in corporate assembly with God's people, whether on a Sunday morning or in a small group during the week, what are your expectations with regard to God? Do you view God's presence as a theological doctrine to be extolled and explained or do you think of it as a tangible reality to be felt? Those hymns that are more traditional in their focus stress divine transcendence. God is out there, beyond us, above us, and we sing *about* him. The songs you hear in a more charismatic setting stress divine immanence. God is down here, very near us, close to us, and we sing *to* him.

It follows from this that cessationists tend to fear excessive familiarity with God. They're concerned lest we get too chummy with God. Charismatics, on the other hand, tend to fear relational distance. They want nothing to do with an impersonal religion that relegates God to a remote and deistic heaven. Their longing is for the nearness and now-ness of God.

The spiritual atmosphere cessationists cultivate is characterized more by *fear and reverence* when compared to the charismatic desire for *joy and love*. Again, the former prizes form, the latter freedom. A cessationist service is somewhat controlled, both in terms of what is regarded as acceptable physical posture and the length of time devoted to corporate singing. Charismatic worship is emotionally free and physically expressive, with the characteristic lifting of hands and dancing.

There is a humble solemnity in most cessationist services versus the exuberant celebration among charismatics. This invariably elicits criticism from both sides. The cessationist is offended by what appears to be an overly casual, if not presumptuous, approach to God. Is not our God a consuming fire, holy and righteous? The charismatic sees in cessationist worship an excessively formal, if not lifeless, approach to God, if they dare approach him at all. And without denying that

God is holy, the charismatic is emboldened by what he believes is God's own passionate longing for relational intimacy.

The Holy Spirit and How We Worship

As you can see from the biblical texts cited at the beginning of this chapter, there is a very clear and direct relationship between the ministry of the Holy Spirit and proclamation and praise. Our worship is certainly to be grounded in God's Word and to be an accurate theological reflection of the truth of Scripture. But true worship must also be characterized by the presence and power of the Spirit. And when people are filled with the Spirit they break out spontaneously in praise and celebration, and occasionally during those times the Spirit speaks and imparts spiritual gifts and perhaps even brings healing to those in need.

We could spend several chapters exploring this subject alone. When I talk on this, there are many questions that come up. But in this chapter I want to focus on two primary issues. Both of these have practically impacted how we worship at our church, Bridgeway Church in Oklahoma City. In directing your attention to our approach (which is by no means the only approach to worship), I hope to encourage you in pursuing the praise of God in a way that will more readily facilitate your experience of the Spirit's power and gifts.

Singing in the Spirit

> And do not get drunk with wine, for that is debauchery, but be filled with the Spirit, addressing one another in psalms and hymns and spiritual songs, singing and making melody to the Lord with your heart, giving thanks always and for everything to God the Father in the name of our Lord Jesus Christ, submitting to one another out of reverence for Christ. (Ephesians 5:18–21)

Earlier in this chapter I mentioned the biblical idea of spiritual songs. Here I'd like to unpack that idea a bit more for you. The first thing we need to observe in what Paul says is the relationship between being "filled with the Spirit" and worship or singing. Here we see that being filled with the Holy Spirit is vividly contrasted with being drunk with wine. The issue is one of influence, control, or power. Paul is essentially saying to the Ephesian church: "If you insist on getting drunk, be inebriated with the Spirit!" Please note, however, that the force of this exhortation is not that Christians should stagger and slur their speech as those drunk with wine do. The influence of the infilling Spirit is *moral* in nature, the results and tangible evidence of which are the spiritual and relational fruit that Paul describes in Galatians 5. Paul envisions a community of people (the church) whose lives are so totally given over to the Spirit that his presence and fruit are as obvious in their behavior as the effects of excessive alcohol are in the other.

Notice that Paul does not say, "be full of the Spirit," as though one were full of the Spirit in the same way one is full of wine. He says, "be filled by/with the Spirit." The emphasis is on being filled to the full by the Spirit's presence. This is similar to Ephesians 3:19, where Paul speaks of being "filled with all the fullness of God," i.e., of being filled up with God himself.

This raises a question: Does Paul mean we are to be filled "with" the Spirit, as if the Spirit is himself the content with which we are filled? Or does he mean we are to be filled "by" the Spirit, the content of which is not clearly specified? This may seem like a fine distinction to some, and though we can't be certain, my sense is that it is the Spirit himself who fills us or empowers us.

We should also note that the verb, "be filled," is imperative; which is to say, it is a *command*. This is not a suggestion or a mild recommendation or a polite piece of advice. Being filled with the Holy Spirit is not optional. It is obligatory. And the verb in the original Greek is also plural. Paul would never have countenanced the idea that the fullness of the Spirit was a special privilege for a unique and privileged few. This is a responsibility that falls on each and every one of us. The exhortation has primarily to do with community life, i.e., the need for God's people to be so collectively full of God's presence that their worship is transformed, their relationships are transformed, and their lives as a totality are transformed.

Some Greek scholars downplay the significance of the present tense of the verb in this passage, but I am persuaded that Paul envisions this as a continuous, ongoing experience. This is not a dramatic or decisive one-time experience that settles things but a daily appropriation. It is a command that is relevant to all Christians throughout the course of their lives. Short of death itself, we are to continually seek the filling and empowering of the Spirit!

The mere fact that we are commanded to be filled implies that a Christian faces the danger of being low (but never empty!). We are always in need of refreshing and renewal. Therefore, in view of this command, we should cease speaking of the "second" blessing and begin to seek God for a "third" and a "fourth" and a "fifth" and for as many subsequent blessings or encounters with the person and power of the Spirit as God is pleased to bestow.

Finally, be careful to note what Paul says is the *consequential evidence* of being filled with/by the Holy Spirit. In other words, what happens when one is filled with the Spirit? What indication is there that this has actually happened? The answer is found in Ephesians 5:18ff. I'll break it into four key parts, but we'll focus most of our attention on the first two—speaking to one another in ministry and singing:

1. Speaking to one another in ministry
2. Singing to God (wholehearted worship in corporate fellowship)
3. Gratitude (for all things at all times)
4. Mutual submission (as over against being self-assertive and demanding)

In this chapter our concern is with verses 19–20 where Paul speaks of various ways of speaking to one another and singing to God. Paul envisions believers communicating truth, knowledge, and instruction by means of these various forms of speaking and singing. But what's the difference, if any, between "psalms" and "hymns" and "spiritual songs"? Some insist there is no difference between these items. But if Paul meant only one thing, what is the point of employing three different words? Most likely Paul had a distinction in mind, one that's important for us to note.

"Psalms" most likely refers to those inspired compositions in the Old Testament book of that name. Luke uses the word in this way in his writings (Luke 20:42; 24:44; Acts 1:20; 13:33) and Paul encouraged Christians to come to corporate worship with a "psalm" to offer (1 Corinthians 14:26 NASB). The word literally meant "to pluck" or "to strike or twitch the fingers on a string" and thus could possibly refer to singing with instrumental accompaniment (although we shouldn't restrict it to that).

The word *hymns* would refer to any human composition that focuses on God or Christ. Hannah's song in 1 Samuel 2 or the Song of Moses in Exodus 15 would qualify, as would Mary's Magnificat in Luke 1. Perhaps the most explicit examples would be what some call the Christ Hymns in Philippians 2:6–11, Colossians 1:15–20, and 1 Timothy 3:16.

This brings us to the third expression of singing, something that is designated not simply as *songs* but as *spiritual songs*. Could this be Paul's way of differentiating between those songs that are previously composed as over against those that are spontaneously evoked by the Spirit himself? As I mentioned earlier, I think so. I believe that *spiritual songs* are most likely *unrehearsed and improvised*, perhaps short melodies or choruses extolling the beauty of Christ. They aren't prepared in advance but are *prompted by the Spirit* and thus are uniquely and especially appropriate to the occasion or the emphasis of the moment.

These are songs that we sing under the immediate prompting

and infilling of the Holy Spirit. I have in mind spontaneous songs that break out unexpectedly in the midst of our worship. In other words, there is a difference between those songs that a worship leader rehearses and practices before we gather together (for which words appear on the screen), and the unplanned melodies and phrases and short choruses that break out spontaneously.

This interpretation strikes many today as strange for the simple fact that, outside of charismatic churches, there are virtually no opportunities for expressions of spontaneous praise. The only songs permitted in most churches today are those listed in the bulletin, the words of which are either in the hymnbook or included in the liturgy. In these churches, singing is highly structured, orchestrated, and carefully controlled (but not for that reason any less godly or edifying, of course). There is typically a distinct beginning and ending without the possibility of improvisation or free vocalization. People are expected to sing what is written in the hymnal or projected on a screen, nothing more and nothing less.

But let's look at the context of the early church again. Paul seems to envision a "singing" in which the individual is given *freedom to vocalize his/her own passions, prayers, and declarations of praise*. Although this may strike some as chaotic and aimless the first time it is heard (it certainly did me!), it can quickly become a beautiful and inspiring experience, as the Spirit is given free rein in the hearts of Christ's people. As the instrumentalists play a simple chord progression or perhaps even the melody of a familiar song, the people spontaneously supply whatever words are most appropriate to their state of mind and heart.

On countless occasions I have been blessed and edified by what some have called *prophetic singing* (so named because it is believed the Spirit reveals something to the person who in turn puts it to music). Typically an individual who is part of a worship team is led by the Spirit into a spontaneous song that may well evoke another to respond antiphonally. Such "spiritual songs" can last a few seconds or several minutes. Often, what one person sings will stir up yet another with a similar refrain, which on occasion will lead back into a verse or the chorus of a hymn previously sung.

More important still is the fact that such singing, whether psalms, hymns, or spiritual songs, are designed not simply to extol God but to educate his people. By means of them we "teach" and "admonish" one another. Clearly Paul envisioned songs that were biblically grounded and theologically substantive, songs that both communicated truth and called for heartfelt consecration, repentance, and devotion to the Lord. Let's not forget that Paul is describing a situation far in advance of the printing press and hymnbooks. Thus these various expressions of singing were an invaluable means for transmitting and inculcating Christian truth.

Although many today may never experience a worship service that incorporates these elements in the way I described, the educational and convicting power in music and song cannot be denied. In his book *Real Worship*, Warren Wiersbe wrote:

> I am convinced that congregations learn more theology (good and bad) from the songs they sing than from the sermons they hear. Many sermons are doctrinally sound and contain a fair amount of biblical information, but they lack that necessary emotional content that gets hold of the listener's heart. Music, however, reaches the mind and the heart at the same time. It has power to touch and move the emotions, and for that reason can become a wonderful tool in the hands of the Spirit or a terrible weapon in the hands of the Adversary.[7]

Not long ago one of the men in our church approached me with a concern. He was slightly uncomfortable with the way in

---

7 Warren Wiersbe, *Real Worship: It Will Transform Your Life* (Nashville: Thomas Nelson, 1986), 137.

which one of our worship leaders would spontaneously deviate from the song list and engage in free vocalization. His objection wasn't theological in nature. He had no qualms about what was being sung, as if it were unbiblical, but only that it was being sung while he perceived others to have disengaged.

"They don't know what to do," he said. "So many of them just sit down." The incorporation of such "spiritual songs" in our time of corporate praise was obviously unsettling to him. He asked: "Why can't he do that when he's in his car or somewhere other than in front of hundreds of people who are attempting to follow his lead?"

That's not an illegitimate question. I suspect that not a few others were wondering the same thing. So at the first opportunity, I seized the moment to instruct our people on what one should do when worship took this unexpected turn. I told them that one must resist disengaging, on the false assumption that this expression of praise is only for the benefit of the person singing and has nothing to do with anyone else. Instead, I provided several suggestions, which are instructive for all of us, as we think about worshiping in our local context.

Listen and Learn

First of all, we should listen to the singing, and we should learn from it. Note again Ephesians 5:19 where Paul says that we are "addressing one another" in "spiritual songs." At your church during worship, meditate on what is being sung. Focus on the words. Turn them over again and again in your mind. Ask the Spirit to quicken in your own heart the truth of what is being sung and to stir your affections with joy and love. Be open to being taught in those times of prophetic worship. The Spirit may well have prepared something uniquely and especially for you!

Sing the Same Song

As you listen, pay attention to recurring phrases and the melody line and if it lasts long enough, join the singer in whatever "spiritual song" he/she is singing. This may feel uncomfortable for you, especially if you have never tried it before! But I've found that with practice and experience it can become a significant means by which the Holy Spirit opens up our heart to enjoy God in worship.

Sing Your Own "Spiritual Song"

You can also take whatever truth about God or Jesus the Spirit has awakened in your heart and put it in your own words, adapting it to the melody of the leader. It may be a short, simple phrase of praise or thanksgiving or proclamation or prayer. Those, such as yours truly, who possess the spiritual gift of speaking in tongues, will often take advantage of such times to sing in tongues. This is surely what Paul had in mind when he made known his resolve to "sing praise with my spirit" (1 Corinthians 14:15; see also Acts 2:11; 10:46).

Pray and Give Thanks

Use this time to intercede for yourself or others. Or perhaps take the truth of what is being sung and let that shape and form the content of your prayers. Turn their spiritual song into your own personal intercession! And if you aren't sure what to pray for, spend time giving thanks (v. 20), thanking God (either in prayer or in song) for all that he has done.

Postures of Praise[8]

In addition to spiritual songs, one of the more important factors in creating an atmosphere where people are open to the movement of God's Spirit are what I call the postures of praise. Worship involves

8 For more on this subject, see my book *More Precious than Gold: 50 Daily Meditations on the Psalms* (Wheaton, Ill.: Crossway Books, 2009), 148–152.

our bodies as well as our hearts and minds, and our posture communicates something to God and to others. It tells a story. It makes a statement to God and to others about the state of our souls and the affections and passions of our heart.

If you were to visit Bridgeway, you would immediately recognize that we freely and frequently lift our hands when we worship. Some people may be seen kneeling. Some sit throughout the course of a service, either by preference or due to some physical limitation. Some just stand. And yes, some even dance. But for the sake of time and space, I'll forego talking of the other postures and restrict my comments to one key posture—the lifting of hands and its significance for worship.

On more than one occasion, I've been asked: "Sam, why do you lift your hands when you worship?" My answer is twofold. First, I raise my hands when I pray and praise because I have *explicit biblical precedent* for doing so. I don't know if I've found all biblical instances of it, but consider this smattering of texts.

> *So I will bless you as long as I live;*
> *in your name I will lift up my hands.* (Psalm 63:4)

> *To you, O Lord, I call;*
> *my rock, be not deaf to me,*
> *lest, if you be silent to me,*
> *I become like those who go down to the pit.*
>
> *Hear the voice of my pleas for mercy,*
> *when I cry to you for help,*
> *when I lift up my hands*
> *toward your most holy sanctuary.* (Psalm 28:1–2)

> *Every day I call upon you, O Lord;*
> *I spread out my hands to you.* (Psalm 88:9)

I will lift up my hands toward your commandments, which I love,
and I will meditate on your statutes. (Psalm 119:48)

Lift up your hands to the holy place
and bless the LORD! (Psalm 134:2)

O LORD, *I call upon you; hasten to me!*
Give ear to my voice when I call to you!
Let my prayer be counted as incense before you,
and the lifting up of my hands as the evening sacrifice!
(Psalm 141:1–2)

I stretch out my hands to you;
my soul thirsts for you like a parched land. (Psalm 143:6)

Then Solomon stood before the altar of the LORD in the presence of all the assembly of Israel and spread out his hands. Solomon had made a bronze platform five cubits long, five cubits wide, and three cubits high, and had set it in the court, and he stood on it. Then he knelt on his knees in the presence of all the assembly of Israel, and spread out his hands toward heaven. (2 Chronicles 6:12–13)

And at the evening sacrifice I rose from my fasting, with my garment and my cloak torn, and fell upon my knees and spread out my hands to the LORD my God. (Ezra 9:5)

And Ezra blessed the LORD, the great God, and all the people answered, "Amen, Amen," lifting up their hands. And they bowed their heads and worshiped the LORD with their faces to the ground. (Nehemiah 8:6)

Let us lift up our hearts and hands
to God in heaven. (Lamentations 3:41)

> I desire then that in every place the men should pray, lifting holy hands without anger or quarreling. (1 Timothy 2:8)

If someone should object and say that few of these texts speak explicitly of worship (see Psalms 63:4; 134:2), but only of prayer (as if a rigid distinction can even be made between the two; indeed, I can't recall ever worshiping God without praying to him; and prayer is itself a form of worship), my question is simply this: Why do you assume that the appropriate place for your hands is at your side and you need an explicit biblical warrant for raising them? Wouldn't it be just as reasonable to assume that the appropriate place for one's hands is raised toward heaven, calling for an explicit biblical warrant (other than gravity or physical exhaustion) to keep them low?

The second answer I give to the question, "Why do you lift your hands when you worship?" is: "Because I'm not a Gnostic!" Gnosticism, both in its ancient and modern forms, disparages the body. Among other things, it endorses a hyperspirituality that minimizes the goodness of physical reality. Gnostics focus almost exclusively on the nonmaterial or "spiritual" dimensions of human existence and experience. The body is evil and corrupt. The body must be controlled and suppressed and kept in check lest it defile the pure praise of one's spirit. The body, they say, is little more than a temporary prison for the soul that longs to escape into a pure, ethereal, altogether spiritual mode of being. Nonsense!

In one particular wedding ceremony I performed, the woman was from England and asked that I include in the vows one particular part that goes as follows:

> *With my body I thee honor.*
> *My body will adore you,*
> *and your body alone will I cherish.*
> *I will with my body, declare your worth.*

Biblical Christianity celebrates God's creation of physical reality (after all, he did pronounce it "good" in Genesis 1). We are more than immaterial creatures. We are embodied souls, and are to worship God with our whole being. We should "honor" God with our bodies. We "adore" God with our bodies. With our bodies we "declare" his worth. Paul couldn't have been more to the point when he exhorted us to present our "*bodies* as a living sacrifice, holy and acceptable to God," which is our "spiritual worship" (Romans 12:1, emphasis mine).

By all means, we must worship with understanding. We must think rightly of God and love him with our heart and soul and mind (see Matthew 22:37). But we are not, for that reason, any less physical beings. We will have glorified bodies forever in which to honor and adore our great God. If we are commanded to dance, kneel, sing and speak when we worship, what possible reason could there be for not engaging our hands as well?

The human hand gives visible expression to so many of our beliefs, feelings, and intentions. When I taught homiletics (how to preach), one of the most difficult tasks was getting young preachers to use their hands properly. Either from embarrassment or fear, they would keep them stuffed in their pockets, hidden from sight behind their backs, or nervously twiddle them in a variety of annoying ways.

Our hands speak loudly. When angry, we clinch our fists, threatening harm to others. When guilty, we hide our hands or hold incriminating evidence from view. When uneasy, we sit on them to obscure our inner selves. When worried, we wring them. When afraid, we use them to cover our face or hold tightly to someone for protection. When desperate or frustrated, we throw them wildly in the air, perhaps also in resignation or dismay. When confused, we extend them in bewilderment, as if asking for advice and direction. When hospitable, we use them to warmly receive those in our presence. When suspicious, we use them to keep someone at bay, or perhaps point an accusing finger in their direction.

Does it not seem wholly appropriate, therefore, to raise them to God when we seek him in prayer or celebrate him with praise? So again, why do I worship with hands raised?

Because like one who *surrenders* to a higher authority, I yield to God's will and ways and submit to his guidance and power and purpose in my life. It is my way of saying: "God, I am yours to do with as you please."

Because like one who expresses utter *vulnerability*, I say to the Lord: "I have nothing to hide. I come to you open handed, concealing nothing. My life is yours to search and sanctify. I'm holding nothing back. My heart, soul, spirit, body and will are an open book to you."

Because like one who needs help, I confess my utter *dependence* on God for everything. I cry out: "O God, I entrust my life to you. If you don't take hold and uplift me, I will surely sink into the abyss of sin and death. I rely on your strength alone. Preserve me. Sustain me. Deliver me."

Because like one who happily and expectantly *receives* a gift from another, I declare to the Lord: "Father, I gratefully embrace all you want to give. I'm a spiritual beggar. I have nothing to offer other than my need of all that you are for me in Jesus. So glorify yourself by satisfying me wholly with you alone."

Because like one who aspires to direct *attention* away from self to the Savior, I say: "O God, yours is the glory; yours is the power; yours is the majesty alone!"

Because as the *beloved* of God, I say tenderly and intimately to the Lover of my soul: "Abba, hold me. Protect me. Reveal your heart to me. I am yours! You are mine! Draw near and enable me to know and feel the affection in your heart for this one sinful soul."

For those many years when I kept my hands rigidly at my side or safely tucked away in the pockets of my pants, I knew that no one would take notice of my praise of God or my prayers of desperation. No one would dare mistake me for a fanatic! I felt in control, dignified, sophisticated, and, above all else, safe. These matter no more to me.

Please understand: These are not words of condemnation but confession. I know no one's heart but my own. I judge no one's motives but mine. I'm not telling you how to worship but simply sharing how I do and why. I'm at that point in life where I honestly couldn't care less what the immovable evangelical is thinking or the crazy charismatic is feeling. What matters to me is that God have my all: my mind, will, feet, eyes, ears, tongue, heart, affections, and yes, my hands.

No, you need not raise your hands to worship God. But why wouldn't you want to?

CONCLUSION

The three words I fear beyond all others are: "*Some assembly required.*" Whether it comes in the form of instructions on how to piece together my new office chair or the meticulous steps that must be followed to construct my grandson's favorite Lego® space station, I react negatively to virtually all pamphlets that call for some measure of mechanical know-how and manual dexterity. When I make a purchase of anything, I want to pull it from the box ready-made and fully functional.

I suspect that some of you feel the same way when it comes to the Holy Spirit and the many gifts that he supplies to individual Christians. You may feel a bit overwhelmed by the precise, practical suggestions, recommendations, and guidelines, together with the somber warnings, that I've articulated in this book. You may be inclined to join the chorus of voices I've often heard who repeatedly say: "Why does effective ministry in the gifts of the Spirit so often require such things as persistent prayer and fasting and study of the Bible and other forms of detailed spiritual preparation? Couldn't God have made it a lot easier than it is?"

I suppose he could have. But he didn't. The gift and gifts of the Holy Spirit are precious, and must be handled according to the instructions the Spirit himself has given to us in the Bible. In virtually every arena of Christian ministry, and especially when it comes to spiritual gifts, we are confronted with the warning: "Some assembly required." Of course, it doesn't have to be all that difficult (unlike some of those incredibly complex Lego® projects in which my grandson revels and excels). God's aim isn't to confuse us but to guard us and guide us into the most effective and Christ-exalting exercise of the many manifestations of his Holy Spirit.

So let's briefly take stock of where we've been before I close with a story of how the Spirit brought miraculous healing to a lady in our church.

Now that you've finished the book, it would probably be wise for you to revisit my opening comments concerning the challenges that lie ahead. There is a price to pay to move forward in the pursuit and practice of the charismata. Are you willing to pay it? If you are, God will more than abundantly provide whatever is needed.

Never think that you can pull ready-made from the box the fullness of the Spirit's supernatural work in the lives of God's people. Yes, some assembly is required. And the instruction manual that we call the Bible is quite clear. Whether it be in the form of incessant and heart-felt prayer, or through fasting, or in the recasting of the structure, style, and rhythm of your small group gatherings as well as your corporate worship services, there are steps that cannot be avoided if you hope to arrive successfully at your destination.

One thing must be stated again with even greater intensity. Very little authentic change will come about in the absence of consistent and unrelenting teaching on this subject from God's Word. The foundation for the experience of spiritual gifts is and always must be the inerrant truths articulated in the Bible. Any attempt to move forward apart from the parameters set for us in the NT will likely lead to experiential excess, theological error, and an unbridled fanaticism that will serve only to bring disgrace on the name of Christ and do damage to those very people you are trying to serve and help.

Ask yourself yet again: How hungry am I for the gifts of the Spirit in my life? How desperate am I for their accurate exercise in the local church? If you feel fairly full and don't crave for more of God's miraculous power in your life, little if any, of what I've said will make a dent in your understanding of the Holy Spirit or your pursuit of the manifestation of his presence. Pray yet again that God would increase your spiritual hunger pangs, that he would intensify your thirst for godly power, that he would never allow you to settle for the status quo.

Satan, of course, will never sit still for this. Plan on pushback. That is why I included a chapter on the power and authority given to us by Christ, in Christ.

Be willing to put your reputation on the line. Don't fear looking foolish. (But never seek to look foolish for its own sake!) John Wimber, founder of the Association of Vineyard Churches, was fond of saying that FAITH is a four-letter word spelled: R-I-S-K! There is little in the ministry of spiritual gifts that comes with an advanced guarantee, a promise that failures will never happen and that no one will ever feel ill at ease or be embarrassed by those who go too far. But that reality must never be allowed to cripple our zeal or paralyze our pursuit of what God has clearly told us to seek and to experience.

Don't minimize the critical importance of the final chapter on worship. If you are still wondering why it was included in this book, the simple answer comes in two words: presence and power. When God's people praise him, God's presence is felt and sensed and enjoyed. And when God is extraordinarily present among us, his power is invariably at work. The hunger for God that I've encouraged and the prayer life that I've outlined and the authority over the enemy that we've been given are all magnified and expanded when our hearts and minds are filled with exalted thoughts of God and our mouths are loudly and passionately proclaiming his excellencies (1 Peter 2:9–10).

One More Story of Miraculous Healing

This final story is not a fable or a fabrication. These are real people, not unlike you and me.[1]

My sermon series on the book of James was coming to a close. We had finally arrived in chapter five when I decided to devote four

1 The names of the people involved have been altered. They have given me permission to tell the story of what happened.

messages to James 5:13–18, the famous passage on praying for the sick to be healed. After each of the four messages, I invited anyone in the congregation who had a physical affliction of any sort to stand. Patience is essential in such matters, so I waited silently for people to respond. First one stood, then another, so that after about two to three minutes, there were upwards of fifty who were requesting prayer. This happened much the same way after each of these four concluding sermons. There are numerous stories of miraculous healing and prophetic words that ministered powerfully to those asking for prayer, but here I mention only one. Aside from my having changed the names of those involved, the following is their testimony in their own words.

> My wife, Julie, and I have been attending Bridgeway for the past several years. I am an ER doctor and Julie is a stay-at-home mother of four children, ages 3–7. Julie has been suffering with severe back pain for the past several years. Her back has hurt her to some degree essentially every day, with intermittent periods of worsening severity for a week or two at a time.
>
> She had an MRI of her lumbar spine (low back) in 2012 that showed an annular disk tear at L5-S1. This means that the disk between those vertebrae has leaked fluid into an area that causes pain. She went through a course of physical therapy and then home exercises that produced some short-term improvement but certainly not resolution.
>
> Lately, her back pain has been increasing in severity. Over the last several years, this has caused lifestyle limitations, and it certainly has put a damper on her general wellbeing. Some days, her back pain was very problematic. She was taking over-the-counter medication on an almost daily basis to treat her back pain and, when severe, had to take prescription medication. I, too, was growing frustrated on her behalf that such a healthy young woman (whom I love deeply) was experiencing such

debilitating pain, and I was overall unable to help her to a great degree.

Two Sundays ago in church, Sam had a call to prayer for healing. I was sitting next to Julie and felt compelled to pray for her. I prayed very specifically for the healing of the annular disk tear in her lower back, and as I prayed, I felt a powerful warmth and sense of confidence that her back was going to be healed. I prayed that she would be healed of her back pain and that she would no longer suffer. She also has had frequent migraine headaches for most of her life. Several years ago we went through a medical evaluation and course of treatment that produced some degree of improvement but, again, no resolution.

As we were finishing our prayer, another couple came to pray with us as well. Julie came to me later that week and told me that since we prayed for her back, she has had NO LOWER BACK PAIN for the first time in years! Also, she has not had any headaches! I was overjoyed to hear of the Lord's healing touch on my wife! After years of doing everything that I could to help her medically with her headaches and back pain (short of back surgery), specific prayer is the only thing that has provided complete relief. This is incredibly encouraging to me as a physician that oftentimes sees the limitations of modern-day medicine. I am so grateful to God for his love, his concern with the seemingly minute details of our lives, and his omnipotence. I am especially grateful that my wife finally has relief from physical ailments that have been plaguing her for years! God is Good![2]

I wish I could tell you that everyone for whom we pray at Bridgeway is healed in this manner, but I can't. However, many are. But even if they were not, we remain committed to obeying

---

2 As of the publication date for this book, "Julie" is still completely healed.

the command of Scripture as found in James 5:16—"Therefore, confess your sins to one another and pray for one another, that you may be healed. The prayer of a righteous person has great power as it is working."

What's important for all of us to remember is that loving, Christ-exalting, Bible-honoring ministry in the power of the Holy Spirit and his gifts, absent manipulation and devoid of hype, *is* possible today. My prayer is that this book has made a small contribution to describing how it might be done. So, I concur with Paul (and I hope you do so as well) when he says:

> Pursue love, and earnestly desire the spiritual gifts, especially that you may prophesy.
>
> 1 CORINTHIANS 14:1

APPENDIX 1

AN ALTERNATIVE INTERPRETATION OF 1 CORINTHIANS 14:33–35

There has been much said about Paul's instructions in 1 Corinthians that a woman not speak in church, a passage that has given way too much controversy. It is a particularly puzzling passage, especially when taken with other verses that portray women sometimes sharing in public settings. When Paul tells women in this passage to "keep silent," he is not prohibiting them from making a verbal contribution to the meeting, whether in the form of worship or praying or prophesying or reading Scripture or sharing a testimony or similar activities. The view held by most is that Paul is saying that no woman is permitted to speak responsively in judgment of a man's prophetic utterance. However, some have argued that *Paul is prohibiting women from engaging in a public interrogation of another woman's husband*. Two reasons are cited for this.

The first reason is found in verse 35. There Paul says that their speaking was motivated by a desire to "learn." The "speaking" that Paul silences was their asking of questions in an attempt to gain knowledge and insight. If they want to learn, and it is perfectly right and good that they should, they must wait and ask their husbands at home. Note well: Paul does *not* say, "If they have something to *contribute* they should *tell* their husbands later at home," but rather, "If they wish to *learn* something they should *ask* their husbands later at home."

But why would it be inappropriate for women, in the church meeting, to ask questions in their pursuit of knowledge? The answer is found in the second possible key to understanding this passage. It is the word translated "shameful" (ESV) in verse 35 or "improper" (NASB).

Why would it be "shameful" or "improper" for women to publicly interrogate or ask probing questions of men other than their husbands in the public assembly of the church? Christopher Forbes says, "There existed in the Graeco-Roman world in [the first century] . . . a strong prejudice against women speaking in public, and especially against their speaking to other women's husbands. In a society with strictly defined gender and social roles, and a strong view of the rights of the man over his wife, such behaviour was treated as totally inappropriate."[1]

Therefore, according to this view, women are free to pray and prophesy within the assembly. But when issues arise that they don't understand, they must refrain from making probing inquiry. Why? For one thing, there is a limited time in any one meeting, and Paul does not want anyone or any group to dominate the gathering (which seems to be at least part of the reason for his instruction in verses 27–31 where he puts limits on how many can speak in tongues and prophesy). But more important, "To ask questions of the husbands of other women (especially as this might lead to extended discussions) would be grossly improper, and as such is not to be permitted."[2]

One could reasonably argue that, if this view is correct (and I'm not entirely confident it is), Paul's prohibition in verse 34 on women speaking is no longer applicable. For all will acknowledge, at least in Western society, that today there is no shame or impropriety in a woman asking a question in public of another woman's husband. At the same time, if this interpretation proves to be correct, the restriction Paul places on women teaching and exercising authority over men would remain unaffected (1 Timothy 2:12–15).

---

1 Christopher Forbes, *Prophecy and Inspired Speech: In Early Christianity and Its Hellenistic Environment* (Peabody, Mass.: Hendrickson Publishers, 1997), 274–75.

2 Ibid., 276.

APPENDIX 2

ARE MIRACULOUS GIFTS FOR TODAY?[1]

This is a question that deserves a book-length response. Thankfully, that has been done elsewhere, and I'd encourage you to investigate it there in far greater detail. This is just a brief introduction to the subject.[2]

In this shorter essay, I'm going to answer this question by giving twelve bad reasons for being a cessationist, followed by twelve good reasons for being a continuationist. And I'll begin by defining those terms for you. A *cessationist* is not a person who believes the South had a right to secede from the Union in the middle of the nineteenth century. That would be a *secessionist!* A *cessationist* is someone who believes that certain spiritual gifts, typically those of a more overtly supernatural nature, *ceased* to be given by God to the church sometime late in the first century AD. A *continuationist*, on the other hand, is a person who believes that all the gifts of the Spirit *continue* to be given by God and are therefore operative in the church today and should be prayed for and sought after. In case you hadn't guessed it, I'm a continuationist. That being said, here is why.

---

1 This material is taken from chapter 18 in my book *Tough Topics* (Crossway) and is used here with permission of the publisher. Some new material has been added in the section concerned with spiritual gifts in church history.

2 Among the many books on this topic, I'll recommend only two. The first, and truly the best, is Jack Deere's book *Surprised by the Power of the Spirit* (Grand Rapids: Zondervan, 1996). Another helpful book to which I contributed is edited by Wayne Grudem and entitled *Are Miraculous Gifts for Today? Four Views* (Grand Rapids: Zondervan, 1996). Much of what I write in this chapter has been adapted from the much longer treatment that I contributed to the four views in the book.

Twelve Bad Reasons for Being a Cessationist

(1) The first bad reason for being a cessationist is an appeal to 1 Corinthians 13:8–12 on the assumption that the "perfect" is something other or less than the fullness of the eternal state ushered in at the second coming of Jesus Christ. Even most cessationists now agree that the "perfect" cannot be a reference to the canon of Scripture or the alleged maturity of the church in the first century. The "perfect" is that glorious state of final consummation when, as Paul says, we will see "face to face" and "know fully" (v. 12), as over against the limitations imposed by our life now where we see as "in a mirror dimly" and know only "in part" (v. 12).

There is simply no evidence that even Paul anticipated the formation of a "canon" of Scripture following the death of the apostles. In fact, Paul seems to have expected that he himself might survive until the coming of the Lord (1 Thessalonians 4:15–16; 1 Corinthians 15:51). Furthermore, there is no reason to think that Paul could have expected the Corinthians to figure out that he meant the canon when he used the term *teleion*. "In any case," notes Max Turner, "the completed canon of Scripture would hardly signify for the Corinthians the *passing away of merely 'partial' knowledge* (and prophecy and tongues with it), and the arrival of 'full knowledge,' for the Corinthians already had the Old Testament, the gospel tradition (presumably), and (almost certainly) more Pauline teaching than finally got into the canon."[3]

We must also take note of verse 12b where Paul says that with the coming of the "perfect" our "partial knowledge" will give way to a depth of knowledge that is only matched by the way we are known by God. That is to say, when the perfect comes we will then see "face to face" and will know even as we are now known by God. Few people any longer dispute that this is language descriptive of our

---

3 Max Turner, *The Holy Spirit and Spiritual Gifts, Then and Now* (Carlisle, England: Paternoster Press, 1996), 294.

experience in the eternal state, subsequent to the return of Christ. As Turner says, "However much we respect the New Testament canon, Paul can only be accused of the wildest exaggeration in verse 12 if that is what he was talking about."[4] Finally, this view rests on the assumption that prophecy was a form of divine revelation designed to serve the church in the interim, until such time as the canon was formed. But a careful examination of the New Testament reveals that prophecy had a much broader purpose that would not in the least be affected by the completion of the canon.

(2) Another bad or illegitimate reason for being a cessationist is the belief that signs and wonders, as well as certain spiritual gifts, served only to confirm or authenticate the original company of apostles, so that when the apostles passed away so also did the gifts. The fact is, no biblical text (not even Hebrews 2:4) ever says that signs and wonders or spiritual gifts of a particular sort authenticated the apostles. Signs and wonders authenticated Jesus and the apostolic message about him. If signs and wonders were designed exclusively to authenticate apostles, we have no explanation why nonapostolic believers (such as Philip and Stephen) were empowered to perform them.

Therefore, this is a good reason for being a cessationist only if you can demonstrate that authentication or attestation of the apostolic message was the *sole and exclusive purpose* of such displays of divine power. However, *nowhere in the NT is the purpose or function of the miraculous or the charismata reduced to that of attestation.*

The miraculous, in whatever form in which it appeared, served several other distinct purposes: *doxological* (to glorify God—Matthew 15:29–31; John 2:11; 9:3; 11:4, 40); *evangelistic* (to prepare the way for the gospel to be made known—see Acts 9:32–43); *pastoral* (as an expression of compassion and love and care for the sheep—Matthew 14:14; Mark 1:40–41); and *edification* (that is, to

4 Ibid., 295.

build up and strengthen believers—1 Corinthians 12:7 and "common good"; 1 Corinthians 14:3–5, 26).

My point is this: *all* the gifts of the Spirit, whether tongues or teaching, whether prophecy or mercy, whether healing or helps, were given, among other reasons, for the edification and building up and encouraging and instructing and consoling and sanctifying of the body of Christ. Therefore, even if the ministry of the miraculous gifts to attest and authenticate has ceased, a point I concede only for the sake of argument, such gifts would continue to function in the church for the other reasons cited.

Someone might object to this by saying: But weren't miraculous gifts "signs of an apostle" such that when apostleship ceased, so too did the signs? No, in fact 2 Corinthians 12:12 says no such thing. Paul does *not* say the insignia or marks of an apostle *are* signs, wonders and miracles. Rather, as the NASB more accurately translates, he asserts that "the signs of a true apostle were performed among you with all perseverance, *by* [or better still, *accompanied by*] signs and wonders and miracles." Paul's point is that miraculous phenomena accompanied his ministry in Corinth. Signs, wonders, and miracles were attendant elements in his apostolic work. But they were not themselves the "signs of an apostle."

(3) A third bad reason for being a cessationist is the belief that since we now have the completed canon of Scripture, we no longer need the operation of so-called miraculous gifts. However, the Bible itself quite simply never says this. In fact, as will become evident below, it says precisely the opposite. It is the Bible itself that gives us warrant for believing that all spiritual gifts are designed by God for the church in the present age.

No biblical author ever claims that written Scripture has replaced or in some sense supplanted the need for signs, wonders, and the like. Why would the presence of the completed canon preclude the need for miraculous phenomena? If signs, wonders, and the power of the Holy Spirit were essential in bearing witness to the truth of the gospel *then*, why not *now*? In other words, it seems reasonable to assume that the miracles which confirmed the gospel in the first century, wherever it was preached, would serve no less to confirm the gospel in subsequent centuries, even our own.

If signs, wonders, and miracles were essential in the physical presence of the Son of God, how much more essential are they now in his absence? Surely we are not prepared to suggest that the Bible, for all its glory, is sufficient to do what Jesus couldn't. Jesus thought it necessary to utilize the miraculous phenomena of the Holy Spirit to attest and confirm his ministry. If it was essential for him, how much more so for us? In other words, if the glorious presence of the Son of God himself did not preclude the need for miraculous phenomena, how can we suggest that our possession of the Bible does?

(4) A fourth bad reason for being a cessationist is the belief that to embrace the validity of all spiritual gifts today requires that one embrace classical Pentecostalism and its belief in Spirit-baptism as separate from and subsequent to conversion, as well as their doctrine that speaking in tongues is the initial physical evidence of having experienced this Spirit-baptism. One can be a continuationist, as I am, and affirm that Spirit-baptism happens for all believers at the moment of their faith and conversion to Christ and affirm that speaking in tongues is a gift for some, but not all, believers.

(5) Another bad reason for being a cessationist is the idea that if one spiritual gift, such as apostleship, has ceased to be operative in the church that other, and perhaps all, miraculous gifts have ceased to be operative in the church. But is "apostleship" a spiritual gift? I doubt it. Even if it is, there is nothing inconsistent about acknowledging that one gift might have ceased while others continue. If you can make an exegetical case for the cessation of apostleship, fine. But then you must proceed and make an equally persuasive exegetical case for the cessation of other gifts. That is what I contend you cannot do. I'm more than happy to concede that *every* spiritual gift has ceased and is no longer operative if you

can provide me with biblical evidence to that effect. In the meantime, the mere potential for one or more gifts to have ceased is no argument that others definitely have.

(6) A sixth bad reason for being a cessationist is the fear that to acknowledge the validity today of revelatory gifts such as prophecy and word of knowledge would necessarily undermine the finality and sufficiency of Holy Scripture. But this argument is based on the false assumption that revelatory gifts such as prophecy and word of knowledge provide us with infallible truths that are equal in authority to the biblical text itself.

(7) A seventh bad reason for being a cessationist is the appeal to Ephesians 2:20 on the assumption that revelatory gifts such as *prophecy* were uniquely linked to the apostles and therefore designed to function only during the so-called *foundational* period in the early church.

A closer look at Scripture indicates that there are numerous instances where prophecy was not linked to the apostles and never functioned foundationally. Not everyone who ministered prophetically was apostolic! In other words, Ephesians 2:20 clearly does not have in view all prophetic ministry. Consider, for example, Acts 2 (where men and women, young and old, from all walks of life are expected to prophesy in the new covenant age); Acts 11 (the ministry of Agabus); Acts 21:9 (the four daughters of Philip who prophesied); Romans 12; as well as 1 Corinthians 12:7–10; 14:1, 26, 39 (in these two texts all believers are exhorted to earnestly desire to prophesy); and 1 Thessalonians 5:19–22.

In summary, both the nature of the prophetic gift, as well as its widespread distribution among Christians, clearly indicates that there was far more to this gift than simply the apostles laying the foundation of the church. Therefore, neither the passing of the apostles nor the movement of the church beyond its foundational years has any bearing whatsoever on the validity of prophecy today.

(8) An eighth bad reason for being a cessationist is the argument

that since we typically don't see miracles or gifts today equal in *quality or intensity* to those in the ministries of *Jesus* and the *apostles*, God doesn't intend for *any* miraculous gifts of a *lesser quality or intensity* to operate in the church among ordinary Christians. (Although many texts would refute this. See 1 Corinthians 12–14; Romans 12; 1 Thessalonians 5:19–22; James 5:13–18).

However, no one denies that Jesus and the apostles operated at a far superior level of the supernatural than others. But why should that be an argument against the validity of the spiritual gifts listed in 1 Corinthians 12? If we are going to insist that the apostles set the standard by which we are to judge the validity of all spiritual gifts, such as those in 1 Corinthians 12 and Romans 12, then we might be forced to conclude that no spiritual gift of any sort is valid today, for who would claim to teach like Paul or evangelize like Paul? No one measures up to the apostles in any respect.

The most that we may conclude from our not seeing apostolic healing or apostolic miracles is that we are not seeing healing/miracles at the level and with the frequency that they occurred in the ministry of the apostles. It does not mean that God has withdrawn gifts of healing or the gift of working miracles from the church at large.

(9) A ninth bad reason for being a cessationist is the so-called cluster argument. According to this argument, miracles and supernatural phenomena were concentrated or "clustered" at specific times in biblical history and therefore should not be expected to appear as a regular or normal phenomenon in other periods of history. My first response is to direct you to Jack Deere's book *Surprised by the Power of the Spirit*, referenced in an earlier footnote. Jack provides an extensive and detailed refutation of this argument. I only wish space allowed me to reproduce his findings here.

Also, this argument, even if true, only demonstrates that miracles, signs, and wonders were more prevalent in some seasons than at other times, but not that they were non-existent during other seasons or that we shouldn't pray for them today. One must also explain not only why miraculous phenomena were prevalent in these three periods (assuming they were) but also why they were, allegedly, infrequent or isolated in all other periods. (See Psalms 74:9–11; 77:7–14; and Mark 6:5.)

We must also not forget that there were no cessationists in the Old Testament! No one during the time of the old covenant appealed to the alleged "clustering" of supernatural phenomena as grounds for arguing that such had altogether ceased. And, of course, as I hinted at above, the cluster argument is simply unbiblical and false. Miracles, signs, and wonders occur consistently throughout the OT (as Deere demonstrates in his extensive survey of the OT; see especially Jeremiah 32:20 as well as the miraculous and supernatural activity during the Babylonian captivity as recorded in the book of Daniel). Prophecy in particular was prevalent through most of the OT, being absent or comparatively less active only because of the idolatry of Israel.

(10) A tenth bad reason for being a cessationist is the appeal to the alleged absence of miraculous gifts in church history subsequent to the first century. I'll have more to say about this below.

(11) Eleventh, it is a bad reason to be a cessationist because of the absence of good experiences with spiritual gifts and the often fanatical excess of certain TV evangelists and some of those involved in the Word of Faith or Prosperity Gospel movements (as well as the anti-intellectualism often found in those movements).

(12) Finally, a twelfth bad reason for being a cessationist is fear of what embracing continuationism might entail for your life personally and the wellbeing of your church corporately.

Twelve Good Reasons for Being a Continuationist

(1) This may sound strange, but the first good reason for being a continuationist is the twelve bad reasons for being a cessationist! In

other words, no convincing biblical, theological, historical, or experiential argument that either in isolation or in conjunction with any other arguments gives reason to believe that what God did in the first century he will not do in the twenty-first.

(2) A second good reason for being a continuationist is the consistent, indeed pervasive, and altogether positive presence throughout the NT of all spiritual gifts.[5] Beginning with Pentecost and continuing throughout the book of Acts, whenever the Spirit is poured out on new believers, they experience the manifestation of his charismata. There is nothing to indicate this phenomenon was restricted to them and then. Such signs appear to be both widespread and common in the NT church. Christians in Rome (Romans 12), Corinth (1 Corinthians 12–14), Samaria (Acts 8), Caesarea (Acts 10), Antioch (Acts 13), Ephesus (Acts 19; 1 Timothy 1), Thessalonica (1 Thessalonians 5), and Galatia (Galatians 3) experienced the miraculous and revelatory gifts. It is difficult to imagine how the NT authors could have said any more clearly than *this* what new covenant Christianity is supposed to look like. In other words, the burden of proof rests with the cessationist. If certain gifts of a special class have ceased, the responsibility is his to prove it.

(3) A third good reason for being a continuationist is the extensive NT evidence of the operation of so-called miraculous gifts among Christians who are not apostles. In other words, numerous nonapostolic men and women, young and old, across the breadth of the Roman Empire consistently exercised these gifts of the Spirit (and Stephen and Philip ministered in the power of signs and wonders).

Others aside from the apostles who exercised miraculous gifts include (a) the seventy who were commissioned in Luke 10:9,

5 The problems that emerged in the church at Corinth were not due to spiritual gifts, but to unspiritual people. It was not the gifts of God but the immature, ambitious, and prideful distortion of gifts on the part of some in that church that accounts for Paul's corrective comments. Let's not forget that whatever else one may think or say about spiritual gifts, they were God's idea!

19–20; (b) at least 108 people among the 120 who were gathered in the upper room on the day of Pentecost; (c) Stephen (Acts 6–7); (d) Phillip (Acts 8); (e) Ananias (Acts 9); (f) church members in Antioch (Acts 13:1–3); (g) new converts in Ephesus (Acts 19:6); (h) women at Caesarea (Acts 21:8–9); (i) the unnamed brethren of Galatians 3:5; (j) believers in Rome (Romans 12:6–8); (k) believers in Corinth (1 Corinthians 12–14, especially 12:7–10); and (l) Christians in Thessalonica (1 Thessalonians 5:19–20).

(4) A fourth good reason for being a continuationist is the explicit and oft-repeated purpose of the charismata: namely, the edification of the body of Christ (1 Corinthians 12:7; 14:3, 26). Nothing that I read in the NT nor see in the condition of the church in any age, past or present, leads me to believe we have progressed beyond the need for edification and therefore beyond the need for the contribution of the charismata. I freely admit that spiritual gifts were essential for the birth of the church, but why would they be any less important or needful for its continued growth and maturation?

(5) The fifth good reason for being a continuationist is the fundamental continuity or spiritually organic relationship between the church in Acts and the church in subsequent centuries. No one denies that there was an era or period in the early church that we might call "apostolic." We must acknowledge the significance of the personal physical presence of the apostles and their unique role in laying the foundation for the early church. But nowhere does the NT ever suggest that certain spiritual gifts were uniquely and exclusively tied to them or that with their passing the gifts passed as well. The universal church or body of Christ that was established and gifted through the ministry of the apostles is the same universal church and body of Christ that exists today (something that only the most extreme of hyper-Dispensationalists would deny). We are together with Paul and Peter and Silas and Lydia and Priscilla and Luke members of the same one body of Christ.

(6) Very much related to the fifth point, a sixth good reason

for being a continuationist is because of what Luke recorded Peter saying in Acts 2 concerning the operation of so-called miraculous gifts as characteristic of the new covenant age of the church. As D. A. Carson has said, "The coming of the Spirit is not associated merely with the *dawning* of the new age but with its *presence*, not merely with Pentecost but with the entire period from Pentecost to the return of Jesus the Messiah."[6] Or again, the gifts of prophecy and tongues (Acts 2) are not portrayed as merely *inaugurating* the new covenant age but as *characterizing* it (and let us not forget that the present church age = the latter days).

(7) The seventh good reason for being a continuationist is because of what Paul says in 1 Corinthians 13:8–12. As noted above, here Paul asserts that spiritual gifts will not "pass away" (vv. 8–10) until the coming of the "perfect." If the "perfect" is indeed the consummation of God's redemptive purposes as expressed in the new heaven and new earth following Christ's return, we can confidently expect him to continue to bless and empower his church with the gifts until that time.

(8) The eighth good reason for being a continuationist is because of what Paul says in Ephesians 4:11–13. There he speaks of the bestowal of spiritual gifts (together with the office of apostle), and in particular the gifts of prophecy, evangelism, pastor, and teacher, as functioning in the building up of the church "until we all attain to the unity of the faith and of the knowledge of the Son of God, to mature manhood, to the measure of the stature of the fullness of Christ" (v. 13). Since the latter most assuredly has not yet been attained by the church, we can confidently anticipate the presence and power of such gifts until that day arrives.

(9) A ninth good reason for being a continuationist is because the Holy Spirit in Christ is the Holy Spirit in Christians. We are

---

6 D. A. Carson, *Showing the Spirit: A Theological Exposition of 1 Corinthians 12–14* (Grand Rapids: Baker, 1987), 155.

indwelt, anointed, filled, and empowered by the same Spirit as was Jesus. His ministry is (with certain obvious limitations) the model for our ministry (cf. Acts 10:38).

(10) A tenth reason to be a continuationist is the absence of any explicit or implicit notion that we should view spiritual gifts any differently than we do other NT practices and ministries that are portrayed as essential for the life and wellbeing of the church. When we read the NT, it seems evident on the surface of things that church discipline is to be practiced in our assemblies today and that we are to celebrate the Lord's Table and water baptism, and that the requirements for the office of elder as set forth in the pastoral epistles are still guidelines for how life in the church is to be pursued, just to mention a few. What good exegetical or theological reasons can be given why we should treat the presence and operation of spiritual gifts any differently? None, so far as I can see.

(11) An eleventh good reason for being a continuationist is the testimony throughout most of church history concerning the operation of the miraculous gifts of the Spirit. Contrary to what many cessationists have suggested, the gifts did not cease or disappear from early church life following the death of the last apostle.[7] Here are just a few examples.[8]

Justin Martyr (100–165) boasted to the Jewish Trypho "that the prophetic gifts remain with us" (*Dialogue with Trypho*, 82).

Irenaeus (120–200) also bears witness to the presence of the gifts of the Spirit. He writes:

---

7 There are numerous resources that document the presence of the gifts in history, several of which are cited in my contribution to the book *Are Miraculous Gifts for Today? Four Views*, 200–204. See especially note 32, p. 201. After studying the documentation for claims to the presence of these gifts, D. A. Carson's conclusion is that "there is enough evidence that some form of 'charismatic' gifts continued sporadically across the centuries of church history that it is futile to insist on doctrinaire grounds that every report is spurious or the fruit of demonic activity or psychological aberration" (*Showing the Spirit*, 166).

8 For full documentation, see Ronald A. N. Kydd's book, *Charismatic Gifts in the Early Church* (Peabody, Mass.: Hendriksen Publishers, 1984).

> We have heard of many of the brethren who have foreknowledge of the future, visions, and prophetic utterances; others, by laying-on of hands, heal the sick and restore them to health (*Against Heresies*, 2:32, 4).
>
> We hear of many members of the church who have prophetic gifts, and, by the Spirit speak with all kinds of tongues, and bring men's secret thoughts to light for their own good, and expound the mysteries of God (*Against Heresies*, 5:6, 1).
>
> It is impossible to enumerate the charisms which throughout the world the church has received from God (*Against Heresies*, 2:32, 4).

Eusebius concludes that the charismata were all still in operation down to the time in which Irenaeus lived (*Ecclesiastical History*, 5:7, 6).

Apollinarius is quoted by Eusebius as saying that "the prophetic gifts must continue in the church until the final coming, as the apostle insists" (*Ecclesiastical History*, 5:16, 7).

Epiphanius, perhaps the most vocal opponent of the Montanists, did not attack them because they practiced the gifts of the Spirit. Indeed, he declared that "the charism [of prophecy] is not inoperative in the church. Quite the opposite. . . . The holy church of God welcomes the same [charisms] as the Montanists, but ours are real charisms, authenticated for the church by the Holy Spirit" (*Panarion*, 48).

The work of Theodotus (late second century) is preserved for us in Clement of Alexandria's *Excerpta ex Theodoto*. In 24:1 we read: "The Valentinians say that the excellent Spirit which each of the prophets had for his ministry was poured out upon all those of the church. Therefore the signs of the Spirit, healings and prophecies, are being performed by the church."

Clement of Alexandria (d. 215; *The Instructor*, iv.21, ANF, 2:434) spoke explicitly of the operation in his day of those spiritual gifts listed by Paul in 1 Corinthians 12:7–10.

Origen (d. 254) acknowledges that the operation of the gifts in his day is not as extensive as was true in the NT, but they are still present and powerful: "And there are still preserved among Christians traces of that Holy Spirit which appeared in the form of a dove. They expel evil spirits, and perform many cures, and foresee certain events, according to the will of the Logos" (*Against Celsus*, i.46, ANF, 4:415).

The pagan Celsus sought to discredit the gifts of the Spirit exercised in churches in Origen's day, yet the latter pointed to the "demonstration" of the validity of the Gospel, "more divine than any established by Grecian dialectics," namely that which is called by the apostle the "manifestations of the Spirit and of power." Not only were signs and wonders performed in the days of Jesus, but "traces of them are still preserved among those who regulate their lives by the precepts of the Gospel" (*Against Celsus*, i.2, ANF 4:397–98).

Hippolytus (d. 236) sets forth guidelines for the exercise of healing gifts, insisting that "if anyone says, 'I have received the gift of healing,' hands shall not be laid upon him: the deed shall make manifest if he speaks the truth" (*Apostolic Tradition*, xv, Easton, 41).

Novatian writes in *Treatise Concerning the Trinity* (ca. 245):

> Indeed this is he who appoints prophets in the church, instructs teachers, directs tongues, brings into being powers and conditions of health, carries on extraordinary works, furnishes discernment of spirits, incorporates administrations in the church, establishes plans, brings together and arranges all other gifts there are of the charismata and by reason of this makes the Church of God everywhere perfect in everything and complete. (29, 10)

Cyprian, Bishop of Carthage (248–258) spoke and wrote often of the gift of prophecy and the receiving of visions from the Spirit (*The Epistles of Cyprian*, vii.3–6, ANF, 5:286–87; vii.7, ANF, 5:287; lxviii.9–10, ANF, 5:375; iv.4, ANF, 5:290).

Gregory Thaumaturgus (213–270) is reported by many to have ministered in the power of numerous miraculous gifts and to have performed signs and wonders.

Eusebius of Caesarea (260–339), theologian and church historian in the court of Constantine, opposed the Montanists' abuse of the gift of prophecy, but not its reality. He affirmed repeatedly the legitimacy of spiritual gifts but resisted the Montanists who operated outside the mainstream church and thus contributed, said Eusebius, to its disunity.

Cyril of Jerusalem (d. 386) wrote often of the gifts in his day: "For He [the Holy Spirit] employs the tongue of one man for wisdom; the soul of another He enlightens by Prophecy, to another He gives power to drive away devils, to another he gives to interpret the divine Scriptures" (*Catechetical Lectures*, xvi.12, NPF 2nd Series, 7:118).

Although Athanasius nowhere explicitly addressed the issue of charismatic gifts, many believe he is the anonymous author of *Vita S. Antoni* or "The Life of St. Anthony." Anthony was a monk who embraced an ascetic lifestyle in 285 and remained in the desert for some twenty years. The author of his life describes numerous supernatural healings, visions, prophetic utterances, and other signs and wonders. Even if one rejects Athanasius as its author, the document does portray an approach to the charismatic gifts that many, evidently, embraced in the church of the late third and early fourth centuries.

The influential and highly regarded Cappadocian Fathers (mid-to-late fourth century) must also be considered. Basil of Caesarea (born 330) spoke often of the operation in his day of prophecy and healing. He appeals to Paul's description in 1 Corinthians 12 of "word of wisdom" and "gifts of healing" as representative of those gifts that are necessary for the common good of the church (*The Longer Rules*, vii).

> Is it not plain and incontestable that the ordering of the Church is effected through the Spirit? For He gave, it is said, "in the church, first Apostles, secondarily prophets, thirdly teachers, after that miracles, then gifts of healing, helps, governments, diversities of tongues," for this order is ordained in accordance with the division of the gifts that are of the Spirit (*On the Holy Spirit*, xvi.39, NPF 2nd Series 8:25).

Spiritual leaders in the church, such as bishops or presbyters, says Basil, possess the gift of discernment of spirits, healing, and foreseeing the future (one expression of prophecy) (*The Longer Rule*, xxiv, xxxv, xlii, lv).

Gregory of Nyssa (born 336; Basil's younger brother) speaks on Paul's words in 1 Corinthians 13:

> Even if someone receives the other gifts which the Spirit furnishes (I mean the tongues of angels and prophecy and knowledge and the grace of healing), but has never been entirely cleansed of the troubling passions within him through the charity of the Spirit, he is in danger of failing. (*The Life of St. Macrina*, FC 58:175)

The final Cappadocian, Gregory of Nazianzen (born 330), provides extensive descriptions of the physical healing that both his father and mother experienced as well as several visions that accompanied them (*On the Death of His Father*, xxviii-xxix, NPF 2nd Series 7:263–64; xxxi, NPF 2nd Series 7:264).

Hilary of Poitiers (356) speaks of "the gift of healings" and "the working of miracles" that "what we do may be understood to be the power of God" as well as "prophecy" and the "discerning of spirits." He also refers to the importance of "speaking in tongues" as a "sign of the gift of the Holy Spirit" together with "the interpretation of tongues," so "that the faith of those that hear may not be imperiled through ignorance, since the interpreter of a tongue explains the tongue to those who are ignorant of it" (*On the Trinity*, viii.30, NPF 2nd Series 9:146).

By the late fourth century, the gifts of the Spirit were increasingly found among ascetics and those involved in the monastic movements. The various compromises and accommodations to the wider culture that infiltrated the church subsequent to the formal legalization of Christianity under Constantine drove many of the more spiritually minded leaders into the desert.

Something must be said about Augustine (354–430), who early in his ministry espoused cessationism, especially with regard to the gift of tongues. However, in his later writings he retracted his denial of the ongoing reality of the miraculous and carefully documented no fewer than seventy instances of divine healing in his own diocese during a two-year span (see his *City of God*, Book XXII, chs. 8–10). After describing numerous miracles of healing and even resurrections from the dead, Augustine writes:

> What am I to do? I am so pressed by the promise of finishing this work, that I cannot record all the miracles I know; and doubtless several of our adherents, when they read what I have narrated, will regret that I have omitted so many which they, as well as I, certainly know. Even now I beg, these persons to excuse me, and to consider how long it would take me to relate all those miracles, which the necessity of finishing the work I have undertaken forces me to omit. (*City of God*, Book XXII, ch. 8, p. 489)

Again, writing his *Retractions* at the close of life and ministry (ca. 426–27), he concedes that tongues and the more spectacular miracles such as people being healed "by the mere shadow of Christ's preachers as they pass by" have ceased. He then says, "But what I said should not be understood as though no miracles should be believed to be performed nowadays in Christ's name. For I myself, when I was writing this very book, knew a blind man who had been given his sight in the same city near the bodies of the martyrs of Milan. I knew of some other miracles as well; so many of them occur even in these times that we would be unable either to be aware of all of them or to number those of which we are aware."

Although there is less evidence as we enter the period of the Middle Ages (the reasons for which I've already noted), at no time did the gifts disappear altogether. Due to limitations of space I will only be able to list the names of those in whose ministries are numerous documented instances of the revelatory gifts of prophecy, healing, discerning of spirits, miracles, together with vivid accounts of dreams and visions.[9]

Pachomius (287–346) and John of Egypt (d. 394); Leo the Great (400–461; he served as bishop of Rome from 440 until 461); Genevieve of Paris (422–500); Gregory the Great (540–604); Gregory of Tours (538–594); Aidan, bishop of Lindisfarne (d. 651) and his successor Cuthbert (d. 687; both of whom served as missionaries in Britain); the Venerable Bede (673–735; his *Ecclesiastical History of the English People*, written in 731, contains numerous accounts of miraculous gifts in operation); Bernard of Clairvaux (1090–1153); Bernard's treatise on the *Life and Death of Saint Malachy the Irishman* (1094–1148); Richard of St. Victor (d. 1173); Anthony of Padua (1195–1231); Bonaventure (1217–1274); Francis of Assisi (1182–1226; documented in Bonaventure's *Life of St. Francis*); Thomas Aquinas (1225–1274); together with virtually all of the medieval mystics, among whom are several women: Hildegard of Bingen (1098–1179), Gertrude of Helfta (1256–1301), St. Clare of

---

9 For additional documentation, see Craig S. Keener, *Miracles: The Credibility of the New Testament Accounts*, 2 volumes (Grand Rapids: Baker Academic, 2011); Stanley M. Burgess, *The Holy Spirit: Medieval Roman Catholic and Reformation Traditions (Sixth–Sixteenth Centuries)* (Peabody, Mass.: Hendrickson Publishers, 1997); Paul Thigpen, "Did the Power of the Spirit Ever Leave the Church?" in *Charisma*, September 1992, 20–29; Richard M. Riss, "Tongues and Other Miraculous Gifts in the Second through Nineteenth Centuries," *Basileia*, 1985; and Ronald Kydd, *Charismatic Gifts in the Early Church* (Peabody, Mass.: Hendrickson, 1984).

Montefalco (d. 1308), Bergitta of Sweden (1302–1373), Catherine of Siena (1347–1380), Julian of Norwich (1342–1416), Margery Kempe (1373–1433); Dominican preacher Vincent Ferrer (1350–1419); and Theresa of Avila (1515–1582).

If one should object that these are exclusively Roman Catholics, we must not forget that during this period in history there was hardly anyone else. Aside from a few splinter sects, there was little to no expression of Christianity outside the Church of Rome (the formal split with what became known as Eastern Orthodoxy did not occur until 1054).

One should also not forget Ignatius of Loyola (1491–1556), founder of the Jesuits and author of the *Spiritual Exercises.* Spiritual gifts, especially tongues, are reported to have been common among the Moravians, especially under the leadership of Count von Zinzendorf (1700–1760), as well among the French Huguenots in the late seventeenth century and the Jansenists of the first half of the eighteenth century. John Wesley (1703–1791) defended the ongoing operation of tongues beyond the time of the apostles. One could also cite George Fox (1624–1691) who founded the Quaker church.

Those who insist that revelatory spiritual gifts such as prophecy, discerning of spirits, and word of knowledge ceased to function beyond the first century also have a difficult time accounting for the operation of these gifts in the lives of many who were involved in the Scottish Reformation, as well several who ministered in its aftermath. Jack Deere, in his book *Surprised by the Voice of God,*[10] has provided extensive documentation of the gift of prophecy at work in and through such men as George Wishart (1513–1546; mentor of John Knox), John Knox himself (1514–1572), John Welsh (1570–1622), Robert Bruce (1554–1631), and Alexander Peden (1626–1686). I strongly encourage you to obtain Deere's book

10 Jack Deere, *Surprised by the Voice of God* (Grand Rapids: Zondervan, 1996), 64–93.

and read the account of their supernatural ministries, not only in prophecy but often in gifts of healing. Deere also draws our attention to one of the historians of the seventeenth century, Robert Fleming (1630–1694), as well as one of the major architects of the Westminster Confession of Faith, Samuel Rutherford (1600–1661), both of whom acknowledged the operation of the gifts in their day.

It may surprise some to discover that we have extensive knowledge of but a small fraction of what happened in the history of the church. It is terribly presumptuous to conclude that the gifts of the Spirit were absent from the lives of people about whom we know virtually nothing. We simply don't know what was happening in the thousands upon thousands of churches and home meetings of Christians in centuries past. I cannot say with confidence that believers regularly prayed for the sick and saw them healed any more than you can say they didn't. Cessationists cannot say they never prophesied to the comfort, exhortation, and consolation of the church (1 Corinthians 14:3) any more than I can say they did. Neither of us can say with any confidence whether countless thousands of Christians throughout the inhabited earth prayed in tongues in their private devotions. That is hardly the sort of thing for which we could expect extensive documentation. We must remember that this was long before the printing press or the advantages of mass media. The absence of documented evidence for spiritual gifts in a time when documented evidence for most of church life was, at best, sparse is hardly good grounds for concluding that such gifts did not exist.

If the gifts were sporadic, there may be an explanation other than the theory that they were restricted to the first century. We must remember that prior to the Protestant Reformation in the sixteenth century the average Christian did not have access to the Bible in his own language. Biblical ignorance was rampant. That is hardly the sort of atmosphere in which people would be aware of spiritual gifts (their name, nature, and function) and thus hardly the sort of atmosphere in which we would expect them to seek and pray for such phenomena or to recognize them, were they to be manifest. If the gifts were sparse, and this again we cannot know, it could have been due as much to ignorance and the spiritual lethargy it breeds as to any theological principle that limits the gifts to the lifetime of the apostles.

Related to this previous point is the fact that God mercifully blesses us both with what we don't deserve and what we refuse or are unable to recognize. I am persuaded that numerous churches today who advocate cessationism experience these gifts but dismiss them as something less than the miraculous manifestation of the Holy Spirit. For example, someone with the gift of discerning spirits may be described as "possessing remarkable sensitivity and insight." Someone with the gift of word of knowledge is rather said to have "deep understanding of spiritual truths." Someone who prophesies is said to have "spoken with timely encouragement to the needs of the congregation." Someone who lays hands on the sick and prays successfully for healing is told that God still answers prayer but that gifts of healing are no longer operative. These churches wouldn't be caught dead labeling such phenomena by the names given them in 1 Corinthians 12:7–10 because they are committed to the theory that such phenomena don't exist.

If this occurs today (and it does, as it did in a church in which I ministered for several years), there is every reason to think it has occurred repeatedly throughout the course of history subsequent to the first century. Consider this hypothetical example. Let us suppose that a man had been assigned to write a descriptive history of church life in what is now southern France in, say, 845 AD. How might he label what he saw and heard? If he were ignorant of spiritual gifts, being untaught or perhaps a well-educated cessationist, his record would make no reference to prophecy, healing, miracles, word of knowledge, etc. Such phenomena might well exist, perhaps even flourish, but would be identified and explained in other terms by our hypothetical historian. Centuries later we discover his manuscript. Would it be fair to conclude from his observations that certain spiritual gifts had ceased subsequent to the apostolic age? Of course not! My point in this is simply that in both the distant past and present the Holy Spirit can empower God's people with gifts for ministry which they either do not recognize or, for whatever reason, explain in terms other than those of 1 Corinthians 12:7–10. The absence of explicit reference to certain charismata is therefore a weak basis on which to argue for their permanent withdrawal from church life.

The ministry of Charles Spurgeon is a case in point. Read carefully the following account taken from his autobiography:

> While preaching in the hall, on one occasion, I deliberately pointed to a man in the midst of the crowd, and said, "There is a man sitting there, who is a shoemaker; he keeps his shop open on Sundays, it was open last Sabbath morning, he took ninepence, and there was fourpence profit out of it; his soul is sold to Satan for fourpence!" A city missionary, when going his rounds, met with this man, and seeing that he was reading one of my sermons, he asked the question, "Do you know Mr. Spurgeon?" "Yes," replied the man, "I have every reason to know him, I have been to hear him; and, under his preaching, by God's grace I have become a new creature in Christ Jesus. Shall I tell you how it happened? I went to the Music Hall, and took my seat in the middle of the place; Mr. Spurgeon looked at me as if he knew me, and in his sermon he pointed to me, and told the congregation that I was a shoemaker, and that I kept my shop open on Sundays; and I did, sir. I should not have minded that; but he also said that I took ninepence the Sunday before, and that there was fourpence profit out of it. I did take ninepence that day, and fourpence was just the profit; but how he should know that, I could not tell. Then it struck me that it was God who had spoken

> to my soul though him, so I shut up my shop the next Sunday. At first, I was afraid to go again to hear him, lest he should tell the people more about me; but afterwards I went, and the Lord met with me, and saved my soul."

Spurgeon then adds this comment:

> I could tell as many as a *dozen* similar cases in which I pointed at somebody in the hall without having the slightest knowledge of the person, or any idea that what I said was right, except that I believed I was moved by the Spirit to say it; and so striking has been my description, that the persons have gone away, and said to their friends, "Come, see a man that told me all things that ever I did; beyond a doubt, he must have been sent of God to my soul, or else he could not have described me so exactly." And not only so, but I have known many instances in which the thoughts of men have been revealed from the pulpit. I have sometimes seen persons nudge their neighbours with their elbow, because they had got a smart hit, and they have been heard to say, when they were going out, "The preacher told us just what we said to one another when we went in at the door."[11]

What are we to make of this? My opinion is that this is a perfect and not uncommon example of what the apostle Paul described in 1 Corinthians 14:24–25. Spurgeon exercised the gift of *prophecy*. He did not label it as such, but that does not alter the reality of what the Holy Spirit accomplished through him. If one were to examine Spurgeon's theology and ministry, as well as recorded accounts of it by his contemporaries and subsequent biographers, most would conclude from the absence of explicit reference to miraculous

11 *The Autobiography of Charles H. Spurgeon* Vol. II (Curts & Jennings, 1899), 226–227.

charismata, such as prophecy and the word of knowledge, that such gifts had been withdrawn from church life. But Spurgeon's own testimony inadvertently says otherwise!

If we concede that certain spiritual gifts were less prevalent than others in the history of the church, their absence may well be due to unbelief, apostasy, and other sins that serve only to quench and grieve the Holy Spirit. If Israel experienced the loss of power because of repeated rebellion, if Jesus himself "could do no miracle there except that He laid His hands upon a few sick people and healed them," all because of their "unbelief" (Mark 6:5–6), we should hardly be surprised at the infrequency of the miraculous in periods of church history marked by theological ignorance and personal immorality.

The argument we are considering is this: if the Holy Spirit wanted the church to experience the miraculous gifts, they would not be so conspicuously absent from church history. Let's take the principle underlying that argument and apply it to several other issues. We all believe that the Holy Spirit is the *teacher* of the church. We all believe that the NT describes his ministry of *enlightening* our hearts and *illuminating* our minds to understand the truths of Scripture (see 1 John 2:20, 27). Yet within the first generation after the death of the apostles, the doctrine of justification by faith was under attack. Salvation by faith plus works soon became standard doctrine and was not successfully challenged until Martin Luther's courageous stand in the sixteenth century. My question, then, is this: If God intended for the Holy Spirit to continue to teach and enlighten Christians concerning vital biblical truths beyond the death of the apostles, why did the church languish in ignorance of this most fundamental truth for almost 1,000 years? If God intended for the Holy Spirit to illumine the minds of his people concerning biblical truths after the death of the apostles, why did the church languish in ignorance of the doctrine of the priesthood of all believers for almost 1,000 years? Why did Christians suffer from the absence of those experiential blessings this vital truth might otherwise have brought to their church life? Those of you who believe in a pretribulational rapture of the church must also explain the absence of this truth from the collective knowledge of the church for almost 1,900 years!

Undoubtedly, your response will be that none of this proves the Holy Spirit ceased his ministry of teaching and illumination. None of this proves that God ceased to want his people to understand such vital doctrinal principles. Precisely! And the alleged relative infrequency or absence of certain spiritual gifts during the same period of church history does not prove that God was opposed to their use or had negated their validity for the remainder of the present age.

Both theological ignorance of certain biblical truths and a loss of experiential blessings provided by spiritual gifts can be, and should be, attributed to factors other than the suggestion that God intended such knowledge and power only for believers in the early church.

Finally, and most important of all, is the fact that what has or has not occurred in church history is ultimately irrelevant to what *we* should pursue, pray for, and expect in the life of our churches today. The final criterion for deciding whether God wants to bestow certain spiritual gifts on his people today is the Word of God. I am continually shocked and grieved to hear people cite the alleged absence of a particular experience in the life of an admired saint from the church's past as reason for doubting its present validity. As much as I respect the giants of the Reformation and of other periods in church history, I intend to emulate the giants of the NT who wrote under the inspiration of the Holy Spirit. I admire John Calvin, but I obey the apostle Paul.

In sum, neither the failure nor success of Christians in days past is the ultimate standard by which we determine what God wants for us today. We can learn from their mistakes as well as their achievements. But the only question of ultimate relevance for us and for this issue is: "What saith the Scripture?"

(12) Twelfth, and finally (although it is technically not a *reason* or argument for being a continuationist like the previous eleven), I cannot ignore personal experience. The fact is that I've seen all spiritual gifts in operation, tested and confirmed them, and experienced them firsthand on countless occasions. As stated, this is less a *reason* to become a continuationist and more a *confirmation* (although not an infallible one) of the validity of that decision. Experience, in isolation from the biblical text, proves little. But experience must be noted, especially if it *illustrates* or *embodies* what we see in the text.[12]

So, to sum up as briefly as I can, are miraculous gifts for today? Yes!

---

12 In this regard, I would recommend my book, *Convergence*, where I describe in detail several of these personal experiences.